VNWORTHY CREATVRE:

A Punjabi Daughter's Memoir of Honour, Shame and Love

By

Aruna Papp with Barbara Kay

FR**3**DOM PRESS
CANADA INC.

Freedom Press
12-111 Fourth Ave., Suite 185
St. Catharines, ON L2S 3P5

ISBN 978-0-9812767-6-2

Book design by David Bolton
Front cover photo Eric Vardy
Aruna's photo Pamela Elle
Outfit on the front cover provided by *Design Hut* Brampton, Ontario

"For Elizabeth Shafqat (Aunt Liz in chapter 12) who believed in my dream before she met me. "

Contents

Acknowledgements

ARUNA PAPP

My life has been an amazing journey on which I have met incredible people who have held my hand during the darkest moments and have stood with me during the celebrations. It is difficult to mention everyone, but Elizabeth Shafqut, Elspeth Hayworth, Shobah Mendiratta, Zarina Sharazee, Baldev Mutta, Veena Dutta, and Pamela Elle were there when I needed them most.

Barbara Kay held my hand through some of the darkest times in my life, when I was forced to dig up and relive some of the unbearable events of the past. She was not just a co-writer, but an excellent therapist. This project would not have been completed if it had not been for Barbara's gentle and kind guidance. Barbara believed that this story needed to be told in order to reach out and help others in need. I found the same spirit of generosity in Ronny Kay, Barbara's husband, and her son Jonathan, as well as her sisters Anne and Nancy.

My parents were hardworking people who sacrificed everything they had, and left behind all that was familiar to give their children a better life in Canada, and for that I will be eternally grateful. My father was a proud, honourable man whom I adored. I am grateful that he allowed me to witness the change in him. He supported my work by attending many events with me and participating in a teaching video. I am grateful to my mother for the long chats we had when she was hooked up to a dialysis machine. It gave me an opportunity to get to know her better. My sisters and my daughters and son, I acknowledge them as well. Even in their silence, they have always wished me well.

Gregory Papp, you are my hero, my motivator and a wonderful stepson. An unfortunate accident left you quadriplegic at age 28. I had such misgivings and fears about what life might be for you after that. You returned to school, became a fantastic architect and showed us all how to play the cards we are dealt and how to live a life of dignity.

Finally, and most important, I have no words to express my feelings for, and gratitude to David Papp, my husband, a kind, gentle, unselfish man. David picked me and my children off the street and literally gave us shelter, love and unconditional acceptance. It is he who has taught me what it is to be loved and respected for myself. His sense of humour, his nurturing and unselfish generosity have been poured into our child, Christina, without whom I would be nothing. She allowed me to be the mother I always wanted to be. God has been good to me. I feel very blessed.

I am grateful above all to Aruna, whose need for a professional writer coincided with my emergent interest in honour-based culture and its implications for Canadian society. This collaboration has been a deeply fulfilling project for me.

I thank my family – my husband Ronny, and my children Jonathan and Joanne – for their encouragement and practical advice, as well as for their patience when my long stints at the computer cut into time that should have been theirs and my four granddaughters'.

A number of friends, including my sisters, Anne Golden and Nancy Kumer, read portions of the manuscript in progress and offered warm feedback. I am especially indebted to two cherished long-time friends, fellow literature student and writer David Saunders and former teaching colleague Marilyn Sims, for their attentive close reading of the manuscript and their valuable editorial suggestions.

INTRODUCTION

On June 30, 2009, three teenage girls from Montreal – Zainab, Sahar and Geeti Shafia – along with their father's first wife, Rona Amir Mohammad, were found dead in a Nissan Sentra, submerged under the waters of a Kingston, Ontario canal.

During the fall of 2011, and into the winter of 2012, Canadians were riveted by courtroom testimony in the criminal trials of the girls' father, mother and brother – Mohammad Shafia, Tooba Mohammad Yahya and Hamed Shafia – on four counts of first-degree murder. All were convicted.

In response to the prosecutor's relentless grilling of the defendants, a sickening tale of domestic terrorism emerged, which made it clear that the lives of three beautiful young women were cut short because their modest bids for social autonomy, such as dressing fashionably, and dating boys of their choosing, were perceived by their parents and brother as a defilement of the family's honour.

The multiple horror, the fact that the Shafia girls had begged for help from a system that could not compete with a cultural imperative, and the compelling tape-recordings of the father's vicious references to the girls as "filth" and "whores," served to awaken unprecedented indignation and disgust amongst Canadians.

And yet this is by no means a first in Canada. In the last two decades there have been about thirteen other occasions when a father, or a father and a son, and occasionally a mother, with the collusion of other family members, has not only killed a daughter, but admitted to doing so as a necessary means of redressing family shame.

In the years leading to the Shafia case, 16-year old Aqsa Parvez was killed by her father and brother because she wanted to be like other Canadian girls, and because she was resisting a forced marriage with a Pakistani relative. Bahar Ebrahimi, 19, came home late one night and was stabbed to death by her mother for her perceived loose morals. Farah Khan, five, was killed and dismembered by her father with the complicity of his wife, because he believed Farah was the "bastard child" of his first wife in Pakistan. Jaswinder Kaur Sidhu, 25, Khatera Sadiqi, 20 and Amandeep Atwal, 17 were killed because they dared to love men their fathers did not approve of. Unhappy wife Amandeep Dhillion, 22, was killed rather than be allowed to bring dishonour to her in-laws by leaving her husband.

Killing in the name of honour – *"Izzat"* in most of South Asia, or *"sharam"* in Punjabi, a concept that crosses almost all religious lines – is only the most dramatic element in a whole matrix of behavioural codes that condemn many girls and women from honour cultures to entire lives of quiet desperation:

before marriage in thrall to their parents, and after marriage in thrall to their husbands and in-laws.

I know something of what the Shafia girls experienced, because I grew up in a similar household in India. I know the fear that gripped Zainab, Sahar and Geeti. Like them I knew from my earliest youth that I had been born the wrong sex, that I was an "unworthy creature," words I heard over and over again from my mother and grandmother. I knew that my life was expendable if I did not meet the draconian standards for chastity that would ensure my marriageable status, because marriage and motherhood, hopefully of sons, was all I was good for.

Until I came to Canada as a young mother of two little girls, trapped in a loveless arranged marriage, I had no reason to believe life had treated me unfairly. I had never met any woman of my own culture who was considered the moral or social equal of a man. I never questioned the privileges, like a good education, that sons could expect, but not daughters. I never resented my father, a Christian pastor, for the beatings I frequently endured at his hands, nor did I resent the disparity between my mother's warm indulgence of my brother's wishes and the grudging scraps of attention that were my portion.

Gradually I awoke to the opportunities and rights that were available to Canadian women, and realized that my dream of a proper education was within my grasp, if I had the courage to break my cultural shackles. I finally left my abusive marriage and got my education, but like all women from honour cultures who manage to escape, I paid a heavy price for my freedom.

When western women leave a marriage, they leave one man. When South Asian women walk away from their marriage, they are often excommunicated by their disapproving parents, siblings and extended family because they have stepped out of their family role. Unlike Canadian women, they must choose between their individual needs and rights, and the expectations of their community that they play the role they were born to: daughter, sister, wife, mother, daughter-in-law.

Those who choose independence over cultural obligations are amongst the loneliest women in the world. As a consequence of leaving my husband, I suffered estrangement from my family and a sometimes frightening wave of hostility from many male South Asians who vilified me for my "self-hating" public critiques of honour-motivated abuse in our community.

Drawing on my own intimate experience with the behavioural codes governing the lives of South Asian girls and women, I have devoted myself for the past thirty years to helping South Asian families in crisis, men and women torn between honour culture and Canadian principles of gender equality. I counsel not only those of the immigrating generation, but – so tenacious are these ancient honour codes – even seemingly integrated girls and women in the second and third generation.

I am proud that South Asian Family Services, now called South Asian Settlement Services, which I founded, has blossomed into one of Toronto's largest social service agencies, with a budget of $4 million and 65 staff. I am as well gratified by the public recognition my advocacy work has brought me.

But I have had some heartbreaking failures too. I have attended too many funerals of girls who have committed suicide, or young women who have died in "accidents." As this book goes to press, I have three clients in hospital who have lost the will to live as a direct result of the same stressors that fuelled the Shafia family tragedy.

I have long wanted to write this memoir as a way of showing, rather than telling, what it is like to grow up in a family schooled in honour-based culture. But English is not my first language. I knew I needed to collaborate with a sympathetic professional writer, preferably somebody who shared my passion for exposing the iniquities so many South Asian girls and women are prey to.

I had no idea where I should look for such a collaborator. Then, a few years ago, at a point when I was feeling particularly disheartened in my work, I happened to read an article on honour killings in the *National Post* newspaper by columnist Barbara Kay.

I was agreeably surprised at Barbara's understanding of the difference between domestic violence and honour-motivated violence, two distinct phenomena that are almost invariably lumped together by naïve observers. Up until then I had not come across any other commentator on this issue in the mainstream media who was ignoring the taboo against 'racist' criticism of minority cultural customs, even when such customs conflict with the most basic principles of democracy and human rights.

I contacted Barbara and said, "You 'get it'. Thank you for writing about this problem. You have no idea how deep and hidden it is and the extent of abuse that is going on in the name of family honour." That was the day the idea for this book took root.

Writing this memoir has been like making my way through a maze. I have been forced to revisit scenes that had been sealed from the light of memory and that I wished would remain so. There were periods when I was not sure if I was on the right track. At such times I turned to my elders – my mother, my uncles and aunts, who thought my work with abused women was important. Occasionally the pain of reliving events was so difficult that it sent me back to the therapist who had helped me through the lowest period of my life.

My ambition in writing this book was first and foremost to capture the story of an immigrant family as well as to honour my parents. They were humble people, but hardworking, and unswervingly religious Seventh Day Adventists, committed to education and higher learning for their children in principle, if not always in practice. I wanted to celebrate the fact that as their first born, not only was I there with them during the years of their hardships, but that I also witnessed many of their successes, and the great difficulties they overcame in adapting to life in Canada.

This memoir is my life as I remember it. Doubtless my relationship with my parents and my memories of family life differ in kind and quality from those of my siblings, children and other family members. Many of the episodes I have recounted occurred when my siblings or children were very young or not even born yet. It has never been my intention to hurt or humiliate anyone. I have tried hard to keep the lives of my siblings and my children out of the book, because each one of them chose not to be included, and I respect their wishes.

It is my hope that this book will help Canadians and other westerners to understand what it is like to grow up in an honour-based culture, in which, from the day she is born to the day she dies, a female's every waking moment is consecrated to sustaining family honour. I also hope that my book will encourage community leaders from all countries where these gendered iniquities flourish to break the silence on, and the cycle of, honour-motivated abuse.

It is too late for the Shafia girls and their stepmother. But it is not too late for the thousands of girls at risk of similar fates. I do not know their names. But this book is dedicated to them.

Chapter One

Unworthy Creatures

Delhi, 1964

I was fourteen. A horrifying scream made me leap from my *charpoy,* my cot, and lunge to the low boundary wall of the rooftop where our family slept in summer. I saw a young woman engulfed in flames, radiantly aglow in a glittering red bridal sari. Her glossy black hair, crowned with a garland of white flowers, was pulled into a neat bun. Head thrown back, wrists bound with thick rope, her arms, sparkling with glass and metal bangles, reached up beseechingly to the stars.

She had only screamed that once. The moment I looked over the wall I knew, I was sure it was Kiran. The girl writhing in her furnace was as dazzling in death as she had been in life. Oddly, I remember thinking: But why are her feet bare? Where are her *chapals*? She forgot her sandals.

Kiran lived on the first floor below us, where her family lodged in one part of a courtyard divided by an eight-foot high wall between four families. She was special. Tall, with a beautiful figure. And educated. Kiran had graduated from university with honours and found a good job in one of the posh American Hotels. Every morning a taxi collected her and two other similarly-endowed girls and delivered them to the hotel. One of them, we learned with awe, had been sent to Russia by Delhi University and she had learned to speak that language. Every evening around six they were delivered home by the same taxi.

And every morning and evening many of the neighbourhood women and teenage girls like me found an excuse to stick our heads out and gape at these neighbourhood princesses. We couldn't wait to see how they were dressed each day. We would estimate the height of their sandal heels, linger over the cut and quality of their clothes, assess the impact of their toes' nail colour. For unlike the far-away beautiful film stars they resembled, these neighbourhood girls were real and present. They excited our imaginations and fed the illusion that such a glamorous life might one day be ours.

During these hot summer days, as the sun began to go down, and we had eaten our last meal of the day, our mother would take us all – myself, and the three younger siblings who weren't away at boarding school – to the rooftop to play until it was time to go to bed on our charpoys under the open sky. On this night Miss Rawat, a spinster, who was the principal of a local English grade school, and her friend, my Auntie Sheila, a nurse, were there as well.

Whenever my mother and her friends visited, I was expected to look after the children. Every now and then mother would ask me to bring up tea or cold water for her friends. Usually I would do so and loiter, listening to the latest gossip.

I was hypnotized. I don't know how long I had been standing there watching Kiran burn, when suddenly my hair was yanked from behind. My mother dragged me backward, screaming at me, "Get away from the wall! Get back to your charpoy and stay there. If I see you out of it I will break your legs." This was followed by a hard slap on the back of my neck that sent me flying on to the cot. "You stay there and keep an eye on the children," she barked, and rushed back to the wall to join the other women.

I lay quietly, seething with inward agitation, straining to hear every word *Ma Ji* and her friends were saying. As a school principal, Miss Rawat was always a trusted source of neighbourhood gossip. She seemed to know everyone by name.

2

Now she yelled to someone below, "Call the police, Baapray, call someone. Do something. Don't just stand there – can't you see there is a girl on fire!"

I heard activity below. Then Ma Ji was looming over me crying, "Take the children downstairs. We are going to sleep in the rooms downstairs." As I picked up one of my sleeping sisters, I peeked over the wall. Kiran and her red sari had subsided into a charred heap of smoking rubbish. I wanted to linger and keep watching, but Ma Ji ssnapped at me again to get myself and the other children down. I could no longer see Kiran as I chivvied the children down the stairs, but the odour of roasting flesh, rare in that vegetarian neighbourhood, followed us down.

Many stories circulated about Kiran's death. In the most common rumour her older brothers became enraged by their sister's rebelliousness, specifically her decision to marry a man she had met at work and fallen in love with. Her brothers, it seemed, had already promised her to a wealthy man twice her age, and he in turn had promised the brothers help with a business venture. When Kiran insisted she was leaving home to be with her beloved…

All that summer I would try to get the younger ones to sleep as early as I could, so that I could listen to what Ma Ji and her friends were saying about Kiran and the police investigation. I expected to hear at least some sympathy for Kiran. Instead, I was stabbed to the quick by the women's facile chatter, all of them agreeing that it was "very difficult to raise girls in this day and age," and complaining about how helpless they sometimes felt to safeguard their family honour.

I was upset for Kiran's sake, because she had been beautiful and happy, and because she seemed lucky and successful, but mostly, I suppose, because she had given so much vicarious pleasure to me, a gangly, ugly, earth-dark tomboy who even in fantasy could not have imagined such personal glory.

I should not have been shocked at these women cursing the bad luck a baby girl represented. After all, I can't remember a time when I didn't understand that even shiny, sophisticated girls were a burden to their families, even, it seemed, those who had made something of themselves and brought money home. These gossipers' disparagement of girls therefore seemed to me entirely reasonable. Yes, of course it was terrible for my mother to have so many girls, really quite unbelievable bad luck.

Ma Ji said to her friends, "I have all these girls. I don't know how I am going to protect them. If one of them became the subject of such scandalous gossip or rumours, my husband would have to break their bones. If anything worse were to happen" – no Indian woman would have to spell out that "worse" meant pregnancy – "he would have to kill her. As a man of honour, what choice would he have? Our good name means everything to him. There would be nothing I could do."

Our family name meant everything to her too. As I and every other girl I knew understood, none of our mothers would protect us in such a situation. "Yes," Ma Ji went on, "If any of my daughters did something like Kiran, I would open her legs, pour gasoline on the part of her that got us in trouble and set her on fire." I believed her.

Shortly afterward, one of Kiran's brothers got married. I stood by the same rooftop wall and watched. Tents had been erected with imitation grass carpets laid down inside for the banquet. There was a space between the tent roof and the wall, enough for me to see everything going on inside. The party went on all night long. The band played loudly, the beat insistent, irresistible. The same women who had stood silently in a circle around Kiran as she burned did not resist the music. They clapped their hands and danced around the celebrating family, and their bracelets glittered in the torchlight as they held their arms up high, beseeching the heavens to bless the union of Kiran's killer and his bride.

Delhi, 1959

Although we lived in a largely Hindu area, we were Christians, Seventh Day Adventists. We had therefore been given Christian – that is to say, western – names. My father had changed his last name, Sindhu, a common surname indicating one of the lower castes, to Abraham. I was given the western name Irene, suggested to my father by a missionary who trained him. I hated it.

Early one Saturday morning when I was eight, my father was rushing us to the bus so we would not be late for church yet again. The mission's pastor had a habit of standing just outside the church door and shaking hands with everyone as they came into the church. He would say, "Good morning, thank you for being on time this morning. I know God appreciates your efforts."

I did not understand English, so Papa would translate to Urdu, explaining that every time we were late, it was noted to his discredit. Papa hated being embarrassed in this way. It was humiliating, and one more stain, however small, on his honour.

As we hurried towards the bus, we passed a hill of garbage. A large flock of crows circling above it were making a terrific racket, clearly fighting over something edible. As we came closer I saw that the crows were tearing at the flesh of a naked baby girl. I let go of my younger sister's hand and ran to have a better look. I thought I saw the infant move. Papa lunged at me for letting go of my sister. He slapped me on my head and shoved me on to an already overcrowded bus.

4

I cried out that I had seen a baby in the garbage. "It's a baby girl," I pleaded. "I think she's still alive! "I was immediately smacked again and told to shut up because I was going to make the family late for church. I stood in the bus, crying from pain and wondering if the baby girl was in pain as well. The woman on the seat next to me said, "Don't pay any attention to the garbage. It happens every day. Just be glad your parents decided to keep you." She beamed at my parents with a big toothless grin, aware that she had paid them a great compliment.

Growing up, I had always known that I was dispensable. I was vaguely aware that this expendability was my fault. Whatever was wrong with me, there was no way to fix it. Girls were worthless. My father's mother, Dadi Ji, had told me this many times. Getting rid of me or one of my sisters would not be difficult, she used to tell us. It all made sense to me. After all, look how easy it was to get rid of Kiran and the baby girl being eaten by birds.

From earliest childhood in our society everyone was exposed to a constant stream of allusions to the worthlessness of girls and the preciousness of boys. Poems, songs, bedtime stories, gossip – the yearning for sons and contempt for girls was the air we breathed. Prayer and supplication to God or our neighbours' deities was considered the only strategy for success in delivering a boy, even though it so often failed.

One day, as Ma Ji and I and my younger sisters stood by the local vegetable vendor's cart estimating her precise need for precious coriander – although considered a culinary necessity, it was quite expensive – a woman walking by said to her, "You have these four cows to feed. I would never put coriander in my dhal for such cows. Pray, woman, pray so that your stars may change."

"Your stars." At these words a long-forgotten memory rushed in. I was five years old. I was asleep in the bed I shared with two of my younger sisters, but was awakened by the sound of my father's voice. Lifting my head I saw both Papa and Ma Ji kneeling by my bed. Papa had his hand on Ma Ji's bowed head, as if he were blessing her. Their eyes were closed. Ma Ji's hands were folded, and tears ran down her face.

I knew that Papa was going to be leaving in the morning on one of the many trips our Church called upon him to make. I had lovingly polished both his brown and his black shoes the day before, a ritual pre-voyage task I cherished, and I had seen his freshly laundered and ironed clothes packed neatly into his travel box.

I was about to open my eyes and wish him a good journey, but he began to speak. Something in his tone troubled me, so I stayed silent, eyes closed. Papa was praying to God in Urdu, his voice soft and urgent. "I am leaving this family in your hands, Lord. Please take care of them, and this time around please bless

5

your servant woman with a son. You have seen fit to burden me, your ever-faithful servant, with four daughters. Now I beg you to give me a son, so that I might have the strength to shoulder the burdens you have seen fit to place on me.

"We, your servants, need a son. You know I have served you as best I can, but bearing the burden alone is so heavy. If you give me a son, O Lord, I will name him Samuel and he will give his life to you as your servant. Please hear our prayers and bless us."

Praying for a son was nothing new to me. I had been taught to pray for a brother at every meal and every bedtime. And making deals with God was nothing new to me either. I believed God could do anything, even answer my nightly prayer with a baby brother the next morning.

What frightened me was the supplicating tone that exposed his naked dread of never having the only child he really wanted. When he rose to leave, I wanted to run after him, to tell him that he had forgotten to pray for us. But watching Ma Ji weep, I couldn't find the courage to move.

My father behaved as though it was my fault he had no son. It appeared that it was my fault he had to thrash me for no reason – or rather for the good reason that I was "God's mistake." Clearly I was the wrong sex for an Indian father's love. But, ever optimistic, always seeking to absolve my adored father of blame for anything he did or said that caused me pain, I did not blame him for his obsession. After all, had he not concluded that it was *God* Who had made the mistake? I chose to believe that in spite of his sorrow in being denied a son, my father bore me no personal ill will that I was the wrong sex.

To increase the liklihood of Ma Ji delivering a son, our Hindu neighbours would advise her to visit a certain temple, or make an offering to a holy man, cleanse her heart and pray. When Papa returned from his frequent tours with the missionaries, the neighbourhood men would shout out to him, "This time it will be a boy. You will see, it will be a boy." Papa would respond to their greetings with laughter and shout back, "From your mouth to God's ears. God willing, this time it will surely be a boy."

My sisters and I prayed at each mealtime and at bedtime. The youngest being only two years old, I would show her how to fold her hands and close her eyes, while I said the words for her when it was her turn to pray. I prayed with real conviction. I knew that if Ma Ji gave birth to a boy, it would in some way mean safety for the rest of us.

The prayer would usually start with, "Dear Jesus, please give us a baby brother this time. I promise to be very good if you give us a baby brother." When Papa was home, the tension mounted, and on those nights I would lie in bed and make deals with God. *Please can you give us a baby brother this time? I promise*

6

not to steal coins from the Hindu temples. I promise not to get into fights with the neighbourhood boys. I promise I will stop playing marbles. I promise I will be a good Christian. I promise not to ask for more food than I already get.

God wearied of our petitions at last. The saviour of our honour and family name was born at 5:20 a.m. on October 18 of my eighth year of life. I had been asleep when Papa came and shook me by the shoulder, exulting, "Wake up, wake up! The baby brother you have been praying for is here. God has heard our prayers!" He was crying, sobbing as he repeated the good news.

I jumped from my bed and ran out to spread the glad tidings around the neighbourhood. In my excitement I forgot to put shoes on. I was scampering over garbage, oblivious to the cow dung and dog shit I stepped through, even unaware that I had somehow cut my foot, so intent was I on banging against doors to announce the news: "We have a baby brother, we have our saviour, we have a boy who will save our family honour. Wake up! Wake up! We have a baby brother. Come to our house, come see our baby brother."

Throughout that day neighbours stopped by the house, stood outside and offered my father congratulations. He beamed. By noon, bursting to share his joy and gratitude, Papa had gone to the local confectionary and bought a large tray of *laddos*, the sweet yellow balls made with lentil flour that are traditionally distributed to friends to mark an Indian celebration.

Of course, our Hindu neighbours would not eat these laddos, or anything else from our house. As Christians who ate meat, we were unclean, low caste. Hindu mothers would smack their children if they were seen playing with us. So there was no question of them breaking bread with us. But Papa was so eager for their good wishes that he announced to them he would have the fellows at the sweet shop deliver laddos directly to their homes. To my father it was a matter of family name and honour, not to mention personal pride, that even high caste Hindus should, by hook or by crook, participate in our joy.

However, the latrine sweeper – *Jamadarnee*– and the launderer – *dhobe* – were happy to accept father's laddos and gifts of cloth. Likewise the milkman who sold me milk from his few cows on mornings we could afford it. He too paid his respects and was given a bit of money. The man with the vegetable cart, the fellow who walked around sharpening household knives and the man who fixed broken shoes – all got money and laddos as well.

As for me, on this day I did not care what our caste was, who played with us, or who ate from our house and who didn't. I knew that everything was going to be all right now that our saviour was born and our family honour had been saved.

Chapter Two

Dadi Ji

My happiest childhood memories are linked to the long summers I spent in my father's native Punjab village. Chukwal is about 200 miles from the bustling ancient city of Jullandhar, where my father's church duties had brought us. The climate there is as hot as in Jullandhar, but Chukwal is surrounded by enormous bodies of water, which makes the heat more bearable. There I could run wild and dance barefoot through the fields instead of trudging shoebound on the city's broiling cement. I could send monkeys fleeing when I climbed the Peepal trees like a boy. And I could cool my baking skin in the vigorous River Beas, whose frigid waters tumbled down from the snow-capped Himalayas to wend their way past my grandparents' little mudbrick home.

Getting to Chukwal from Jullandhar was an adventure. A bus took us most of the way, but for the last 25 miles we transferred to an oxcart, and that part, rumbling along a rough, unpaved road, took a full day. We packed enough food so we didn't have to stop for meals. When we had to answer calls of nature, we jumped off, squatted by the side of the road, and then ran to catch up with the cart. Occasionally the driver would pull up to water the ox.

I adored those rides. The cart was stacked high with bulging bags of rice, flour, salt, lentils, sugar, and a big can of cooking oil. We children sat happily perched on top of the sacks as the cart creaked and swayed its leisurely way forward. To pass the time I would sing. Sometimes the cart driver would ask for a tune from a popular film. All Indian films are musicals, and I loved the sound tracks indiscriminately, so was happy to oblige.

I knew all the words of the latest hits, which shocked my parents. I remember belting out *hum panchhi ek daal ke, ek daal ke, hum sung sung chume sung sung chume*, lyrics to a song from a sentimental 1957 film about a bunch of orphaned children. Another, just as popular, *Ek Se Bhale Do, Do Se Bhale Char munzil apani dur,* philosophized on the wisdom, pleasure and safety of travelling with other companions. It was really about life, I later came to realize, not travelling.

Of course, as an Adventist child I never saw the films themselves – that would have been a great scandal – but it was easy to pick up the tunes by osmosis. Indians are surrounded by music day and night. In that era everyone had a radio. Owning one was a point of pride. Humble transistor radios sat beside shopkeepers and cobblers and oxcart drivers, all of them blaring the pop tunes of the day.

Nourished by five Himalayan rivers, Punjab is the food basket of India. Its fertile soil yields an indescribable bounty. As we neared Chukwal, my heart would swell with rapture at the sight and rich, loamy smells of the surrounding farmland, level to the horizon, a colourful checkerboard, riotous with lush growth: field after field of wheat, mustard and all kinds of vegetables, branches bowed by the weight of plump, blushing mangoes, and fat stalks of *jaamu*, sugar cane ripe for harvest. I often thought the Garden of Eden must have looked just like the countryside around Chukwal.

The road narrowed to a lane, and then finally we would arrive at Dadi's mud hut with its cheerful, bright blue painted door. Young boys playing nearby recognized us, ran over to help unload our provisions and bring everything inside.

Dadi, or *Dadi Ji* more formally, as we called my father's mother, was widowed when I was six years old. I was just old enough to remember my grandfather – Dada Ji – as always sick and never engaged in anything resembling gainful employment. I recall him sitting for long periods on his charpoy with his hookah. In its clay bowl he would set gluey tobacco, topped by red-hot pieces of wood. I was fascinated by his long, deep inhalations and the smoke billowing from his mouth. He could smoke for hours. Sometimes when he fell asleep, I would suck on the hookah pipe, but was disappointed when no smoke emerged from my mouth.

People from our Sindhu caste were also referred to as Jatts, and the Jatts were a clan of farmers and landlords, the employment category assigned to them by their gods. But after they became Christians, they were considered Untouchables in the village. Family members disagreed on what Dada Ji did before he fell ill, depending on whether the motive for telling the story was to burnish or diminish his image. Dada Ji lost his farm to a famous flood. Afterward, my grandfather seems to have turned a listless hand to a variety of tasks that led nowhere.

The massive 1934 flood from the river Beas that claimed Dada Ji's family land was a consequence of British dams and canal-building. Family gossip has it that the British advised Dada Ji's family to move to the other side of the river. Dada Ji complied, which resulted in a probably traumatic further loss, for his brothers refused to join him. He grew ill and smoked his hookah – or perhaps smoked his hookah and grew ill – and died at the age of 56 from some kind of a tumour.

He was buried in Jammu, in the province of Kashmir, but we observed mourning rituals in Chukwal for the benefit of his relatives who did not attend the funeral. At these ceremonies were professional grievers, women dressed in black, with covered heads and face, who wept on cue for money. In India emotion is not a private affair, as it is for westerners. It is public, highly ritualized and performance-like. Extravagant mourning lamentation is closely tied to status. The more important the mourner paying respect to the family – a local politician, a person of higher caste – the more screaming and weeping was expected as the visitor embraced the family member. The wealthier the mourners, the more professional wailers were hired.

Our hired chorus keened loudly as each notable mourner was pointed out to them. One of my cousins and I enjoyed this spectacle, so began lying to them about who was a mourner in order to crank them up, not realizing each performance cost our families more. We both had our ears pulled later for this naughtiness.

One thing everyone seems to agree on is that if Dada Ji had been able to provide for his family, he might not have allowed his sons to go off with the missionaries to be educated in a Christian boarding school, in which case they would not have become Christians, and our lives would have taken a completely different turn.

Although Dada Ji left her materially poor, Dadi had compensating personal capital that contributed to her defining air of high status. She was very fair-skinned, an accident of birth, but one that conferred a lot of social cachet. And her only brother was educated, and employed as a minor civil servant who taught at a boys' high school.

But her sense of superiority was mainly due to treasure that in our culture was far more important than mere money. Dadi had only three daughters, but six sons. Her sons were her wealth, her protection from abuse by her husband – she was a sly and rather manipulative woman, practiced at pitting her protective sons against their father – and her justification for flaunting her authority over lesser women like her daughters-in-law.

And so the Chukwal summers were a vacation for me, but not for my mother. She would be stressed and argumentative with Papa every time we packed up for the trip. She knew what was in store for her. As a daughter-in-law, she was bound to submit to the demands of a mother-in-law who held her in contempt because she only had daughters.

Chukwal freed my father to set off on book-selling tours as a way to pay off debts, some incurred on his mother's behalf. As a pastor, Papa made only 300 rupees a month, about $32 Canadian, from which he had to feed and clothe his children, and of course send money to his mother. The church paid the rent and Papa received a travel allowance, including meals. But it wasn't enough. We ran up tabs with shopkeepers all winter.

So after dropping us off in Chukwal, Papa would set off on his two months' church-paid vacation to sell books all over the Punjab. We knew Papa would bring back a suitcase full of money. We held our breath until he flung it open with a proud flourish to genuinely excited oohs and aahs from his admiring family. The year would begin with new clothes for all and storage tins heavy with food.

Papa's stock in trade were books called "Bedtime Stories" and "Bible Stories," as well as health books featuring research done at Loma Linda University and Hospital in California, a Seventh Day Adventist institution. Most of them were written in English, but some children's storybooks had been translated into Urdu and Hindi. People were drawn to these books, with their colourful, washable Mylar covers, a novelty in India then. Possession of such exotic objects became something of a status symbol, as well as an aid to teaching children English, which the Sikhs were particularly keen on.

The biggest sellers were the health books. Adventists promote a vegetarian diet, which most native Adventists observed more in the breach than the practice, so those books were not of particular interest to the meat-eating Sikhs, but like-minded Hindus appreciated the latest research.

Although unsuccessful in many other endeavours, Papa was always a very good salesman. Punjabi men like poetry and they like ambitious men. Papa's extroverted charm and love of poetry gained him entry into some of the more prominent Punjabi families. He would greet the owner of the house with rhetorical flourishes, like "The essence of his lordship has drawn me, this humble educator, to this blessed doorstep." Naturally the flattered man would invite him in, and not only would Papa make a sale, he would ferret out information about nearby relatives "worthy in my opinion of sharing the same status as the owner of these remarkable books."

My father was intimately familiar with Punjabi fathers' hopes and dreams for their sons, and rather cunning in his exploitation of family rivalries. Punjabis were eager to educate their sons, and to them the West was the measure of all prosperity-building knowledge. Papa would say to a potential customer, "When your son is ready to go to America or England, he will be ahead of everyone else because of these books." After he had made a sale, he would then go to that man's brother, and say to him, "Your younger brother has bought these books. How will it look to others if you don't have them for your children?" It never failed. I loved hearing Papa's stories about how he was invited into a provincial Minister's home and how he sold thousands of rupees' worth of books. But no matter how much he earned during those two months, supporting his own family and his extended family meant that he'd be hard up again before the end of the year.

Like most other homes in the neighbourhood, Dadi Ji's had only two rooms. Some years that humble dwelling accommodated up to a dozen people during our long sojourns, not an uncommon situation in India, where the English words "crowded" or "privacy" have no meaning. During the summer I am remembering, when I was eight, there were only eight of us resident there. Dadi and Ma Ji, of course. Then there were Papa's brothers – my uncles, or *chachas*; there was Chacha Raja, who was in his early twenties, and six-year old Chacha Prem. There was also Papa's sister, my aunt, *Phuphi* Madhu, eleven. And finally there were me and my sisters: six-year old Mary, a bit sickly and perhaps for that reason mother's favourite, born the same month and year as Chacha Prem – and four-year old Jessica. But Aunt Sharifa would often show up from her nearby village to stay for a few days with her three children.

Logistically life was quite well organized. Our belongings were kept in metal boxes stacked one upon another. Food was secured in other rat-proof boxes. Bedding was stored or pinned up in the sun all day. Our rope-woven charpoys were hung on long wooden pegs attached to the walls of the house outside during the day. At night we would take them down, line them up and top them with thin mattresses and sheets, retrieved from their *paytee* – their tin box. Depending on our size, we kids would sleep two or three to a charpoy under mosquito nets we'd brought with us from the city. When it rained, the men would sleep in one room on the floor, the women in the other.

Before going to sleep, we would need to be sure the rooms were free of snakes and scorpions. They were everywhere, and especially fond of hiding amongst the food tins. One of the men would go in with a stick and lantern. It was rather frightening, but also exciting when a snake was cornered, as there would be a great deal of screaming and commotion amongst the onlookers jumping up and down on the charpoys. Uncle Raja preferred just to chase the snake out, but if Papa was on snake patrol, he would kill it.

I would have liked to be the one to hunt snakes, but Ma Ji would not allow it. When we finally got an outhouse of our own at the far end of the yard, the coolness and dampness from the well water run-off seemed to attract them. As the eldest, it was my job to take the younger children to do their business. I was courageous in the daytime, but at night I made them go on newspapers closer to the house. Then I would roll them up and toss them into the big hole.

At suppertime we would exchange stories about who had been bitten by what. Chacha Raja always came up with exciting narratives, like the one about a woman cutting greenery with her sickle, who grabbed a handful of grass and found herself staring into the eyes of a cobra, its scaly body writhing in her grip. She had little choice but to cut the head off the snake off while screaming for help. Such tales gave me goose bumps, and I begged Uncle Raja to tell me more.

Monkeys could be a nuisance too, but they were a benign problem compared to snakes. In front of Dadi's house there was a large yard, perhaps 100 ft by 50 ft. Around it was a mud brick wall about four ft high. Inside the wall my mother had planted rose bushes, some jasmine and a herb garden. The cow or water buffalo – whichever we had that year – was tied up next to the garden under our beloved, thickly-leaved Peepal tree, the only shade-providing tree on the property. Both the animal and the garden would have died from the heat without its protection. It was also my playhouse, and I shinnied up into it whenever I had time to myself. The monkeys enjoyed the tree too. They didn't attack people, but had a habit of scampering down to steal our snacks, so I delighted in scaring them away when we were in possession of the tree and its priceless shade.

In those days Chuckwal was an adventure in roughing it for children, but primitive for those running a household. There was neither plumbing nor electricity in the village. Water was drawn for crops and domestic needs by two white oxen roped together, plodding in endless circles around a well. Food was cooked in a *chula*, a fireplace-like attachment to the yard wall. The fires were fuelled by cow patties. I used to enjoy running after the cows and picking up the dung while it was still almost too hot to hold, but I had to be nimble to beat other little girls intent on the same mission.

Punjabi villages are all self-sufficient, with basic provisions produced locally, and goods from the larger cities sold in shops. Some Chukwal shop owners were Hindu, others Muslim, particularly devoted to supplying their co-religionists with *halal* meat, but most of the shop owners were Sikhs. Hindus would never enter any shop where meat was sold, but we Christians shopped wherever we liked.

Each religious group also had its own well. Every morning the temple *pandit* would bless the Hindu well and leave behind flowers, fruit and sometimes sweets as offerings to their gods. All the religions co-existed in harmony, but there were firm and clear social dividing lines that ran according to an inflexible caste ladder, and we Christians were on the bottom rung.

Without electricity, our lives were dictated by the sun. We went to bed when it got dark. At dawn, in a timeless ritual order followed by the villagers – women go first – all the mothers would rise and wake their daughters. Those who didn't have an outhouse, regardless of faith, would walk to the cornfield near the river and relieve themselves in gossipy proximity amidst tall stalks. Then we would rinse our bottoms in the river and come home. On our return, the men would rise and do likewise.

In later years we had our own outhouse and a well, so we could wash our clothes and do our proper bathing at home. The "bathroom" was four posts stuck in the ground, covered with burlap. The well's hand pump finally broke after years of use and abuse, so we would fill our buckets of water from the well, haul it to the burlap bathroom and wash ourselves. Mother attacked our hair with her precious brick of Sunlight soap that she brought with her from the city. It was like being scrubbed by a slippery stone, and it hurt. If the house was very full with extended family, an aunt kept watch to warn off stray males. When we were finished, it was the men's turn.

Before the sun came up, Ma Ji coaxed the fire to life in the chula and started making the *rotis*, a simple flatbread. Breakfast consisted of a cup of tea, two rotis, and a fistful of raw brown sugar we called *jaggery*. Sometimes, when my father was home, milk from the cow was set out to make yogourt. Whatever animals we had that year were seen to, and all the cooking was finished early, before the sun's withering incandescence made any cooking unbearable. By 9 a.m. the entire household was all washed and fed. Then the grown-ups would settle into their routines.

Ma Ji cleaned and cooked some more, and washed clothes. By noon she could sit under the Peepal tree with Dadi and the other village women who didn't have their own tree. They would gossip – as the daughter-in-law, Ma Ji was expected to contribute very little to such conversations – and nap a bit, then it was back to work as the fiery sun subsided, perhaps sewing an outfit by hand, after that cleaning lentils and rice, grinding wheat for rotis and more cooking.

Raja would go off to the village, supposedly looking for work from a local farmer, but happy enough just to sit under a tree and smoke pot. For hours every afternoon, we children escaped the heat, lightly slumbering and dreaming vividly in the sweet coolness provided by the Peepal tree's thick canopy of leaves.

I was too young for meaningful domestic work, so I was put in charge of the children all morning, a common occupation for girls my age. Far from resenting such a big responsibility, I enjoyed my job, because I got to plan adventures with

15

the local boys. And anyway, it suited my confident and rather bossy disposition. Mostly I think I liked feeling useful. I was helping to take care of our family, as Papa would have wanted me to.

Villages in the Punjab in those days were peaceful communities to grow up in, where everyone knew each other, so we were perfectly safe no matter where we roamed. The adults were all very busy, with no time to supervise us, and so my decisions were law. I would take the little girls and Prem for excursions. I'd put Jessica on my hip with Mary clutching my tunic, and off we'd go. I was the leader. Everyone listened to me, even the boys and older kids. If they didn't, I'd beat them up.

A little gang of village boys liked to follow me as I led them on adventures, which might include raiding temples and graveyards for sweets and fruit offerings. I was a faithful Christian, and I was sure there was no way I could offend any of these lesser Indian deities by taking away their offerings. I believed what my parents had taught me – that Christ was the all-mighty God and since I was his child, these heathen gods would never come after me. So I was free to rob them of their gifts and share them with my siblings and friends. This made me quite popular with the children, but not with my Dadi Ji or the rest of the family. I would bring what I stole to Mary and Jessica's doll wedding parties as a gift for the doll bride and groom. I myself never played with dolls. I preferred boys' games.

Sometimes we'd squat under the trees in the graveyard, waiting for the farmer to leave his field so we could steal some corn. Or we'd wander down to the river. We weren't supposed to go near it unsupervised, as none of us could swim, so we'd watch other people bathing and swimming. But if it was unbearably hot, I'd instruct the younger children to sit down away from the water, then fetch the cow or the water buffalo, and after splashing her in the shallows to cool her off, clamber up on her back and trail my feet in the chilly stream as the beast lumbered sedately through the water.

On the days Raja did actually get work, either cutting sugar cane, cropping wheat or picking corn, Madhu and I would bring his lunch to him. It might mean walking for an hour there and back. She would carry the food and I would carry water in a brass bucket. I enjoyed this grown-up activity, and it gave me a break from my babysitting responsibilities. We'd dawdle as long as possible on these sojourns, picking water lilies and gathering fallen mangoes.

On the way home, we might steal a cabbage, a cauliflower or some mustard greens. That would be dinner, along with rotis and dhal. I seem to remember we were always hungry and on the lookout for food, because it was too hot at midday for cooking, so we only ate two real meals a day.

Occasionally Madhu and I came upon a lost chicken. Between us we would grab it and kill it with a neat twist of its neck and throw it in the bag. I was also very good at catching pigeons, with an upside-down basket on a stick. When the pigeons pecked at the grain I'd scattered underneath, I would pull a string and capture them inside the basket. Some days I caught a dozen or more pigeons this way, which made a good meal for all of us and sometimes for Papa's visiting older sister Sharifa and her family.

Chukwal was in many ways an idyllic time for us children, but I missed not having Papa around. When he was there, the atmosphere was festive, more people came to visit, two or even three chickens were killed in his honour, and everyone had enough to eat. Sometimes his presence over-excited me and I would forget to behave like a decorous girl, which would earn me a thrashing – or worse, Papa's disapproving glare.

When he wasn't there, though, nobody in Chukwal thrashed me. My mother had made it clear to my father that neither Dadi nor Raja nor anyone else could beat her children. Only she could. Once she took a vicious stick to Raja when he kicked me. She looked quite mad, and rather scary, as if she were thinking of impaling him. I wonder if she wouldn't have hurt him seriously if he hadn't run away. But it worked, because nobody ever touched me after that. Nor did Ma Ji herself, almost ever, in Chukwal. Although she never once said that she appreciated it or complimented me, I think she was grateful that I looked after the little ones, and helped her to draw water and start the fire when I was old enough.

I used to think my mother must have been grateful for this respite from the tensions in the city of entertaining church members who often dropped by without notice. But Dadi's imperious management of her household meant Ma Ji enjoyed little in the way of leisure or pleasure. We children had no pleasure from Dadi either. I knew that Dadi did not like Ma Ji, or me or my sisters. She was cold to us, and we never felt we were anything but a burden to her. She never touched or kissed us, or told us stories or gave us treats. If there were tidbits available, if Raja brought home some bits of sugar cane, for example, Dadi would give them to Prem first, then Madhu, then to any visiting cousins, and only then, if there was any left, to us.

If I tried to challenge Dadi openly, threatening to tell my father that she was mean to us, she would just laugh and say, "Don't be ridiculous. He is my son and he loves me. That is why mothers must have sons, to love them and care for them." Of course she made sure Ma Ji heard this exchange. So I had to find more subtle ways to subvert Dadi. Once I caught and killed a chicken that I knew would be fed to her children first, and possibly all of it, with none left for us. So I distracted her with animated chatter, giving Ma Ji the time to feed the younger girls and hide some meat for me and herself. Dadi called me a "cheat" and said I was "too clever," not meant as flattery. But I didn't care. I liked these power jousts.

And although I had plenty of reason to, I didn't dislike my Dadi. She was the way she was. I worked around her, bringing her tea, doing what she told me to do – mostly – and harboured no ill will towards her, even when she treated my mother like dirt. It was how things were. But I was protectively alert for danger to my mother and my sisters.

Dadi was sly, as I mentioned. It was her nature, and she inspired the same craftiness in her daughters. When my father was around, Dadi and her daughters would make a great show of helping with the household chores. The minute he was gone, the performance ended. They made it clear that they had no intention of working to feed my mother's "stones," as Dadi frequently called us. Ma Ji must cook for her daughters, Dadi said, and once she was at it, she might as well cook for everyone.

So Ma Ji did cook for everyone, and she was an excellent cook, too, but she got no credit for it. I remember at one dinner Dadi took a bite of dhal and announced there was too much salt in it. Not once, but over and over. Ma Ji said nothing, but finally after the tenth time, she burst out, "Well, eat it or pour it on my head." Then Dadi gleefully fired back, "Your mother must have poured it on your head quite often, yet you did not learn to cook – you, with your educated mother, and still so stupid you never learned to cook."

I found the thought that dhal might at any moment be poured on someone's head very funny, and started to laugh. Ma Ji naturally took her fury out on me with a rare thrashing. I was a slow learner, for on his return I told Papa that Dadi Ji wanted to throw dhal on Ma Ji's head and got another smack for being a troublemaker.

Just as Papa knew exactly what cultural buttons to push to pique the desire of his customers for his books, Dadi Ji knew exactly what cultural buttons to press in Ma Ji to make her wild with frustration. My mother had already given birth to three daughters, and was pregnant with what she feared was a fourth. She'd suffered many miscarriages and, if what she later told me was true, several abortions. In spite of all our prayers, her whole life revolved around her womb's sadistic denial of the one and only thing she yearned for.

Dadi would sneer at Ma Ji, "You have produced all these stones. If you cared for my son, you would have strangled one or two of them as soon as you gave birth and saw they were girls. My son is going to die feeding the cows you have produced." Dadi did not hesitate to say this and many other similar insults in front of us children. If she had a neighbour or two within hearing distance, she would voice her disappointments even louder, seeking empathy from both men and women, who would all nod their heads in placid agreement with her. "I understand your suffering," they would say in comforting tones.

Every so often Dadi would pick up one of the younger girls, hold her at arm's length, drop her on the ground and say, "It would be simple enough for me to drop one or two of them into the well. After all, accidents do happen. It would give us the opportunity to breathe again."

Ma Ji cried when such exchanges took place. I could never tell if she was crying because she was afraid that harm would come to her daughters, or because she was ashamed she did not have a son, or because she was humiliated to be so pitied by the villagers.

Sometimes Ma Ji would scream at Dadi, other times weep quietly, and occasionally counter with, "It is all in the hands of God," or "If I could, do you not think I would do something about what I produce?" Or "I too am aware of the responsibility of raising girls and the family honour and what can happen to girls in this society. What can I do about what has happened to me?"

So Ma Ji toiled her days away as an unpaid servant and cook to the whole household in Chukwal, and did her best to smother her rage against Dadi and fate. After our saviour Paul was born that fall, though, my mother finally had some say in the disposition of her services. Paul was a sickly child, and there were no hospitals or even decent medical service of any kind in Chukwal. That is, they were decent enough for daughters, but not for a son.

From then on, Papa's family came to stay with us in the city. Ma Ji had status now, and the shoe was on the other foot. But instead of remembering her own misery under the heel of her mother-in-law and turning her experience into Christian love and kindness to others, my culturally conditioned mother continued to view women unblessed by sons with the same disdain Dadi Ji had shown her.

Chapter Three

Naani Ji

As a small child, I would anticipate my father's homecomings like a faithful dog, on the alert for his manly tread on the stairs and that beloved voice calling "*Ija, Ija betah*" – ("betah" in formal speech means a son, but informally it can mean 'dear' or 'darling' for either sex). I would hesitate, just a few more seconds, to taste the thrill of my nickname on his lips as he impatiently called again – "*Ija, Ija*" – and then I could resist no longer, but would fly into his arms. He would kiss my forehead a dozen times before setting me down and turning to greet Ma Ji or, one by one, to lift my sisters into his arms.

This physical intimacy in my father's homecomings ended as I neared puberty, but the effects lingered, giving me confidence in discouraging moments that Papa still loved me. But I can't ever remember receiving warmth or affection from my mother, and have spent most of my life wondering why. What was it about her situation in life that drained her of any love – or willingness to show love – for me?

Paul, her only son, was of course the sun and the moon to her. Yet she was also tender towards Mary and Pamela (Pinky). I would make excuses for her. I would tell myself that Mary had captured her heart with her fair skin and graceful figure, and Pinky because she was Ma Ji's last baby. Deep down, though, even as a child, I suspected the answer lay in her difficulties with her own mother.

I was aware that *Naani Ji* did not love or respect her daughter. When the two of them were together, I saw fear in Ma Ji's eyes. Naani's insults, the way she openly belittled my mother in front of her younger sister and us, her children – I found her cruelty distressing to witness. I have often wondered if Ma Ji envied me. Naani was fond of me and sympathetic to my periodic flashes of rebelliousness that Ma Ji found so threatening. Sometimes I think that Ma Ji beat me to get even with Naani, to punish her for a mother's mysterious, chronic rejection that had permanently disempowered and embittered her daughter.

Naani Ji's Christian name was Daisy. Daisy was a tiny woman, not quite five feet tall. She weighed only 98 pounds, as she would imperiously remind anyone who opened that conversational door. "Have some more of this delicious goat curry," someone might say, and Daisy would smugly reply that at her weight, *98 pounds*, all she needed was a single roti and a bit of dhal to satisfy her birdlike appetite. No one disputed her weight or anything else she pronounced on. Even my father ducked away from arguments with the formidable Naani Ji and did his best to please her.

Naani was born in Lahore, Pakistan in 1917, but of course it was not yet Pakistan then, it was still part of British-ruled India. Naani Ji's house was located in a quarter of Lahore known as "Christian Town," a reference to the several large churches in the area. Her redbrick house was similar to, but slightly bigger than, Dadi Ji's mudbrick house in Chukwal – two spacious rooms, plus a large courtyard in front – with the added conveniences of wood rather than cow patties to fuel the cooking fire, and a verandah that served multiple purposes for rainy days and extended-family visits.

Naani Ji was a restless soul who craved stimulation, and therefore we were treated to all kinds of excursions on our visits to Lahore. From Christian Town we could take a bus to Anarkali Bazaar. The exotic atmosphere of the Bazaar delighted us, as did the panoply of animal life in the famous Lahore Zoo, where we would sometimes spend a long day with an elaborate picnic lunch to see us through.

I looked forward to everything about these adventures, including the bus rides, where I was exposed to the Punjab's rich diversity of custom and traditions. Once a fully covered woman with two fair-skinned, dark-haired children boarded our bus. I was mesmerized by her deep blue silk burqa, whose glass-bead trims I longed to explore with my fingers, but dared not touch. Suddenly the woman lifted her veil, revealing white skin, red hair and blue eyes. I gazed at her in awe. She may have been from Afghanistan, where such colouring was not unheard of, but wherever she was from, she seemed to me a vision of feminine perfection. I believed that if I looked like this woman, my Dadi would never have considered throwing me down a well.

Yet another of Lahore's many attractions was the Lohari Gate, free but for the bus fare to get us there. On the way there Naani would regale us in a loud voice – not very subtly informing our fellow passengers that they were privileged to be fellow-travelling with an unusually well-educated woman – with tales of Lahore when it was the seat of kings who walled the city off against enemies. The huge Gate was the entrance to that ancient royal stronghold.

We'd find a continually shifting profusion of fascinating entertainment milling around the Gate: snake charmers, men striding about on tall stilts, a drama group enacting a morality play. We listened to buskers singing film songs. My curiosity was also aroused by a group of old men sitting under a tree and drinking tea. At intervals, one or another of them would stand and declaim loudly to the others, who would nod and sometimes throw their arms up in the air with flattering shouts of "whaaa" to the speaker. Naani explained that they were poets reading their works to each other. But women would be reprimanded if they stayed to listen, so to my regret, for I found them very interesting, I was hustled away before I had my fill of this amusement.

We could not linger at any other single attraction for long, anyway. Impatient Naani couldn't sit still for more than a few minutes. She always had to be going somewhere or doing something, and I was pulled along in her wake.

During these outings Naani passed along family lore. It was through Naani Ji's cumulative narratives about her parents and her childhood that I came to understand the forces that had shaped her formidable will and independent spirit. Although both my grandmothers dominated their households, and both were very proud of their high social status, they drew their respective feelings of superiority from very different wells. Dadi's positive self-image was grounded in cultural tradition, and wholly connected to her status as the mother of many sons. Naani Ji's inflated self-esteem sprang partly from inherited social caste, but to a far greater extent from a privileged association with her parents' British employers and patrons, the ultimate status symbol for Indians of her class during the Raj.

On the bus, bumping along to the zoo or the bazaar or the Gate, Naani would talk about her father, who had been a cook for a high-ranking British army officer. Employment of any kind under the colonial service, I came to understand, provided a living wage and modest security. But more important, it was valuable social capital in an era and place where the British held the keys to poor Indians' advancement.

Naani Ji also took pride in the fact that her parents were not Punjabi, but Bengali Muslims. In the Punjab both men and women wore the *shalwar kameez* – pajama-like trousers, narrow-bottomed for men, wide for women – and long tunic. Not Naani Ji. She wore a sari all her life. But in the Bengali tradition she did not cover her head, a sign of her advanced education and social finesse. Moreover, unlike Punjabi women, she and her mother wore *brassieres*! As Naani would disdainfully comment over and over again, "Look at these frumpy Punjabi women walking around in their tents, like cows with their flopping breasts. They have no idea of how unsightly they are. They have no class at all."

Christianity, or rather Catholicism, was not new to India. Catholics have lived in India for almost 2000 years, and there are well over twenty million of them there today. But Protestant Christianity was a spinoff of the Raj. Like hundreds of thousands of other Indians, Naani's parents were converted to Christianity during Britain's imperial heyday in the nineteenth century, when waves of Protestant missionaries descended on Britain's 'jewel in the crown' to save as many pagans as they could.

Indians converted to the various branches of evangelical Christianity for all kinds of reasons, including those of belief, I suppose. Naani Ji's family chose to become Baptists. Not for doctrinal reasons, but because her father's employer made it clear he would trust his cook more as a Christian, and the employer happened to be a Baptist. Her father reasoned that Christianity was close enough to Islam that a stubborn fidelity to the latter wasn't worth risking his job over.

It was imperative to Naani Ji that she clarify that last point to all and sundry. It was well understood that most Indians who converted to Christianity – there were perhaps a half million in the Punjab – were motivated by poverty and the desire to escape the grinding rigours of the caste system. Christianity held out to Untouchables and those of other low castes seductive promises of social equality and eternity in Heaven, plus the added enticements of powdered milk, wool blankets and jobs. Conversion was regarded as a sign of good faith and often a qualification for entry into the civil service. So in Naani Ji's eyes, most converts were nobodies, losers, people without status. Not at all like her brilliant father, whose achievements, and later hers, were a product of talent, and whose Christian status was incidental to their success in life.

When Indians converted to Christianity, they chose – or had chosen for them – new first and last names, often taken from the Bible, to broadcast their religious transformation. At the suggestion of his employer, my great-grandfather's last name was changed from Allam to Masih (short for *masiha*, which translates as saviour, meaning Christ). His wife Zarina became Martha Masih. But he balked at changing his first name. His father had chosen Zahoor for him, and Zahoor it remained.

Zahoor was not just any old cook, according to Naani Ji, but a "fantastic" cook, who began his career at the age of twenty. Zahoor had been quick to learn English ways and expectations, and soon ingratiated himself with his boss. Zahoor's wife Zarina/Martha, my *bardi* Naani – my great-grandmother, but literally "older grandmother" – became the army couple's housekeeper. Martha hired and fired the cleaning help, oversaw the laundry and attended to the food marketing. When Zahoor travelled with his boss, Martha cooked for the household. When Zahoor was home and the couple entertained, Martha set the table and greeted the guests.

Because it was not seemly for British women to go about alone in public, and since the husband was frequently away on army business, my bardi Naani was also a kind of lady's companion to the wife, Priscilla, accompanying her on visits to friends and on shopping jaunts, and joining her in the evenings as a chaperone when Priscilla's Muslim tutor came to give her lessons in Urdu.

The employers had no children of their own, so when Naani Ji was born and Martha brought her along to work, she became Priscilla's special pet. It was Priscilla who named Naani Ji Daisy. Priscilla had been a teacher in England before marrying, and she instinctively adopted a mentorship role with her brown-skinned wards.

During the long hot Punjabi days, Priscilla taught Martha how to sew and crochet with silk thread, embroidering sheets and creating beautiful brassieres, tablecloths and handkerchiefs. She taught her English manners and etiquette. She schooled her in the English style of household management, and encouraged Martha to learn how to read and write Urdu during her own evening lessons.

As for Daisy, she learned to speak, read and write good English under Priscilla's tutelage, in turn often serving as the white woman's interpreter. So it happened that Daisy completed eighth grade at a church school in a time and place where girls were not generally permitted to attend school at all, and only wealthy girls learned to read and write with private tutors in their homes.

Daisy emerged from this unusual childhood environment as a cultural hybrid. Superficially she conformed to the same expectations of submission and obedience as all other Indian girls, but internally she was a free spirit: self-assured, confidently opinionated as only the educated can be, and independent in her outlook on life.

Finding a husband was not easy for such a headstrong girl. Still not betrothed at seventeen, alarmingly late for her generation, in spite of a large dowry on offer, she had become a worry to her parents, and doubtless something of an embarrassment. Daisy took matters into her own hands. Her father Zahoor had been assigned to teach future army chefs how to cook. One of them, John Lal, also a convert to Christianity, had taken Daisy's fancy. Family legend has it that she boldly approached him and asked for his hand in marriage. Whoever approached whom, they were soon united in matrimony and embarked on their peripatetic life with the army.

In short order Daisy and John had two daughters, Victoria, my mother, and Venus. Life was good. Then, travelling with the British army in Africa, John fell ill and died, leaving 26-year old Daisy, now a widow with two young children, virtually alone in the world. Daisy's parents had retired to spend their old age with relatives in the land of their ancestors, but Martha had died when Daisy's older child, Victoria, my mother, was only six years old. Zahoor, fearing for his daughter's safety without a male protector, urged her to come live with him amongst his kinsmen, but Daisy stubbornly refused, so there was little he could do for her, and he returned in disappointment to East Bengal.

Daisy put her embroidery and seamstress skills to entrepreneurial purpose, developing a good clientele amongst the British officers' wives and local moneyed families. She also taught Sunday school to women and girls in the Baptist church. In time the missionaries opened a small school for girls in Lahore, installing Daisy as one of its first teachers. In the following years she was moved around from school to school according to the missionaries' dictates.

Here my Naani Ji's history becomes somewhat murky, especially regarding the birth of her next two children, a son and a daughter, five years into her widowhood. My Uncle Matthew and Aunt Esther look nothing like their older sisters, my mother and Aunt Venus. Matthew and Esther are much lighter-skinned, with barely a hint of brown in their complexion.

My mother, when questioned on the matter, was evasive, insisting Naani had remarried twice more. But my father's version was that the father of the children must have been a British missionary or army officer. I know my mother was greatly embarrassed by her mother's social non-conformity, because I could see the mortification in her eyes whenever my father's family indulged their sadistic delight in exploiting Daisy's questionable past for ammunition – they sometimes called her a "whore" when tempers flared – in their constant bickering. To this day, I don't know who fathered those children, but I never did find the courage to ask Naani for an explanation.

When I used to visit her, she was remarried to a fine man, Peter Emmanuel, whom we called *Nana Ji*. They had a rather unorthodox arrangement, which I was too obtuse to notice at the time, in that they lived in separate houses. It was Naani's idea. She did not want to have her teenage daughters living with a man who was biologically unrelated to them. So Naani Ji left them in the care of their older brother while she and Peter would spend the night at Peter's house, then arrive at Naani Ji's house early in the morning and spend the day there, except when my father was around. Then Naani Ji stayed in her own home and Peter came and went.

Naani Ji joined the Seventh Day Adventist Church when my mother was about thirteen years old. The Adventists were new to the area and therefore unaware

26

of her personal history. She saw in the SDA Church an opportunity for a fresh start, a clean break from the ugly rumours circulating around the mystery of her pale-skinned children's paternity.

The Adventists had opened a school in a North Punjab village near Jullandhar, and Naani was transferred there to teach. She sent my mother and her younger sister Venus to an Adventist boarding school, one that my father had previously attended. It was there, visiting his younger brother, my Chacha Sadiq, that Papa first crossed paths with my mother when she was seventeen. He saw and heard her singing in the Church choir. He was smitten.

My mother was poor and my father was poorer. She brought no dowry with her. But even though the marriage was essentially arranged – my father made inquiries about a possible betrothal after that first encounter – they fell in love with each other after the wedding. Until they had children, they enjoyed their life together. Both had beautiful voices and a passion for singing, which I inherited, and after Ma Ji learned to play the harmonium and Papa the tabala, they became minor celebrities on the Adventist circuit in India.

I only know about the happy part of their life from stories, of course. I dearly wish I could have shared in the glory of their salad days. The thought of my mother and father singing in partnership, feeling joy in each other's company, smiling, – perhaps laughing! – and gazing at each other with affection and trust… I can't put such scenes together with the Ma Ji I knew: a grim, sharp-eyed, joyless overseer of our household, whose only ambition seemed to lie in scaling new heights of personal and domestic hygiene.

I never ever remember my mother in a dirty sari. Her face was always spotless, soft and shiny from the white petroleum jelly she applied to her skin (and ours) every day of her life. It was as though she were lavishing on her appearance the tenderness and protectiveness she couldn't give to her children. For she had no instinct or appetite for intimacy, apart from the calculated affection she lavished on my brother, who would be her surety for a secure old age.

To be fair, she had little time for anything besides the endless cycle of tasks involved in running a large household on a limited budget, a household moreover in which the burden of both arranged and spontaneous hospitality to extended family and Church colleagues fell entirely into her busy hands. My intuition is that because she was not naturally gregarious, she disliked and resented the continuous social flow in which my expansive father delighted. But although she often grumbled before us children, when my father was present I never heard a word of complaint from her lips on that or any other perceived hardship attached to her rigidly defined role as a woman of that time and place.

Much of Ma Ji's considerable energy flowed into the endless struggle against dirt. Every morning she scoured our home, whether it was a modern flat in

Delhi, Papa's village house, or a shack in the back of beyond. She scrubbed us children to such shining outward perfection that no visitor could ever find fault and shame her before other women. She was also a superb cook who could somehow find a way to make two eggs and a bit of rice or lentils feed seven children. To the people whose good opinion determined her social status, she was a virtuous woman, wife and mother. And that, in a nutshell, was what mattered to her.

Perhaps, even though I was only a girl, my mother had warm feelings for me as a baby. I was after all her first, and every first child is special to a mother. I'd like to think so. But I have no memory of it.

Like Dadi Ji, Naani Ji had a tree in her courtyard. Naani's produced a tropical fruit called *Jamun*, and in the summers this massive tree was loaded with juicy, sweet-sour berries that turned our tongues purple. I loved that tree and lived in it throughout our visits to Lahore, where I had no cousins or neighbourhood children to play with. There were many children about, but Naani said they were not fit to socialize with, often referring to them as *janglees*, complete hicks.

At nine years old I was as agile and sure-footed as a monkey, but my mother fretted about my passion for tree-climbing, constantly nagging me about its dangers, frequently calling up to protest that I had climbed too high and would surely come to grief in a fall. But Naani, sitting under the tree and nimbly plying her crochet hook, would look up at her, and comment with calm sarcasm, "The only reason the child may fall out of the tree is because you are frightening her with your screaming," or "In order to prove you right, the child will have to fall out of the tree."

Naani Ji seemed to delight in undermining my mother's authority. It seemed to me she disapproved of my mother in a wholesale way, as her criticisms were so eclectic: My mother lacked motivation, she had poor parenting skills, she showed insufficient appreciation of her husband. There seemed no end to Naani Ji's complaints about Ma Ji.

In particular, Naani felt my mother imposed too much responsibility on me, that she was robbing me of my childhood. If Ma Ji told me to get down from the courtyard wall and play with my sisters, Naani would retort, "Why must Irene play with them when they are old enough to amuse themselves?"

I think she was especially irritated by the fact that my mother did not allow me to make any choices for myself. Ma Ji believed allowing children any freedom inevitably led to their getting into trouble. But Naani was of the opinion that making choices was the way children learn right from wrong. When my mother told me to do one thing and Naani gave me tacit permission not to obey her, I felt torn. At such times Ma Ji would never argue with her mother, but later perhaps, while combing my long hair, she would lash out and smack my head

28

for no reason, at which point Naani would step in and demand that one of my aunts braid my hair.

Naani Ji was unpredictable, and at times frightening in her volatility. In the afternoons an ice cream man would come around, with a cycle pulling what looked like a freezer on wheels. The first time I saw him, Naani Ji bought us ice cream. The next day, when the peddler came around, I innocently asked Naani Ji to buy me another ice cream. Out of the blue she smacked me across the face saying, "Don't ever ask for anything from anybody as long as you live, especially food. If you can't earn it, then better to die of hunger." I was shocked because she almost never hit me.

But Naani redeemed herself. Without spelling it out, she somehow gave me to understand that if I picked the ripe Jamuun berries and managed to sell them, this was money that belonged to me, and I could use it for ice cream. And so I did. I sold the berries to church people and relatives, the neighbours not being worthy customers in Naani's eyes, and savoured the joy of self-sufficiency, as sweet and refreshing to my spirit as the taste of the ice cream on my tongue.

This ambivalence in Naani – her drive to make us psychologically independent warring with her wish to show her love and protectiveness – played out in other food-related ways. She had rigid meal rules, and would never back down on them. If I arrived late for dinner from my playing, I would get no food that evening, even when, or perhaps because, my mother pleaded on my behalf. So I would go to bed hungry, but was still included in Naani's story-telling ritual. If I said I could not pay attention to the stories because I was so hungry, she would say, "Why can't you hear the stories just because you are hungry? Did your hunger block your ears?"

I think Naani was perfectly aware that one of my aunts was sneaking food to me during the night, but she never let on that she knew. In fact I think Naani knew everything that was going on everywhere, under her roof and under the roofs of her neighbours, who visited her, even though she did not deign to visit them back. Aunt Venus used to say, "Naani even knows how many flies are buzzing in the house." Everyone feared her, including me.

But my fear of Naani Ji paled beside my respect for her and my gratitude for the work ethic and yearning for an education and the self-respect it represented that she instilled in me. Both were to stand me in good stead later on in troubled times. My feelings for Dadi Ji and Naani Ji were polar opposites. I felt alienated from Dadi Ji, who never showed in word or deed that I meant anything to her, other than that my sex made me a burden to my family. But I loved Naani Ji who, in her disinterested and unsentimental way, treated me as a human being with value apart from my sex. The more I reflect on my Naani Ji, the more I have come to believe that she is the wind beneath the wings it took me so many years to grow.

Chapter Four

School Days

By the middle of the twentieth century, the Seventh Day Adventists were operating one of the largest Protestant school systems in the world. In 1961 Adventist missionaries opened a new English-language middle school in Harpur, a small village in the province of Uttar Pradesh. At the time we were living quite far away, in Amritsar, a city in the Punjab. We had spent the previous year in Simla. That was where it came to the missionaries' attention that we had never been to school. One day that spring, without preamble, Papa informed us that six-year old Jessica, eight-year old Mary and I, now ten, were being sent to the Harpur school to be educated, which also meant we would board there for ten months a year.

None of us had ever yet attended any school, let alone a boarding school. Nor did any of us speak English, which was to be the only language of instruction there. So this was earth-shattering news. Ma Ji had not been prepared for the bombshell either, and was visibly agitated by Papa's detailed instructions about the bedding and clothes and shoes we would need.

Taking her cue from our mother, Jessica began sobbing in the corner. I asked why she was crying and she said in Urdu, the language of our home, "Ma Ji does not speak English either. She should go to boarding school with us as well."

These were exciting times in India. In January of 1961, five months before my father's dramatic announcement, Jawaharlal Nehru, the newly independent India's first Prime Minister, had welcomed Queen Elizabeth and Prince Philip to India, and Prime Minister Nehru and his daughter had visited President Kennedy in Washington. My father and his colleagues in the missionary movement were deeply stirred by this historical watershed.

Nehru was a passionate advocate of education for India's children and youth. Encouraged by his vision to expand their already considerable ambitions – for the SDA movement was imbued with belief in education as a powerful force for human advancement – the missionaries set about building and staffing world-class English-language schools for the development of national and even global Indian leadership. We had to be very silent when our father was listening to Nehru's ardent radio exhortations on the education of India's youth. Papa was excited to be at the heart of such an important national imperative, and he communicated that excitement to me. But it never occurred to me that the Prime Minister's speeches would lead to a brand-new and important phase of my life, and years of separation from my family.

We three girls would be part of the first cohort attending the Harpur school. We were to make the 250-mile train trip to Delhi with Papa and other area Adventist families, a two-day journey with countless stops along the way, and there we would join other entering students for the last seventy miles to Harpur.

I was thrilled about the coming adventure, but a little nervous too, because I hadn't the vaguest idea of what going to school would entail. While the SDA Church emphasized education for children of both sexes, Papa's mission work had never allowed us to stay in any city long enough to register for school. Usually the house rented for us by the Church wasn't within walking distance to any school anyway. Some families in our neighbourhood collectively rented a rickshaw for six or seven children, but my parents couldn't afford even that inexpensive service.

Our mother was furious. I didn't know it then, but she was expecting her seventh child and felt chronically ill. She pleaded for a local school, so I would still be available to help her at home. Papa refused. The Harpur school had been established as a model institution because the politicians wanted well-run schools, but they had no experience in running them. They didn't want more Catholic schools. The SDA emphasis on health and vegetarian eating appealed to them, and so did the SDA repudiation of the caste system, which Prime Minister Nehru was keen to abolish. The missionaries were hoping that they would be asked to develop more such schools, which in turn would lead to more conversions. Meanwhile the missionaries needed warm bodies to fill the classrooms at Harpur, and we had been recruited for that purpose.

Frustrated at her impotence, Ma Ji redirected onto me her anger at Papa for putting the missionaries' needs above hers. She pulled my hair, slapped my face and scolded me. "There's lots of time for you to go to school. I need you here to help me. You are the most selfish child ever born, only thinking of yourself."

My exhilaration was only temporarily dampened by my mother's displays of temper. I was distracted by the chaos of the preparations and the purchase of new sandals and clothes and sheets. The pleasure I felt in packing our travel boxes made me realize how happy I was to be getting away from my mother.

Then too, I would finally be free of the exasperating caste system, which in those days was still deeply entrenched in our Hindu-dominated neighbourhood. I would no longer be subjected to the local children taunting me. "You are not allowed to play with us, you low caste, meat-eating Untouchable." In the Harpur school everyone would be Christian. We would all be the same. We would all belong together.

At that time I had no idea Christianity had different denominations. The missionaries had taught us about the Jews and why we did not like them, and the Hindus who worshipped 'graven images,' which was a sin, and the Muslims who were descended from Ishmael, an 'illegitimate' child whom God had sent into the desert as an indication of His disfavour. I had learned that we, the Adventists, were the chosen ones and the blessed ones, and now I was on my way to the blessings I was entitled to. There would be no class or caste system at Harpur. Or so I believed.

The train journey from Amritsar to Delhi was one long party for the numerous Adventist boys and girls en route to Harpur. We shared our excited visions of life to come at school, while our parents socialized and swapped food and stories. In Delhi, tributaries of other families swelled our Adventist pool, laden with extra food for those of us from the Punjab. It was all very festive.

To reach the school from the Harpur train station, we had to go by rickshaw along unpaved roads bordered by tall, impenetrable stands of sugar cane. It was rather eerie, like travelling through an endless green tunnel. Finally Papa cheerfully announced, "Well, there it is. We made it." Jessica, snuggled up beside me, woke from her doze with a start, sobbing, "I don't want to go to boarding school," rather spoiling Papa's triumph in the long-anticipated moment.

I remember the campus as a very welcoming place, a group of whitewashed buildings connected to each other by paved pathways curving through manicured lawns bordered with flowerbeds. We were met by Miss Rawat, the girls' Matron, a slim, erect woman with short, neatly bobbed hair, wearing a colourful starched sari with matching shoes. Smiling warmly, she stepped forward to greet Papa and ask why Jessica was crying. But she already knew. Jessica was the youngest child in the school. Miss Rawat took Jessica's hand and told her that she too had been very lonely when she first arrived at the school a few months before, but now she was happy, and especially now because she had been waiting for Jessica to arrive, and she knew they would be great friends. And they were. For the next four years, Miss Rawat was Jessica's surrogate mother, and they remained friends for life.

Papa had to return to Delhi that very night, so once we had been introduced to Miss Rawat, he left in the rickshaw that had brought us to school. Jessica clung to Miss Rawat's hand and Mary and I held on to each other, not sure what was to come next.

We were led to the girls' quarters, which were surrounded with eight-foot walls, topped by pointed glass pieces sticking out of the cement, sparkling like diamonds in the sun. A single large gate was the only way in and out of our compound.

After we had cleaned ourselves up, all fifteen of us were told to stand is a straight line. Miss Rawat said in Hindi that we were going to march in single file to the cafeteria. After dinner we would go to the chapel and attend sunset worship. We would then return to the girls' dorm, when she would explain the dorm rules, and then read us a story before we went to sleep.

We set off behind Miss Rawat and made our way through the beautiful campus. The path's flowering borders backed by papaya trees made me feel like some dignitary on a tour. At the cafeteria we joined a row of about forty-five boys.

On the steps to the main building stood Pastor Christo, the school principal, a dark-skinned muscular man in his late thirties, not very tall, but as handsome as a film star. I was not surprised to learn later that his parents were from Bengal. Next to him stood Mrs. Christo, whose ancestry was not so easily read. She was fair-skinned and dressed like the white missionary women, but there was something oriental in her looks as well. They made a striking couple.

Both Pastor and Mrs. Christo smiled warmly at us. Then Pastor Christo threw his arms open and in a deep booming voice, said, in English, "Welcome children, we are very happy to have you with us." Miss Rawat interpreted what he said for those of us who did not speak English. Pastor Christo continued, looking directly into my eyes, "We see that we have some new family members." As Miss Rawat translated these words, I gazed back at this charismatic man in wonderment. Did my sisters and I belong to Pastor and Mrs Christo now?

Then Mrs. Christo started to speak in English as well. She had the most melodious voice I have ever known in a woman. She was saying that in Harpur Elementary School we would have to learn to eat with a spoon and a fork, and there would be knives on the table as well, but they were only to be used for applying butter to bread. Not rotis. Homemade brown bread.

The dining room was set up with five long tables. Each chair had a dinner setting before it. There was a plate, cloth napkin and, as promised by Mrs. Christo, a spoon, fork and butter knife. The girls and boys sat separately.

Pastor Christo introduced the head cook, Nazir, whom we were to call Mister Nazir. He wore a tall white hat. We learned that he had prepared meals for some very important people around the country and now he was going to cook for us. Mister Nazir had very red lips, a sign that he was in the habit of chewing *paan*, a green leaf filled with sweets and sometimes tobacco, usually served at the end of an Indian meal. Adventists disapprove of paan chewing, and so Mister Nazir became a curiosity to me.

There were two other cafeteria staff, who wheeled in loaded food carts. They stood behind us, lifted our plates, put the food on it and then set it in front of us. We were told to wait until everyone in the room had their filled plate. Then Mrs. Christo picked up a tablespoon and a fork, and demonstrated how we were to shovel rice onto the spoon.

The vegetarian meal was composed of boiled rice with what looked like stew rather than curry, and seemed to be a mess of carrots, potatoes and wheat gluten, meant as a substitute for meat. It was vile.

Food is a serious issue in the Seventh Day Adventist Church. At the heart of the movement are the teachings and works of the American prophet, Mrs. Ellen White. Her messages on health reform, which the Church teaches are direct injunctions from God, were received by Mrs. White in a forty-five minute vision on June 5, 1863, in Otsego, Michigan.

Ellen White was thirty-six years old and, prior to her vision, had been a heavy meat eater, as well as rather sickly. Her epiphany linked physical well-being to sacred duty and spiritual health. She located the devil in tobacco, alcohol, sugar and meat, prescribing natural remedies to heal diseases. On Christmas day, 1865, Mrs. White received a second health vision, guiding her to the establishment of a health reform and research institute – Loma Linda Institute in California – that would care for the sick and teach basic principles of healthful living and preventive medicine.

The American and Canadian missionaries were all strict vegetarians, but the native converts in the Church, specifically those of Muslim ancestry, like ours, found it difficult to give up meat, although we never ate pork or any other animal proscribed in the dietary laws of the Bible. During one of Papa's administrative stints in Delhi, when we lived on the church campus, we had to be very careful about food disposal, because the missionaries would go through the garbage of the native staff checking for meat bones. So when we ate chicken or goat, my mother would wash and dry the bones and we would bring them with us on a walk so we could dispose of them far from the house. Some natives went temporarily vegetarian to please their superiors, and they'd snoop on us too.

Apparently Mrs. White did not like spice either and believed that it made people hot-tempered, so our dinner was bland as well as awful-tasting. The gluten in the stew stuck to my teeth, so I only ate the rice and gravy. But for dessert we were given the novelty of thick custard with embedded bananas. It was the most delicious thing I had ever eaten and I asked for more, but was crisply admonished that to ask for seconds was bad manners, and I was never to do so again.

Meals became a challenge. Every three months parents were allowed to come and visit their children, and every three months a few more children went home because they were losing too much weight, but the missionaries kept finding other children who needed education more than proper nourishment.

Breakfasts were better, consisting of homemade brown bread, a fried or boiled egg and a glass of milk made of powder, which smelled like it had been packed next to gas drums. One day Mrs. Christo announced with excitement the addition of something new that very few children around the world had ever eaten. Nazir came out with "Old Cheddar cheese," horrible stuff that made many of the kids throw up, but they were forced to eat it anyway. I told my sisters to nibble a bit, then I took the rest and stuck it to the bottom of the table. A couple of weeks later I got caught when other children started to do the same.

Learning to speak English was even more of a challenge. Harpur was a pilot project, the focus of a great deal of political and media interest, and the school administrators and staff felt pressured to succeed. Pastor Christo explained to us through Miss Rawat why this was a very special school, why everyone wanted to establish similar schools all over India, and how lucky we were to have been chosen as a role model. We had to learn our manners, but most important, we had to learn to speak in English.

In that inaugural year there were nearly 150 students, which included day school junior kindergarten and senior kindergarten children of local merchants and government employee who wanted their children to learn English. At the age of eleven, I was put into kindergarten, where some of the five year-old children already knew their alphabets and could speak English. Instead of assigning my ignorance to my lack of previous schooling, I inferred that I was stupid, an assumption no teacher ever disabused me of.

I was moved from class to class and grade level to grade level. These arbitrary transfers had less connection to my knowledge than to my increasing height. My relatively gigantic presence amongst small children was an embarrassment to the school. Predictably, in the age-appropriate classes I was at sea most of the time.

In retrospect, I think the main reason why I had so much difficulty learning anything was that my classroom time was constantly disrupted by other duties. My naïve expectation that school would be a respite from childcare and domestic chores was immediately dashed when I arrived at Harpur. In theory I was there to learn, but in reality, because of my age, size and social class, I was less a student than a nanny for the younger children.

As the oldest in my dorm, it was my responsibility every morning to help the younger children wash, dress, make their beds, and present themselves neatly and on time for breakfast. Evenings I saw to their preparation for bed and clothing for the next day. If a child wet her bed, I changed the bedding and aired out the mattress.

In class, where there was only one teacher for thirty children, I helped with discipline, but the greatest disruption to my learning time was continual bathroom escort duty. The washrooms were some distance from the classrooms. Because of the ubiquitous snakes and scorpions, children were not permitted to go to the toilet unaccompanied. I enjoyed helping the teachers out, because they were very grateful, and often complimented me on my usefulness. Since "Take this one to the bathroom, won't you, Irene? Oh, there's a good girl" was about the only kind of positive recognition I ever got at school, I was happy to oblige them. But the constant interruptions played havoc with my acquisition of knowledge. .

When I had learned my alphabet, I was moved up to grade one. The teacher, Mrs. Popkiss, and her husband were Anglo-Indians. She fortunately spoke both English and Hindi, as the local children in her class only spoke Hindi. But we learned to sing a lot of English songs. Some of those songs are still my favourites: *This little light of mine, I'm going to let it shine; I am Jesus, little lamp, little lamp;* and *Wide as the ocean, high as the heavens above.*

Then there were the activity songs, and I loved them too: *Ring around the rosy, pocketful of posies; Ol' Man River, Dat Ol' Man River; Brown girl in the rain;* and *One little, two little, three little Indians.* They were mostly racist songs, including some of the soulful Negro spirituals Pastor Christo used to belt out.

Speaking English endowed a student with enormous social capital. I had supposedly left them behind, but caste and class were in fact pervasive at the Harpur school. While the missionaries instructed new converts that the caste system did not apply to them as Christians, in practice the natives found it difficult to let it go and it showed up in various ways, as in language. Speaking English gave you status; reading and writing gave you more.

Some of the native teachers had chosen Christianity for opportunistic reasons. They had not taken on Christian names, a telling sign of their superficial attachment to their new religion. So at Harpur, for example, I was to find amongst the staff a Mr. Singh, Mr. Khan, Mr. Patel and Mr. Ramsapur, who remained very proud of their caste. These teachers applied the same hierarchal values to the children in their care.

Children from well-off families had better clothes and received regular pocket money and food packages from home. The rest of us had to beg for toothpaste and soap – or steal some – within weeks of our arrival. If your father was an educated man and had an important job assigned by the missionaries, then your family was considered higher class. If a mother was educated and had taught her daughter social skills, how to dress and do her hair and make a fuss about dirt on her toes, she was perceived as better then the rest of us. And if you had already been in school before, and arrived at Harpur able to read and write in English, and were the issue of parents who promoted education, then you were a kind of institutional Brahmin, in a class of your own.

Ranking was done by the teachers. According to their perceived status, the teachers treated certain parents with respect and their children with consideration, and other parents and children on a diminishing scale of kindness and deference,.

And then there were the children of the school's "Untouchables." That was the category my sisters and I fell into. Uneducated themselves, my parents were deemed to be social climbers, and were expected to be grateful that their children had been accepted into this school community. These parents told the teachers to use any means of discipline necessary to educate their offspring. These parents did not visit often and when they did, they brought food packages for the teacher rather than for their children.

We also fell into the despised category of families overrun with daughters. In February of that year, Miss Rawat told us that our sister Pamela had been born. Another girl! We all cried, Mary, Jessica and I. We were too sad to go to dinner. Sympathetic Miss Rawat sent food to the dorm, and the three of us huddled together, eating like mourners after a funeral.

Chapter Five

Loss of innocence

Remembering the ill will with which she had seen me off to boarding school, I wasn't sure what kind of welcome I should expect from my mother when my sisters and I returned home for summer holidays after our first year away. I was poised for resentment, and was therefore surprised when Ma Ji welcomed me with unusual warmth. It made sense when I discovered she was feeling physically fragile, recovering from a coat-hanger abortion (not her first) she'd undergone two weeks earlier. My presence meant more help with child care and hospitality obligations. The newest baby, Pamela, born in 1962, was now six months old. She was to be my parents' seventh and last child. Heather had been born in 1960. Paul, born in 1958, sandwiched between Dorothy, 1956 and Heather, 1960, was to be their only son.

Our house was in a state of social bustle that summer, dominated by frequent meetings of various relatives, chaired by my father, concerning a cousin's broken engagement. Suspicions were raised about both parties, including dark mutterings about the jilted fiancée's chastity. A few lengthy discussions into the night would seem to consolidate a strategic consensus. Then, a week later, the other side of the dispute would show up, and it would begin again. Ma Ji and I were expected to cook for everyone and serve endless cups of tea, but she was only up to making the main curry. After that, she went to bed for most of the day, while Mary and I did the rest.

I didn't mind the extra work. I was perfectly competent to do it, and I felt I was helping Papa create an optimal environment for the exercise of his critical role in a tense family situation.

What did trouble me was my mother's health. Not her physical state. She was weak, but she wasn't suffering from any apparent complications. With two births a year apart, I was far more watchful of her mental condition. Ever since I could remember, my mother's existence had revolved around her reproductive system. She was constantly either pregnant, recouping her strength after a birth, nursing an infant or recovering from abortions. The mental strain of waiting for a son had taken a heavy toll on her. Paul's birth had been an incalculable source of relief and validation. If only they had been satisfied with a single son and not kept hoping for more, I think she might have arrived at a certain serenity and inner contentment.

But after Paul, it was back to the old story of anguished waiting and dashed desires. I hoped Pamela would be the last. The circumstances surrounding Heather's birth had been such a nightmare, it was a miracle she had survived. In fact, it was something of a miracle that our family was still intact and functioning normally after the terrible Simla winter of my ninth year, and Heather's first months, of life.

Simla 1960 -1961

In the spring of 1960 Papa was transferred to Kotgarh, a small village about eight kilometers from the city of Shimla – we called it Simla because that is what the British called it – in the foothills of the Himalayan mountains. Because of its great natural beauty and temperate climate, Simla became the summer capital for the British during the Raj, a welcome respite from southern and central India's intense heat.

The house rented for our family at Kotgarh was built into a hillside near a clear blue stream. Very picturesque through the lens of a camera. But for us it was a frightening place to live. In those days the only means of transporting belongings and provisions was by mule. We had no near neighbours, and the surrounding hills were alive with the throaty mutterings of wild animals. We lived like primitives. Water had to be drawn and carried from the stream and wood chopped for the stove. Our only lighting was provided by oil lamps.

Worship took place at a small chapel in the home of a well-off church member, who owned a number of orchards. To get to the chapel we had to walk about an hour and a half through mountainous terrain. During the eight months we were there, Ma Ji only made it to worship services a few times.

I didn't know it at the time – these matters were never discussed with children – but Ma Ji was pregnant again. As she approached term, she became quite ill, but there were no adequate medical facilities near us. So our family was moved to Simla, where there was a SDA hospital. Ma Ji was so weak she had to be transported down the mountain in a chair borne on the shoulders of four men. She was in the hospital for a few weeks, then came home to await labour.

The SDA Church had bought a large building that had been a summer resort for British families of the colonial service. Its grand staircases, walnut floors and sideboards were evidence of past glory. The Church had divided the building up into small apartments to house people who worked at the hospital, and now several families lived there, including Mr. Devdass, my future math teacher at Harpur, at the time the hospital bookkeeper.

The apartment assigned to our family was at the front of the building. Opening the door to our apartment, you would be in the area where hotel guests had once stowed their winter coats and boots. In the larger of our two living rooms a big bay window offered a beautiful view of the mountains across the valley. In the room were two wide beds. On one, our parents slept with one or two of the younger children, Paul and Dorothy, and in the other I slept with Mary and Jessica, and occasionally Dorothy. A big iron stove dominated one side of this room. On a metal mesh in the stove's belly we would put coal, and under that, wood. The burning wood would light the coal and warm the room. At the far end of our apartment was a room about six feet wide and twenty-five feet long, with a kitchen on one side, and storage and a toilet on the other.

Heather was born in November, and Papa was home with us for two months. But in January he was called out to Jullandhar to deal with some administrative problem at a new SDA hospital there. Once in that lucrative area for book sales, he decided to tack on six selling weeks. There was no way for him to know that a complete mental breakdown of his wife had been in steady progress from the day he left, and that during a good part of his absence, his nine-year old daughter was running his household with no food, money or fuel.

Actually, there was plenty of food – the usual staples of rice, legumes, oil, spices, salt and other dry goods – sealed into mice-proof locked drums, which I couldn't open. And there was money too, if I had known where it was hidden. I couldn't find out, because Ma Ji was disappearing into something like a catatonic state, nursing Baby, as Heather was known for the first months before she was officially named, but otherwise incommunicative, ignoring the rest of us, spending much of the day in bed, sleeping or staring at the walls. Without any comprehension of why she was withdrawing from us, I assumed more and more responsibility for all the children's needs.

I remember the moment when I understood something was seriously wrong. We had run out of food several days previously. We had also run out of wood, because I had burnt too much trying to get our few remaining coals to light.

At one point, through my mismanagement of the stove, the rooms filled with smoke, but the windows were sealed. Ma Ji, usually very annoyed with my incompetence, said nothing. She just sat up against the headboard of her bed and gazed out the window.

We were hungry. There was a family from southern India, the Hevaleys, living in a beautiful apartment on the floor above ours. Both the husband and wife were nurses, and they had two little daughters. They would bring their little girls to a woman near the hospital who looked after them all day, and then all come home together. I had often peeked into their apartment as they came and went, and I remembered they kept fruit in a bowl on the dining table. I climbed up to their back balcony, easily reached because our building, like many others in Simla, backed into a hill, then broke their kitchen window and entered. Once I was inside, I looked around for other food besides the fruit to put into a plastic shopping bag I'd brought with me. I found cooked rice in a pot on the stove, dumped all the rice into the bag, and climbed back out the window.

Unfortunately, monkeys got in after I left, and destroyed the Hevaleys' apartment. If I had not gone back again, they would have believed that the monkeys stole their food. But I did go back after they'd had the window fixed. The second time I broke the upper glass panels of their back door. I took some money from the top drawer in the Hevaleys' bedroom. While I was there, I poked around their drawers and looked at all their interesting things. I liked Mrs. Hevaley's pretty dark blue perfume bottle and sprayed lavish clouds of its contents up and down my body. Later, when the truth came out, the Hevaleys told me the scented air was how they knew it had not been a monkey that stole their food the first time. But after the facts of our situation came to light, nobody wanted to punish me for my thefts, and nothing was said or done about it.

I knew I needed to go farther afield or I would be caught. On a hill not too far from where we lived, a man ran a handy shop that carried candy, cigarettes, betel nuts and other sundries. Over the paneless back window, he had installed a leather flap to keep monkeys out. I would climb the slippery hill until I was level with this window, lift up the flap, steal whatever was within arm's reach, and throw it to Mary. One day I got a kind of candy that looked like gumdrops, but tasted different. Another time I stole a cauliflower, but did not know what to do with it when I got it home.

At first the shopkeepers gave me milk when I told them that Papa would pay them as soon as he got back, but after a few weeks they cut me off. So we had only black tea. My mother was now in bed all the time, and I was looking after the infant as well as seeing to the needs of the other children. When Baby began to cry I would take her to Ma Ji's breast. After she nursed, Mary and I would wrap her up and rock her to sleep. I have no memory of changing her diapers, but we must have done. I do remember washing them in pails in the kitchen and hanging them on a wooden dryer near the fire, until we had no fire, and then they took much longer to dry.

If I had been even a few years older, I might have reached out to some authority figure in our community. But our social isolation was almost complete. Even though our apartment residents would have helped me if we'd asked them, they were all from different parts of India, speaking languages unknown to us. Amongst themselves they had English in common, which neither Ma Ji nor I could speak. I had no relatives in the vicinity to go to with our problems. I didn't know what telephones or telegraphs were, let alone where to find or how to use them. I didn't even know where my father was, although the SDA network would doubtless have found him if I had had the wit to ask them. But I wasn't familiar with Simla's Pastor Jenson and his wife. I don't recall my deductive processes, if any, but I am sure I must have believed that we had no recourse but to wait for Papa's return and manage as best as we could in the meantime.

One night when she was three months old, I was awakened by Baby's screams. It was now late February. There was snow outside, our fuel was gone and the apartment was bitterly cold. Ma Ji was sitting with her back against the headboard as usual. She was holding Baby, naked, upside down by her ankles and spanking her bottom. Then Ma Ji threw the baby towards the end of the bed. I pulled the shivering mite into my quilt and held her to my chest to warm her up. After I soothed her for a while, we both fell asleep.

When we woke up the next morning, I found that Ma Ji had soiled her bed. She was playing with her own feces. Her quilt was covered in shit. It was all over her body and hair. The stench was dreadful. But I cleaned her and her bedding up because there was nobody else to do it. She submitted to my ministrations with total indifference.

That night I was afraid to sleep in the bed next to her, so I arranged the children and myself on the rug. We were still cold with just our quilts, so I went to the front room and brought a small rug, the one we wiped our shoes on, to put on top of our bedding.

I don't know how long we survived this way, whether it was days or weeks. I am told it was six weeks in all, but it felt like years to me. We were alive, so we must have eaten something. Baby was alive, so Ma Ji must have continued nursing her. My mother must have used the toilet, because I don't remember cleaning up her mess on a continuing basis.

Finally my father showed up. I remember we were all sitting on the floor on the carpet when he walked in, with Ma Ji in the bed as usual. He was in a chipper mood. He showed Mother the set of *tabla* – Indian drums – he had brought for Paul. As he turned to hang the drums on a wall nail, Ma Ji jumped off the bed and attacked him. She clung to his back like a monkey, pulling his hair and biting him. Papa staggered, trying to maintain balance and get her off his back, but she hung on, shrieking like the madwoman she had become. It was an astonishing, grotesque tableau, at once terrifying and strangely comical.

Screaming for help, I pounded on all the doors in the building. The Hevaleys were home. They hurried over and others did as well. Someone told me to run to the hospital. I ran out with no shoes. I kept slipping on the hilly streets in my bare feet, so it took me longer than it should have to get there, and the thought that I was delaying help for my mother had me crying as I ran. As soon as I arrived and gasped out my news, the hospital immediately sent people to our apartment. Later, in Harpur, Mr. Devdass told us that he was the first person to arrive with the medics because he knew the address.

The nurses in the hospital told me that I was not in any shape to return and they found some shoes and warm clothes for me. I arrived home just in time to see my mother being taken away. The medics had secured her to the stretcher with ropes, and she had a towel clamped into her mouth. She stared wildly, uncomprehendingly, around her, like a caged animal. Our eyes met and I screamed, "*Ma Ji, Ma Ji.*" Then I saw my father sobbing, and that frightened me more than anything. What was happening to our family?

Ma Ji was in the hospital for two months. We children were not allowed to see her. The hospital sent servants to our apartment, who made our rooms clean and decent again. Now that everyone knew about our situation, kindnesses from church families poured forth. Hot meals were delivered to our apartment every day.

My father was overwhelmed by his world turned upside down. During Ma Ji's hospitalization, a couple, both doctors, who had three sons, offered to adopt Heather. Papa said he would think about it. But he was incapable of making any big decisions at that time, and didn't take them up on it.

Pastor Jenson was a support to my father. His wife and Mrs. Hevaley gave me baby bottles and formula, and showed me how to take proper care of Baby (who was only to get her own name when Pamela was born a year later). By the time my mother came home, Heather was a good weight and thriving.

⁂

Happily, my fears for my mother's mental health in that summer vacation following my first year at Harpur did not materialize. There would be no repetition of the Simla nightmare. It was a great relief to see my mother recovering from her abortion without mishap during that summer vacation. But I was restless after too many weeks of close quarters, cyclical domestic toil and family intensity. I missed my peers and the orderly, purposeful life of

44

a school campus. I longed to go back to school, and my mood brightened in rhythm with my anticipation as the time drew near for my departure.

Then, just days before I was to leave, something terrible happened to me. So terrible I am writhing with shame – and rage at my shame – as I write the words I must. Aalim, seventeen years older than me, was – is, I do not use his real name – a male relative on my father's side. He was a trusted visitor to our home, and I had no fear of being alone with him. A day came when everyone else was out of the house. He grabbed me and raped me. Anally, a common practice in our culture, I was to discover, in order to protect the girl's virginity.

Aalim had good access to me because of his position in the family, and over the years following, he raped me anally again on several other occasions. Each time it was a swift, silent and brutal assault followed by a swift and silent withdrawal from the scene. He was there, pushing me face forward into a pillow to muffle my screams; then there was the shattering pain; then he was not there.

If you ask me how I felt inside, I cannot say. I could not think about my feelings or my emotions. I had far more existential worries. I intuitively knew that I had to suppress any outward manifestations of physical pain so I would not have to explain it. There was no question of telling anyone what I had experienced. I had nobody I could trust to keep such a horrific secret, and even if I had, I was too ashamed to share such a disgusting story with anyone. My parents least of all. They would have killed me on the spot and, whether they believed me or not, they would have apologized to Aalim for my vile accusation.

I was always a practical girl. I had either to give up on my dreams, or get on with life as best I could. What couldn't be changed had to be endured somehow. So I stuffed the first rape, and eventually the others, into a locked mental box, which I stored well below the surface of consciousness. I kept Aalim's crime a secret from every living soul, as though my life depended on it. Which it did.

Chapter Six

Nobody's Child

Everything changed at Harpur when the amiable Pastor and Mrs. Christo left after the first year, and Pastor and Mrs. Wulff took over. The Wulffs were both tall, Canadian-born but of German ancestry. Mrs. Wulff, who was to be the new principal, looked stern.

Mrs. Wulff immediately introduced a rule that students would be punished if they were heard speaking any language but English. Suddenly most of the teachers walked around with wooden rulers, and we were hit on our open palms when we spoke our native languages.

But Mrs. Wulff herself walked around with a rubber hose. She would ask a question in English. If you could not answer, you were sent to stand in a corner until you figured out the answer. If you gave the wrong answer, then you were hit on the legs. So we soon learned to say, "I am sorry, I do not understand."

Mrs. Wulff's other focus for disapproval was ethnic clothing. The parents received letters that the girls were to wear dresses and appropriate shoes. Those of us who did not have any of our own were given dresses donated by American girls our age, and these puffy creations, as well as being unsuited to Harpur's harsh winters, made us look and feel ridiculous.

I was a responsible girl and accustomed to hard work, but I was not submissive by nature, and sometimes that got me into trouble at school.

One day in my second year at Harpur Middle School I was polishing the desks in my classroom. Every student was doing his or her part to make the school shine for a special occasion. Suddenly a boy my age but bigger than me, Peter, a bullying type, grabbed my bottle of polish and ran out with it. I gave chase, and when I caught him, he made a typically insulting remark, this time so crude I just couldn't let it go. Several teachers in the vicinity were shocked to witness me giving the boy a thrashing that left him sobbing and unable to get up.

As a corrective, Mrs. Wulff meted out four lashes to my legs with her beloved rubber hose under the gloating supervision of Peter's mother, Mrs. Stevenson, the dorm housekeeper.

One of the onlookers was Mr. Devdass, our math teacher, whom I had known at Simla. I was hopeless at math. I sat in the first seat of the fifth row in his class. As Mr. Devdass walked into class and made his way to his desk, he had a habit of smacking the neck of those of us sitting in the first seat of each row. He would say, "Johnson, did you do your homework?" Smack. Then, "Will, how about you? You going to stay awake in class?" Smack.

When he got to me, he would pull my ponytail and say, "You're old enough to be married off, why are you killing time?" or "Still here?" and then smack me too. But after he saw me beat up Peter, Mr. Devdass stopped hitting me and saying stupid things. He was not a big man, and I think he was a bit of a coward, but he must also have been something of a fool to believe that I would be crazy enough to attack any adult male for any reason at all, especially one with authority over me.

This was also a difficult year for me because I started menstruating, for which I was entirely unprepared. Our mother had never mentioned anything about it and the older girls in the dorm did not talk about it to the younger ones.

When it began, I was playing marbles with some boys from my class. Miss Rawat was sitting under a tree with some other teachers, and she noticed that I kept running to the dorm room and back. When I ran in for the fourth or the fifth time, she followed and asked me what I was doing. I told her that I was sweating 'down there' and the dirt was turning the sweat red, so I was dusting my panties with talcum powder to dry up the sweat. Miss Rawat understood the situation at once, and insisted that I have a bath. Then she initiated me into the proper management of my periods.

I was devastated to learn that entering the estate of official womanhood meant an end to participation in many of my favourite activities. I was no longer allowed to play marbles. I was not to climb walls or trees or join in any form of play with boys ever again.

Adding insult to injury, these joy-killing restrictions coincided with the donation of the frilly dresses from America we were encouraged to wear. Many of the girls loved them. But I preferred my familiar shalwar kameez, both modest and comfortable, and so much better suited to running and climbing. The absurd dresses, with their fussy layers of hot and itchy petticoats were someone else's idea of femininity, not mine, just as the periods were nature's idea of growing up, but never would have been mine.

Peter Stevenson was not in my class, but after the beating I gave him, he became my nemesis. Every time I turned around he was watching me. He would wait outside for me, and while looking at me, speak to one of my classmates in a very loud voice. "So who got the most smacks in your class today? Anyone retarded in your class?" I was told to walk away from Peter or report him to one of the teachers. But Peter would not leave me alone. One day he stuck his leg out as I passed, and I nearly fell. I'd had enough of this spoiled, sneaky mama's boy. I grabbed him and began to beat him up. Peter's mother saw us and I ended up once again in Mrs Wulff's office.

Mrs. Wulff sat me down. Then she told me how disappointed Jesus was with me. She added that she of course was personally disappointed, and so would my father be when he knew of my misbehaviour. She said that children like me do not go to Heaven. They burn in Hell forever. She went on to say in a sorrowful tone that she had come to India to help save native children, and she was doing the best she could, but dealing with children like me had her feeling very discouraged.

I could not have grasped everything she said with my still rudimentary English, but there was a native teacher beside her relaying everything she said into Hindi. As she translated, my eyes dwelled on the rubber hose in Mrs. Wulff's lap, which she had been gently massaging since I sat down.

Finally Mrs. Wulff asked me to summarize what I had leaned from "our little talk." My mind only had room for two thoughts. One was that no matter what I said, Mrs. Wulff was going to beat me with the rubber hose. But worse, she was going to report the incident to my father, and beside his imagined reaction, the rubber hose seemed almost insignificant. Frightened, I began to cry and sing, *Jesus loves me, this I know, for the Bible tells me so; little ones to Him belong, they are weak but He is strong.*

I seemed to have found the right response. Mrs. Wulff sat back and smiled. Then she said in a mild and kindly voice that this time she would only hit me twice on my legs, but next time it might be more. Mrs. Wulff nodded a dismissal to the interpreter, who promptly left. I breathed a little sigh of relief. Although the rubber hose smarted terribly and its effects were felt for days, I reasoned that two strokes would only be half as bad as the four I had gotten for beating up Peter, so I could cope with that. I did not consider that Mrs. Wulff's public punishments might differ from those she gave in private.

Mrs. Wulff was nearly six feet tall. She was also strong and muscular, the physical reward of a hardworking childhood on a Canadian farm, as she often proudly reminded us. When the rubber hose suddenly came down on my legs with the full force of her manly strength behind it, the shock and searing pain made me lose control of my bladder. She delivered a second agonizing lash, and pushed me out of her office, snarling "filthy urchin."

As I anticipated, on my father's next visit Mrs. Stevenson complained to him about the beating I had dealt her son. In her version, Peter was a good boy with a mischievous sense of humour. Mrs. Stevenson loudly retailed all my deficits, including the suspicion that I was socially unfit for such a good school. Everyone in the vicinity heard her pronouncements, both wandering students and the teachers sitting under the nearby tree drinking their afternoon tea – or rather the nasty soy liquid Adventists substitute for forbidden tea and coffee.

Mrs. Stevenson could afford to publicize her umbrage, because she knew she held the high cards in the ancient Indian game she and my father were playing. For even though she was but a lowly housekeeper and my father a pastor, Mrs. Stevenson was well aware that the shame inflicted on a father by a daughter's unseemly behaviour, no matter the provocation, trumped any embarrassment a mother was expected to feel for a son's incitements.

Mrs. Stevenson had deliberately challenged him in front of witnesses so that my father would be honour-bound to punish me in front of them. I was in my dorm room, but the grapevine had brought me up to date on events within minutes of his arrival. Mary pleaded with me, "Papa is very angry, but don't say anything or he will beat you more. Please cry as soon as he hits you. Scream and scream and then he will stop hitting you."

Several of the girls followed me, watching me silently, like a Greek chorus, as I walked across the lawn toward my father. In spite of what I knew was coming, I felt a tingle of pride at his handsome appearance. He looked like a Somebody, very dapper in his perfectly tailored second-hand grey suit, crisp white shirt and neatly knotted tie. His centre-parted hair was oiled to a brilliant shine. The sole imperfection was that his shoes did not gleam with the same lustre as they did when I polished them.

As I approached, he pulled out his belt, doubled it and without a word raised his arm, bringing it down in rhythmic blows onto my hunched shoulders and back, apologizing to Mrs. Stevenson between strokes. "Sister... this is... the bad seed... in my family. She is... my shame...."

Suddenly Miss Rawat rushed in and grabbed my father's arm. She asked if she could speak with him. She then glanced with narrowed eyes at Mrs. Stevenson, coldly suggesting that if she had no further work in the dorms, it was getting late and she could go home. Miss Rawat asked Papa to follow her, and that was

50

the last I saw of him on that visit. Papa left without a hello or goodbye to me or my sisters. I didn't feel sorry for myself about that, or if I did, I suppressed it. Or about the beating. I understood that if he had been summoned to the school for my bad behaviour, then I was the source of shame for him, and he was obliged to do something to save face.

The Open House, the special occasion for which I had been polishing desks when Peter set these events in motion, was the high point of the school year. Excitement permeated the campus. To dazzle the parents of potential recruits, the administration planned to pull out all the stops that day. The biggest crowd pleaser would be the parade, attended by local dignitaries and politicians. I was exhilarated at the prospect of marching with my dorm mates but, since at twelve years old I was already five foot, four inches tall and quite developed, it was decided that I would look too comical without a girl partner anywhere near my size, so I was cut from the parade roster.

There were also to be dramatic presentations by the various classes, but because I looked more like the mother of the other children than their contemporary, and since there was no part for a mother, I was informed I would have to sit out the plays too.

Of course I quite understood the position of Mr. Popkiss, the drama teacher. All the children taking part in the play were from good families, and the achievements they showcased were a vehicle for attracting more of the kind of students who would enhance the school's prestige. They wore nice clothes and they spoke English. They were, as he put it, very "teachable." Then too, Mr. Popkiss and his wife only spoke English between themselves, so it was natural for them to prefer English-speaking students for all the social programs in the school they oversaw.

The very last item in the day's activities was to be a talent show, which also came under the direction of Mr. and Mrs. Popkiss. Children could choose to read a poem or a story they had written, and there was as well a category for those who could sing. There were to be three prizes awarded for best-in-category performances, and a grand prize for the best performance overall. Some of the children had been practicing their entry for weeks with Mr. Popkiss.

On the big night, a young girl who had worked with Mrs. Popkiss took the stage to read her poem. But stage fright overcame her and she forgot her lines. She was led off the stage sobbing by Mrs. Popkiss, after which there was a bit of a commotion in the hall. I don't know what got into me. I walked up onto the empty stage, looked down at Mr. Popkiss at the piano, and said, "I am going to sing your song, 'Nobody's Child,'" and I plunged in:

As I was slowly passing an orphans' home today
I stopped for just a little while to watch the children play;

51

A lone boy standin', and when I asked him why
He turned with eyes that could not see and he began to cry:
Nobody's child, Nobody's child, just like a flower I am growing wild

No mama's kisses and no Daddy's smile, nobody wants me, I am nobody's child.

I had often heard Mr. Popkiss playing his guitar and singing this song all alone in the music room, and picked it up almost immediately. Something about its mournful lament spoke to my heart. I loved singing, not only because I was good at it and felt confident in performance, but because singing connected me to the stories I'd heard about my parents' choral adventures in their first years as a married couple. Singing was my birthright.

I found out that night that I had the skill to make an audience weep. When I finished my song, I received a standing ovation, and the judges had no choice but to award me the grand prize, which turned out to be a red English dictionary. Hearing the applause, drinking in Mr. Popkiss' astonished pleasure in my rendition of his song, and clutching that dictionary in my hands (even though it was put in the classroom bookshelf afterward and I never got it back) – that was the happiest moment of my years at Harpur Elementary School.

The glow faded soon enough. A terrible miscarriage of justice was waiting in the wings for me, and a few days later the words "nobody's child" would take on personal, and very dark new meaning.

Like just about every girl at Harpur, I developed a crush on a handsome boy with a roguish air. Wilson Mall. I followed Wilson around like a puppy, but I was just another kid to him. Wilson had eyes only for my dorm mate, Norma, at sixteen the oldest female student in the school. It was easy to understand Wilson's fascination with the petite and lushly rounded Norma. She was much more sophisticated than the other students. She had already spent a year in Iran with her Indian missionary parents, and had socialized there with other embassy children from the West. Norma had seen films with her non-Adventist aunts and even owned film magazines! She wore the latest fashions, with beautiful undergarments from England and America. She owned face cream and body lotions, and the soaps she used smelled like fruit.

Norma exuded aristocratic privilege, and others deferred to her. She treated the teaching staff as though they were there to serve her, and they did serve her. Norma could tell Mrs. Stevenson to put her bedding in the sun to freshen it up, and she would do it. Norma would tell Nasir the cook she did not like her meal, and he would run to the kitchen to find something more to her taste. She would say, "I am going for a walk," and then, pointing at some of the younger girls, say "You, you and you are allowed to accompany me." The girls chosen would preen, and Miss Rawat would smile, but say nothing.

Wilson was mad for Norma, but she was out of his league. She was of a higher caste than his, so any idea that theirs could be a meaningful relationship was a hopeless fantasy. In public she treated him with the disdain appropriate to the disparity in their social stations. I was privy to her true feelings, though, because, sworn to secrecy, I was the one chosen to carry letters between them. I loved my job as a runner between these two golden creatures. It was like having a non-speaking, but important role in a film, a romantic tragedy about doomed forbidden love.

It so happened that my bed and Norma's, side by side in the dorm, looked exactly alike, because Norma had given me a companion set of her pretty blue and white striped bed linen to replace my sheet and pillowcase, worn out after years of constant use.

During the Open House celebrations, one of the other girls came to Norma with a note from Wilson. Norma instructed the girl to put it under her pillow. Mrs. Stevenson saw the girl slipping something under my pillow, which she had mistaken for Norma's. As soon as she left, Mrs. Stevenson retrieved the note and read it. It was a handwritten declaration of love for Norma. It began, "My dearest heartthrob," and ended with "I shall love you forever and ever until I die."

Although I had no idea about any of this at the time, circumstances were conspiring against me. For nowhere in the note had Wilson alluded to Norma by name. Mrs. Stevenson still bore me a grudge for shaming her son. She also felt she had been robbed of her proper revenge when Miss Rawat cut short my father's thrashing. Mrs. Stevenson was determined not to lose her opportunity to turn this found nugget of Wilson's youthful indiscretion into the distilled gold of my humiliation and pain. She bypassed her immediate superior, Miss Rawat, who would have gotten to the truth very quickly, and took the note directly to Mrs. Wulff.

As I was to learn later, when the Open House festivities were over and all the visitors had gone, Mrs. Wulff asked the nine-year old child who had delivered the note to show her the bed on which she had placed the note. The girl had by now realized she had put the note under the wrong pillow, but was too afraid to say so.

A few days passed. Then I was summoned, not to Mrs. Wulff's office, but to the Wulffs' home. I had never been inside a missionary's house before. I knew I had done nothing wrong in the last few weeks, so I ran and skipped along with nothing but curiosity in mind. The housekeeper opened the door and showed me into the reception hall.

Peeking into a corner of the living room, I felt as though I were in a palace of some kind. I saw a richly textured curtain, the edge of a glowing silk carpet and the plump round arm of an upholstered divan, furnishings unlike anything I had ever seen before. A novel fragrance emanating from the kitchen – freshly baked pound cake, I later discovered – made my mouth water.

Then I heard a frighteningly familiar voice calling my name from the depths of the living room. Adrenalin flooded my whole body, and my heart began to race. My father! My *father* was here! If my father had been summoned, and had come all this way again, I was in terrible trouble. But why? *Why*? What had I done? Could he have found out about what Aalim had done to me? I dismissed that suspicion at once, though. No Indian father would involve a non-kinsman, let alone a white woman, in the punishment of a crime of that magnitude. I felt slightly dizzy as though all my blood had rushed downward to pool in my feet. I was rooted to the spot.

The housekeeper pushed me forward. "Go in child, your father is calling." Then she opened the front door and left the house. I felt light-headed. I recalled the interpreter leaving Mrs. Wulff's office the last time I had been sent for. Now I knew something bad was about to happen, something the housekeeper did not want to witness, or had been ordered not to witness.

I walked in. My father was standing stiffly in the centre of the room. Mrs. Wulff sat on a richly brocaded wall sofa behind a glass-topped wooden coffee table engraved with elephants. Papa came towards me with the letter Wilson had written to Norma, and asked, "Do you recognize this?" I said truthfully that I did not. Mrs. Wulff said, "That is a love letter written by Wilson Mall to you. It was found under your pillow by Mrs. Stevenson and I know Mrs. Stevenson would never lie to me."

Even after three years of lessons, I could not respond in English, but I understood everything Mrs. Wulff was saying. I told my father in Urdu that it was not my letter, that I had never seen it before. Papa asked me if I had written any letters to any boy. I told him the truth again: that I did not know how to read or write, that I had never written a letter in my life.

When Papa translated what I had said for Mrs. Wulff, Mrs. Wulff picked one of my notebooks up from the table. She pointed to passages in my hand to indicate that I did know how to write. Then I told Papa that Miss Rawat made us practice our penmanship by copying paragraphs from our books. The letter was in Hindi, and the notebook copying was in Hindi. My father did not read Hindi. It was my word against hers.

As my father carried on with this tense interrogation, the uncomprehending Mrs. Wulff's eyes didn't leave my face. But at one point I noticed her fingers groping between the sofa cushions, and then they emerged grasping the rubber hose. My heart hammered. A flutter of nausea swam through my bowels. Finally Papa grabbed me by the hair and shook my head back and forth. In Urdu he said, "Before I go, I am going to have your head shaved, so that everyone will know that you are filth. It is your mother's dirty blood that runs in you. Your Naani was of dirty blood and you are just like her."

Strangely, at that moment my terror drained away, and I felt no emotion at all. This was my karma; this was what I had known was coming to me. We were not talking about a letter anymore. What was happening between my father and me was beyond my youthful capacity to absorb. Words, explanations, the truth – I could see they were of no use to me in this alien place. A curious lassitude possessed me. At that moment I wanted my father to shave my head. I didn't cry. I said very calmly, "I know that I did not do anything wrong, but if you don't believe me, that's okay."

This enraged Papa. He slapped me across the face, yelling, "You want me to believe that all these good people are lying and you are telling the truth?" He grabbed my hair again and pulled my head as far back as it would go. "Tell me how many times you have been with this boy. How many times?" I could not speak with my head so far back. I made gagging sounds and he let go. I told him that I only carried letters from Wilson to Norma.

Mrs. Wulff now cried out to Papa, "Do you see how defiant she is?" But I was not the least bit defiant. I was resigned to whatever was going to happen. I knew that no matter what I said or did, it would not matter. I was probably going to die in that house, I reasoned, so there was no point in fighting my fate.

Papa's hand moved to his belt buckle. A sound, a kind of gasp, issued from Mrs. Wulff's mouth. We both looked at her mottled face and bright, eager eyes, now fixed on Papa. Suddenly she thrust the rubber hose at him across the space between them. He hesitated for a second, then stepped forward and grasped it. Watching the hose being passed, like a baton in a race, a white hand at one end, a brown hand at the other, is the last thing I remember.

My next recollection is waking up in my bed in the dorm and learning that two days had passed since the beating. Miss Rawat was sitting with me, and so was Mrs. Stanley, who ran the cafeteria and lived in a house attached to the girls' dorm. There was a cold towel filled with ice on my forehead. I had a very high fever. The skin on my back had been split open in several places and the wounds had become infected. A local doctor had been called, and he had given me some medication. Mrs. Stanley and Miss Rawat took turns looking after me. I was a long time healing.

There must have been a lot of physical pain, but I have no memory of it. I may have forgotten the pain because I never discussed the beating with anyone, and nobody encouraged me to. Not even kind and sympathetic Miss Rawat. I didn't expect anyone to talk about the beating. Even though this episode was a rather special case, rough corporal punishment of children – canings, open-palm whacks with a ruler, smacks, slaps and hair-pulling – was a commonplace in schools at that time. Even the benevolent teachers used their rulers with casual spontaneity for petty rule breaches.

I was by no means the only student to end up needing medical care after a beating. At Roorkee High School where I went the following year, there was a certain pastor who taught our Bible class. One day he threw a blackboard eraser at a student who wasn't paying attention, but missed, and the student laughed. The pastor attacked the boy in a rage, punching him until he fainted. The boy's life actually hung in the balance for a day. But nobody who witnessed it, including me, talked about it afterward.

My friends and I never confided in each other about the beatings we got from parents, so I don't know whether my experience – apart from this incident – was normal or not. It was understood that parents had absolute rights over our bodies, and that if we were beaten, it was because we had shamed them somehow. We were conditioned to understand beatings as a sign of our parents' love and concern for our reputations, on which all our future happiness rested. In later years I realized that there were girls whose fathers lavished affection on them – my cherished uncle, Chacha Sadiq, had daughters he treated very lovingly, and he never hit them – but in my youth I would have automatically viewed such girls as exceptions to a general rule.

Still, unlike the punishment I had received for humiliating Peter Stevenson, I knew I had been unjustly served. If I had done what my father had accused me of, I would have accepted a death sentence without resentment or judgment. But I had done nothing wrong. I would never have felt anything so articulate as indignation or righteous anger. But for the first time I can remember, I had uncomfortable feelings about my father to which I could not put a name.

Once I was better, Miss Rawat took the extraordinary step of making a special trip to Delhi to see my father and set the record straight for him. She explained to him that the letter had been misplaced, that both Norma and Wilson had owned up to their clandestine romance, and that Wilson had been sent away.

Thirty-nine years later, sitting with my parents in their Toronto home, I finally brought the subject of the beating to their attention for the first time since it happened. Up to then, my father had never explained, let alone apologized for, the brutality of that beating. At that point I wasn't so much interested in arousing remorse, or venting long-suppressed resentment, as I was trying to understand the cultural imperatives behind his behaviour.

During our adult conversation, it became clear that far from feeling gratitude to Miss Rawat for the trouble she had gone to in bringing the truth to light, my father had felt nothing but humiliation. He admitted he believed I was telling the truth at the time, but he had found himself in an untenable position. If he had taken my side, he would have insulted Mrs. Wulff, a white missionary with considerable influence over his fortunes in the SDA movement. In any case, as a native son who came of age in the Raj, it simply wasn't in him to defy a white authority figure. If only she hadn't challenged him with the hose, he would never have beaten me so severely. But she did. What else could he do but take it? He made a case, reasonable from his perspective, for himself as a victim as well, forced to act in the only way possible under the circumstances.

But after Miss Rawat's visit, whose purpose became public knowledge, he could no longer pretend the incident was anything but a farcical mistake that only brought him further shame.

Although I wasn't moved to sympathy, I found a certain satisfaction in finally seeing the incident through my father's eyes. He saw himself as a man trying hard to do the right thing. But his good intentions were foiled at every turn by some female or other. Women! His daughters were nothing but trouble to him. First his sense of honour had been exploited by Mrs. Stevenson. Then a white woman had tapped into a reflexive colonial sycophancy. And now here was yet another woman, this busybody Miss Rawat, to remind him that far from reasserting his family honour in the eyes of those whose good opinion he coveted most, he had made a fool of himself before the entire Indian SDA community.

After my father finished recounting his list of grievances, my mother hastened to add that when Papa arrived home the next day, he wept as he described how he had walked away, leaving me lying unconscious on Mrs. Wulff's urine-soaked carpet. This was not the solace she intended. My father wept to his wife. But he said nothing to me. So I was left to ponder who exactly it was that he was weeping for. The answer was, of course, for himself. No man in our culture ever has to feel guilty for his shabby treatment of girls or women. It's all very simple to men. Women bring their troubles on themselves.

Well, I had asked, and I had my answer.

Mrs. Wulff did not give up on her mission to save my soul. It is the Adventist custom to hold a prayer week every six months in remembrance of the week in 1884 when Ellen White and her followers, believing the Second Coming was upon them, stopped maintaining their farms and livestock, and prayed to God for instructions on how to prepare for Heaven.

Nothing happened, of course, but thereafter prayer weeks became a biannual feature in SDA institutional life, during which Church members re-establish their connection with God and pray for moral guidance under the leadership of a special Guest. At Harpur's spring prayer week, Pastor Christo, our former principal, was the Guest. He led worship services in the mornings and evenings, and oversaw Bible study in the afternoons.

Adventists don't believe in infant baptism. Baptism is supposed to be the result of a conscious, independently arrived-at commitment to the faith. At the end of the prayer week, all those who wanted to be baptized – and many did after a week's immersion in prayer and study – would gather at the river for a group ceremony.

Although teenagers in particular were encouraged to ask for baptism, and although my parents would have been happy if I did, I felt I should be more educated – I should at least be able to read and write properly – before taking such a decisive step. So I had no plans for personal baptism during that Prayer Week.

To round out that year's event, the staff organized a picnic in the woods near the river. Mrs. Wulff told me that if I was baptized, then the Lord's spirit would guide me and make me a better person. I told her I was willing to be baptized in principle, but not just then, because I was wearing my one and only really good outfit, and I explained to her that I did not want to sacrifice that for the Lord.

I stood on the bank to watch the other baptisms. Mrs. Wulff sidled up to me and sweetly asked if I could "feel the Lord's spirit." I was not quite sure what she was talking about, but smiled back and said "yes" to please her. Then Pastor Christo called out in his booming voice for those who had decided to make a public pronouncement to God to come forward.

The riverbank we stood on was a bit slippery. Mrs. Wulff put her hand on the small of my back and pushed hard. I fell into the water. As I struggled to get back out, Pastor Christo congratulated me on my decision, and welcomed me into the fold as an official Adventist. The deceitful, determined Mrs. Wulff had triumphed again.

Chapter Seven

Good times, bad karma

We were told that Harpur was to become a day school in the fall of 1964. Boarding students, including me and my sisters Mary and Jessica, would be transferring en masse to Roorkee High School.

Some of the teachers were staying at Harpur, some were going with us, and some were striking out in new directions. Miss Rawat was leaving to become the principal of am elementary school in Delhi. In fact, she had taken an apartment in the same building as my parents, who had moved for the fourth time to Delhi when my father was assigned to the SDA head office for Northern India. There she developed a friendship with my mother, but my father always kept a frosty distance from her because of her shaming interference in our family's business.

Mr. and Mrs. Singh were coming with us to Roorkee. But many other teachers I had come to love and trust were not, so my mood at this time swung back and forth between excitement and a kind of nostalgia.

I fervently hoped that I would finally get a proper education at Roorkee. At the age of thirteen, after three years of elementary school, I could read and write Hindi at something approaching a Grade Two level; I knew the English alphabet, but could not read in English; I could speak English as well as the average cab driver or servant, but I could not understand a sermon. In math I had learned my times table, but I struggled with algebra and geometry, as Mr. Devdass, the math teacher, spoke only in English.

Mr. Devdass made it clear he thought I was mentally deficient. He would urge me to quit school and get married. He once said, "You are only good for production, like a cow." My English was so uncertain, I heard the word "good" and took it as a compliment. I even thanked him. It wasn't only Mr. Devdass who felt that way, though. It was widely accepted throughout the school that I was somewhat retarded. In adulthood, when I had myself tested, I learned that I was afflicted with dyslexia, but schools in those days knew nothing about diagnosing learning disabilities, much less how to deal with them.

I had been one of the older students at Harpur, but in Roorkee I was in a younger cohort. Some of the students at Roorkee were in their early twenties. The oldest of the Harpur contingent was sixteen, so we were referred to as the Kids. We were already bonded and wanted to keep our identity. The Harpur teachers were "our" teachers. Relationships made at Harpur grew closer at Roorkee, and in fact Harpur friendships persist to this day.

The approximately twenty Harpur girls were housed in two rooms. About five of us had begun menstruating; the rest still looked like children. Our matron was Mrs. Burns from Australia. She lived with her husband and three daughters in a small house attached to the girls' dorm. The Burns family were very large people with funny accents. Both Pastor and Mrs. Burns were over six feet and weighed at least 350 lbs. They liked to sing and Pastor Burns was the choirmaster. But I found them intimidating and never really got to know them. We missed Miss Rawat and wished she had come with us.

I had a great deal more personal freedom at Roorkee than at Harpur. I felt invisible, which I liked. At Roorkee nobody cared whether I spoke English or not, or broke petty rules, as they did at Harpur.

Everything about Roorkee was different from Harpur, and in certain critical respects better. The most obvious cause for the lightening of heart I felt immediately upon arrival there was my liberation from Mrs. Wulff's joyless presence. I was very pleased with our expansive new principal and his wife, the polar opposites of the dour and rancorous Wulffs.

Pastor and Mrs. Streeter had taken over Roorkee school in 1963 with an impressive track record of institution-building to their credit. They were a happy couple from Australia with three daughters and a son, exuberant in their work, open to modern methods of education, always visible on campus, and accessible. Pastor Streeter was a hands-on leader and custodian of his domain, never happier than when drawing up building plans, cutting wood and hammering nails. Cheerful, wholesome Verna Streeter was a champion of equality for girls, or what passed for equality then, and encouraged us to take part, periods and all, in the athletic programs she started.

Pastor Streeter had a wonderful, wry sense of humour, riddled with irony, directed at all and sundry, which I found charming, even though sarcasm is not the average Indian's idea of funny. He had a nickname for me: Aladdin. He said to me one day with a twinkle, "Aladdin, I am certain you are stealing extra bread to give to the younger children. You know you mustn't, but I have to catch you before I can punish you." So we had this joke between us. When I left the cafeteria, he would tell me to open my winter coat so the loot would fall out, but I had cut open the lining, where I stowed thick slices of the delicious whole wheat bread that I considered a treat in our otherwise mundane vegetarian diet. He would scratch his head and I would delight in having tricked him once more. Many years later I met up with him and his wife again. We had some hearty laughs about that and other tricks I pulled on him. He told me he had always enjoyed my "wit." I wish he had told me that back in the days when I was convinced I was a moron.

The native staff didn't appreciate Pastor Streeter's humour or his distaste for corporal punishment, or his familiarity with them and the students. They preferred a more formal relationship with superiors. He was also far too relaxed in their eyes about boys and girls enjoying activities and sports together. And too impulsive for their taste. One night the electricity failed during worship. Pastor Streeter said, "Let's all go out and play catch." He had boys and girls throwing a baseball to each other on the lawn. Baseball was one of the few real sports I actually played and liked, only we called it "rounders," so I was very pleased with this diversion, but the Indian teachers considered the mixed game unseemly.

The staff were also not happy when Pastor Streeter had a beautiful swimming pool built, even though the money for it had been donated by our American brethren. They complained that bathing attire was immodest, and that the boys would watch the girls swimming, which would lead to the obvious bad consequences. In the end a compromise was effected. Only the boys were allowed to use the pool. Even progressive Pastor Streeter had to choose his battles to avoid a staff mutiny.

My father believed that dignity and informality could not co-exist in harmony. Like most Indians he approved of hierarchies. In a pecking order, you always knew where you stood. So he did not like Pastor Streeter. He did not approve of Pastor Streeter's democratic ways and hearty, natural manner. I remember them having a discussion once – I don't recall what the subject was – and Pastor Streeter joshingly said, "Come on, man, you don't really believe that, do you?" I could see from the way my father's face froze over that he considered this matey kind of remark deeply disrespectful. Papa referred to him disparagingly as a "cowboy."

Pastor Streeter had transferred to Roorkee the year before we came. He had been very busy and we arrived at a campus that exuded a festive air. The landscaping had been expanded and beautified, with new roads, more flowerbeds and extended, close-cropped lawns. Freshly painted classrooms welcomed us to our studies.

I was lucky to have been assigned to a room with five other girls I got on well with. Veronica was obsessed with clothes and hairdos worthy of her stunning face and figure, and was failing all her subjects. She felt school was a waste of time for a future film star. Eva was studious, never without a book in her hand, constantly chivvying us to behave more seriously. Evangeline and Parveena divided their time between studying and thinking up pranks to play on unsuspecting victims, usually on our other roommate, Anglo-Indian Rosalind. Rosalind was an amiable girl, and intensely athletic, even though she was nearly blind without her glasses. She was also frequently less than fragrant from her sweaty exertions, and sometimes we simply had to throw a few buckets of water over her, which temporarily solved the problem.

None of us was over-reverent, and we all loved a good laugh. One night around two in the morning we were awakened by heavy footsteps and a buzz of low voices outside our door. The noise seemed to have stopped at the far end of the long hallway. Now all five of us were up and out of our beds, our heads around the door. We were able to identify the gargantuan Pastor and Mrs. Burns, one other female teacher and two male teachers. Pastor Burns was clutching a fat flashlight in his hand and shining it into one of the smallest rooms, which housed two of the most senior girls. Then we heard his stentorian voice calling, "John, we know you are in there. Please put on your pants and come out."

This was all very serious. This boy would have had to climb an eight-foot wall to visit his girlfriend, a terrible act of dishonour worthy of the most severe punishment, and we held our breath to see what would happen next. A very embarrassed young man stepped out, and in the glow of the flashlight we could see him trying to do up his belt on his pants. As he trudged out onto the lawn to join the staff members waiting for him, Pastor Burns said, "Let us pray for wisdom."

As soon as we heard those words, Parveena howled with laughter, followed by Evangeline, and soon all of us were giggling, imagining what John had been up to that needed praying over. It just seemed too funny to us, but it would have been a lot less comical if he had been discovered by native teachers, more inclined to rough justice than to prayer. While the staff were absorbed in dealing with our hapless Romeo and Juliet, we put together a parody of their disrupted tryst.

Parveena started to imitate John's hangdog mortification, Evangeline played the outraged Pastor Burns and I took the role of the girl friend, which only required that I wrap myself in a bed sheet and simper in girlish confusion. Our hilarity at our cleverness had the other girls poking their heads into our room as we replayed the scene over and over, each time to more appreciative laughter.

We had fun like that all the time at Roorkee. I was still a failure as a student, but for many months I was otherwise blissfully happy.

One day I became very ill. I had a throbbing pain in my abdomen area on the right side. Every time I took a deep breath or coughed, it hurt intensely. Vomiting and diarrhea set in. I developed a high fever. Mrs. Burns became concerned and called Mrs. Streeter. The school nurse was quite sure that I was having an appendicitis attack and might need to be operated on. Pastor and Mrs. Streeter decided to take me home.

The drive to Delhi took a full day. We stopped a few times when I needed to relieve myself. Mrs. Streeter had brought food and water, but I couldn't eat. We arrived at my parents' home in the early evening. My father was shocked to see Pastor Streeter, but enraged when he saw me. Pastor Streeter began to explain why we had come. That I was sick and that I might die, and that Roorkee did not have the medical facilities to deal with such an emergency, and that Papa must take me to the hospital.

But Papa wasn't really listening. He had no room in his thoughts for anything but horror that I had been brought home. For him there were only two reasons girls were brought home from school by the principal. Either I had been found in a sexually compromising situation, or I was pregnant. So they were quarrelling at cross-purposes. Pastor Streeter was describing an emergency situation that had to do with an individual girl. He was considering what he would do if it were his child that was sick. And in such a case the only thing that would matter to him would be his child's health. But Papa had already leaped over the news of my illness to the potential for collective ignominy if the reason for my presence was misconstrued, as was not only possible, but probable. At that moment I wasn't a child, I was just a cog in the family wheel. If I were deemed a defective cog, the whole family would break down. He said that Pastor Streeter should have let me die in the school. Because what would people think when they knew he had brought me home?

The two men argued back and forth. Pastor Streeter lost his composure completely, yelling that the life of this girl was more important than what people said, and Papa yelling back no, he had the reputations and the suitability for marriage of his five other girls to consider, and his name would be dirt and no one would believe him. Ma Ji was now huddled behind Papa, weeping, the younger children clinging to her leg.

Eventually it was agreed that I could be brought to the hospital on condition that the Streeters stay with me while Papa rounded up some witnessing relatives and co-workers. Then Pastor Streeter, a white man of high authority, was to inform these people that I really was sick, and not pregnant. At this point I had urgent need of a toilet, but Papa would not allow me into the house. This, I thought for the first time in the drama, was unfair. I had followed with anguish, but not resentment Papa's familiar logic about the permanent damage to a family's honour that gossip over a daughter's purity could wreak. But to refuse me this basic human courtesy was pure spite. What difference would it make to people's opinion of me if I relieved myself in my own home's bathroom?

So the Streeters took me to the hospital suffering needless additional pain and humiliation, and Papa hired a taxi to pick up the people he thought should be there. There were nine or ten of them in the end, amongst them, crucially, Aunt Sheila, known to be a fulltime gossip, who would make sure everyone was informed of my innocence and my father's intact honour.

I was given prompt and very good care at the hospital, probably because I had been brought in by the missionaries: Indian hospitals were very status-conscious, and people of our class would normally not have commanded much respect. Pastor Streeter was so angry with Papa that he asked the doctor to give my father the removed appendix as proof that I really needed this operation. Papa did not receive the gift of the appendix in the ironic, insulting spirit in which it was offered. On the contrary, he felt that his name and his honour had been saved, and the appendix was insurance against false allegations. He kept it in his pocket. Every time someone inquired about my health, he would flourish it with triumphant satisfaction in having the final word on the subject.

❈

To my great disappointment, I did not return to Roorkee after my operation. My mother was happy to have my help at home, and my father doubtless considered the appendix attack a warning to keep me protected from influences beyond his control. Papa wasn't opposed to my continuing my education in principle, though. So he had me placed in a small, private girls' school, run out of his home by a retired college professor in Old Delhi's rundown Daryaganj neighbourhood.

Master Singh's students usually succeeded in passing their "Punjab Matric," the equivalent of a Grade 12 leaving certificate, because he knew the exam questions in advance, and we students only had to memorize the answers. Still, you had to know at least how to read and write, and so I was one of the very few who failed the exams.

Most of the girls were Sikhs. Some were Hindus. I was the only Christian and also the youngest, the lowest in caste, the darkest of complexion, and the most shabbily dressed. At the time I was unaware that in Indian films all the prostitutes and villains were Christians. So I assumed I was being flattered for my good voice, not ridiculed, when my classmates would ask me to sing a popular film song. I didn't realize that the songs they asked me to sing were those sung by the prostitutes in the film, and that in singing them I was only cementing my inferior status in their eyes.

The Hindu girls asked me if I ate meat. When I said yes, it sealed my social fate as well. I was allowed to start the stove and wash the dishes, but most of the girls refused to eat near me. It would not have occurred to me to report them to Master Singh or to complain to my parents. The girls jeered at me, calling me "meat-eater" and other hateful names, like *Kali Mayee* – "Blackie" – or the words for "black skeleton" or "Christian girl."

I had two advantages. I spoke better English than they did, and I had my fine singing voice. Both distinctions brought me to Master Singh's notice. He soon became aware of the harassment without my telling him. In the mornings before class, he would ask me to sing the national anthem. And in English class, I was often called upon to speak before the class on one subject or another. Only Master Singh and I were aware of the sorry state of my English reading and writing.

I desperately wanted to feel as though I belonged. So I began to tell the other girls that my real name was not Irene, but Aruna. I took the name from a Hindu woman doctor I had once seen, a tall, elegant woman, who walked with confidence and always had a long line of patients waiting outside her office.

On the official government exam forms, I signed my name as Aruna. When the results were delivered to our house, my father assumed the exam centre had erred. He said he would go there to have the mistake corrected, but he never got around to it, and as a result I now had a precious official document identifying me as Aruna. After my marriage, where I signed the registry as Aruna, I had a second legal document. When we went to get our passports, I used the two documents as proof of my identity, and so it was that I received a passport with the Hindu name of Aruna, not the Christian name of Irene. One less badge of inferiority to contend with.

Chapter Eight

"You are getting married..."

Most of our Saturday evenings at boarding school were taken up with supervised social activities. But occasionally the staff members wanted a night home with their families, and then we were left to our own devices. We couldn't play outside because of the snakes, scorpions and other poisonous creatures of the night. We had no board games, and our church didn't permit card playing. Sometimes we put on talent shows, but the most popular form of entertainment, one in which every girl could take part, was a wedding play.

We'd divide ourselves into the families of the bride and the groom. One girl would take the role of the minister, another the greeter, others the parents. There was never a question about who was to be the bride. Mina Bose, who owned lovely clothes and expensive makeup, also happened to be the most beautiful and the fairest of complexion amongst us. The groom was chosen with a coin toss. Miss Rawat and Mrs. Stanley would come as the guests, and Mrs. Stanley added a touch of realism by providing the wedding "feast," usually melted cheese on toast and bread pudding.

My sisters and I and a few other girls were always the *Qawwals* – the wedding singers. We sang the *Qawwalis*, music whose origins can be traced back to eighth-century Persia, and popular in South Asia since the eleventh century. We knew them well, because our father loved them. At home we would sit up at night for hours, reverently attentive to Papa's sweet, yearning renderings of those haunting verses.

But in our school wedding skits we sang them for laughs. We would put on baggy pants, twist sheets into turbans, draw pencil moustaches on our upper lip, and strut about the dorm in manly fashion to the hilarity of our friends. Accompanying ourselves instrumentally by slapping upturned buckets and wooden plates, we sang our hearts out with exaggerated gusto.

Of course, none of us had a clue about what it meant to be married in real life. None of us had been educated about sex or reproduction or our obligations to our husband's family. We were kept blissfully ignorant of how profoundly our marriages would change our lives. Mina Bose knew she had to look shy, bewildered and a little frightened while playing the bride, but she had no idea why.

I look back at those scenes of innocent merriment with nostalgia for the fun we had, and chagrin for our ignorance. What a world of difference, I would discover, there was between our childish play-acting and the grim reality I was plunged into when, at the age of seventeen, I became a reluctant participant in my own forced marriage.

❈

All my life I had been told that since I was ugly, uneducated and without dowry prospects, I would have great difficulty in finding a husband. Perhaps that was why unlike other girls I had no romantic notions about weddings in general. Although it was an unacceptable idea for a young girl to entertain in a culture where remaining unmarried was virtually unthinkable, I felt I would have been content to remain a spinster and serve my parents' needs as they aged, and perhaps in time become a beloved aunt to my siblings' children.

But in retrospect I see that really my high-minded indifference to marriage was just a rationalization for deep, inarticulate fears I couldn't allow myself to acknowledge consciously. So it was a shock to me when, about six months after leaving Master Singh's school, I was casually informed by my sister Mary, "You are getting married in three months. To Ralph."

Ralph L., eleven years older than me, was an Anglo-Indian Adventist, whom I had seen in church, but never met alone. It was part of my father's job in the SDA Church to oversee the founding of new schools and even the occasional church. At this time we were living in the green and pleasant city of Bhopal, the capital city of the state of Madhya Pradesh, where my father had started up a small school in which Ralph was a teacher. I had only seen Ralph on a few occasions in church. I remember my first impressions of him: balding, somewhat shy and very slow-moving. I remember he seemed to take forever to stand up in church.

I was never alone with him, but his younger sister visited us once. She was not allowed to attend our wedding, though, because she had given birth to a child out of wedlock, and Papa didn't want that information to get out. That my father would permit an alliance with a family in which such shameful behaviour was tolerated was a sign of how little value I had in the marriage market. I knew Ralph's family were not getting any dowry from my father, so he was no more a catch than I was. I could not foresee having any affection for this man, but since nobody asked me if I thought I might fancy him, it was not something I brooded over or even remember thinking about.

Once we were officially engaged, my father didn't think it was a good idea for me and Ralph to be in the same city before our marriage. Papa was mortally afraid of any gossip arising about improprieties between us. He had nothing to fear on my part, that was certain, but innocence is no proof against malicious gossip in Indian culture. So he had Ralph transferred to Indore, about 200 kilometres away, today a large commercial centre, but then a small town with a single central marketplace.

As the wedding day approached, Papa arranged for us to move to Indore, where he promptly opened a tiny three-room school for the SDA, teaching English to children who would be attending a Catholic convent school afterward. I worked there as the unpaid nanny-cum-janitor. I can never forget my embarrassment when my father, showing around a prospective client he wanted to impress, not only failed to introduce me to her as his daughter, but slightingly referred to me as the school's servant.

My family's move to Indore, the usual household chores and my demanding job at my parents' school were a welcome distraction from the looming wedding, which I tried hard not to think about. When I did, it was with all-consuming dread. I was not fit to be married. I was damaged goods. I was to find out that technically I was still a virgin, but until I had sex with Ralph, I had no idea what that meant. I was ignorant of what marital relations consisted of, but I was quite certain that once they were initiated, my secret would be revealed, and I would have to be killed. Or perhaps forced to kill myself, an equally likely consequence in my culture to a woman who dishonours her family. To add insult to injury, the man who had damaged me was to be an honoured guest at the wedding.

I passed the final weeks leading up to the wedding in a fatalistic fugue. Nobody noticed my lack of affect. Nobody cared that I had no appetite, never smiled or chattered or showed interest in the wedding preparations. As a bride, I was the least important player in the wedding party, even on the day itself. My white bridal sari and trousseau, such as it was – two new shalwar kameezes, one sky blue, one a mustard colour – were bought by my mother and one of her friends. I accompanied them to the tailor, and stood to be measured, staring into space, while they conferred and giggled and fingered materials. My mother and her friend also bought my shoes, which were presented to me when I was dressed for the wedding. They were too small.

Relatives began to arrive in Indore. Neither of my grandmothers came. My father didn't have the money to bring Dadi Ji from Chukwal, and during those days of strife between our countries, it would have been risky for Naani Ji to travel from Pakistan. I hadn't seen either of them in years, so I doubt their presence would have been a comfort to me. But there was no shortage of other kinsmen. A constant stream of visitors flowed in and out of the house. The house hummed with animated talk and movement.

On the day itself, I wasn't allowed to take part in any socializing or even to be seen by anybody. This was a blessing in its way, since putting on a happy face all day would have been torture for me. Our home was a two-room apartment attached to our landlord's house. At the back of the second room, there was a small kitchen and behind that a windowless, closet-like storage cubicle where, on my wedding morning, I was banished, to sit on a mattress and await directions. My sisters darted in and out to keep me up to date on activities and rumours. Mary informed me that some of the women were going to put a mustard paste on my body and then wash me with yogurt as was the custom. I told her that I would box their ears if they tried.

Eventually Aunt Madhu bounced into my little cell and cheerfully ordered me to get up and bathe. She started yanking playfully at my shalwar, but instead of taking it in good humour, I fought her off like an animal.

She yelled back to my mother in the kitchen, "The bride is acting like a mad dog. I don't want to bother with her." Then two women joined her. Strangers to me, they were church members who, in the absence of friends – I hadn't had the inclination or encouragement to even think of inviting friends to my wedding – had offered to act as surrogate intimates in the traditional role of attendants to the bride.

Like a prisoner about to be executed, I was hoping for a reprieve at the last minute. My lack of cooperation was duly reported to my mother, who stormed in and snapped, "Stand up." I stood up. She grabbed my hair with one hand and smacked me with the other, snarling through gritted teeth, "Go and bathe or I will have the door broken down. I will come in and cut you into pieces." I believed she might do just that, so I stopped resisting. There was no mention of mustard pastes or yogurt, at least, so my tantrum was partially effective.

As I washed myself under the taps, I found myself descending into the curious state of lassitude I had experienced at Harpur in the living room of Mrs. Wulff, when it became clear that my father was going to beat me. The marriage would expose my shame. The punishment – and this time I deserved it – would be severe. To cope with my fear, I mentally stepped outside myself. My body was being ritually prepared for my certain doom, but my mind was somewhere else.

I came back to the little room to find that my sari had been laid out on the mattress by Aunt Madhu. I had never worn one before, but I had watched my mother arranging hers many times. I wrapped it around myself in the prescribed manner, pinned it to make it secure and sat down. I let Mary fuss with my hair, but I did not permit her to apply any makeup to my face.

The wedding ceremony was scheduled for 5:00 pm. By 2:00 pm, I was washed and wrapped in my white silk sari, sitting in the airless box room, and sweating profusely. Through the door to the hallway I watched with indifference the comings and goings of all the happy people.

In India people who can't afford banquet halls often put up tents on the road in front of their home. They rent carpets of artificial grass and set up and decorate tables. In our case, a cheaper alternative even than the road, we had rented the rooftop of a neighbour with a big house. The women finally came to get me. They were to accompany me to the rooftop, where a pastor would marry me to Ralph before four male witnesses.

I collected myself. I was ready. But when I stood up, I couldn't seem to catch my breath and felt dizzy. The women helped me to my parents' bedroom, where I collapsed on their bed. I could hear some commotion amongst the women, and then I could hear my mother's angry voice urging me to get up. Feeling very woozy, I closed my eyes.

I was suddenly aware of a male face near mine, a rush of breath to my ear, and a soft, familiar voice whispering, "You had better get up and do as your mother says. After all, you would not want her to think that you have been a bad girl, would you? You would not want your parents to feel humiliated, eh? So get up and get moving. People are waiting for you." It was Aalim, the author of my shame and the sharer of my terrible secret.

The implications of Aalim's whispered words penetrated my dazed mind. He was threatening to expose my shame, even though he couldn't have done so without revealing his role in it. His words had the intended effect. I got up off the bed.

My shoes were too tight. I had to take them off and walk on burning feet with my female escorts along the road to our neighbour's house. My mother met us at the bottom of the stairs. The guests were all gathered in the tent on the rooftop. I thought I was composed and ready, but suddenly panic rose up in my breast. This was my last chance. I tearfully begged my mother not to make me go up. She smacked me across the face, and hissed, "If you think you are going to live in my house as my *sautan*" – in Punjabi this means a father's second wife – "you had better think again. I would carve you limb from limb first. Get upstairs and get married."

What Ma Ji had said was truly unforgivable, implying that I would be vying with her for my father's sexual favours. It was so shocking that I found myself more than willing to go through with the ceremony. Blinded by tears I made my way up the stairs and stood in front of the pastor.

I don't remember the ceremony. I don't remember the vows. I recall that Ralph looked concerned, so my distress must have been evident in my face. His relatives also seemed uneasy. His older sister came to me after the ceremony and hugged me, saying, "He is not such a bad fellow, you know. Don't be so worried."

There were two chairs behind the table which had held the marriage certificate. Ralph and I were seated on them. People began to move the folding chairs around and sit in groups. There was none of the vibrant festivity of Hindu weddings. Without music, dancing or alcohol, SDA weddings are subdued affairs. Ralph asked me in Hindustani, a mix of Hindi and Urdu, if I was all right and I said yes. Thereafter we always spoke in Hindustani. He said something else, I forget what, that made me smile, and instantly Aunt Madhu came and whispered in my ear not to talk so much and look happy or "people will gossip." I was to look solemn, unhappy to leave my parents' home, not joyous lest it be taken as a sign of lascivious anticipation.

When it was time for us to depart, Aunt Madhu and the same two women assembled to walk me to my new husband's home. At this point in Indian movies featuring weddings, the script usually includes a sweet, playful scene, in which the bride's married girlfriends try to quell her anxieties. They remind the bride that she is loved and that this will be the night that begins a long, romantic partnership. Affectionate hugs and assurances of her family's support tell her she is not alone, and that her future life will be shiny and good. In my case there were no hugs or reassurances from my parents. There were no girlfriends. My escorts were fed up with me and couldn't wait to be done with their responsibilities. They delivered me to Ralph's lodgings. As they pushed me through the door, my aunt Madhu said, "Don't fight, do as he says." Then I heard the women giggling as they locked the door and fled.

Ralph had rented a one bedroom apartment, less than four hundred square feet . It didn't take long to explore. It contained two charpoys, a small table with two chairs, a kerosene stove in a corner, two small pots, four plates, a paring knife, four drinking glasses and a few spoons. There was a sink with running water in the cooking area and a separate bathroom with shower and toilet. The apartment was clean, and I could finally use the toilet, a great relief.

I had been distracted by the evening's events, but now I was again gripped by fear. I wasn't sure how Ralph would discover my secret, I just believed that he would. If Ralph sent me home, Papa would have to kill me. I could not be allowed to live in my father's house as though nothing had happened. If he failed to kill me, he would also have failed in his duty to make me an example to my sisters, and then they might become careless of their chastity. Most important to him, he would have lost face in the community.

This couldn't have happened at a worse time in my father's career. After so much struggle he had finally made it to the higher levels of the Church administration. How he had gloried in his new promotion. He was now "President of the Central India Region," the first SDA native to achieve such a distinguished position. And now I was going to bring his career crashing down in ruins around him. I waited for Ralph, churning with dread. How I longed for someone in whom I could confide and be advised by, someone who might help me find a way to save my father's honour without having to die.

Time passed. I tried to think of less hopeless scenarios. There was the faint possibility that Ralph would not find out. Then he would think he was deflowering a virgin. Would it be as terrible as what Aalim had done? If I had to endure a lifetime of that, it seemed to me that being killed by my father was a more pleasant alternative.

Romantic songs about the wedding night one heard on the radio were never very clear about what actually happened. It was all innuendo, the kind of lyrics where the singer coyly pleads with the bumble bee to be gentle when opening the flower bud, because the dew on the petals is precious. Once, when I was about twelve, I was scrubbing the large curry pot with ash from the wood-burning stove and singing my heart out. The film 'Junglee' was popular then, and every rickshaw puller could be heard crooning lyrics which roughly translate from the Hindi as "I am begging to be allowed to say that I have fallen in love with you and so please let me stay where I am always visible to you." My mother heard me singing and grabbed me by my hair and kicked me, shouting, "You want to be seen, you want to stay under a man, I will carve you into pieces before you are under him." I had no idea what she was screaming about.

I sat on the charpoy in my white wedding sari thinking of Papa, and wondering how he would kill me if Ralph sent me home. Strangling? Knife? Poison? I did not feel anger at the thought. I felt very sorry for him. I loved my father so much that the thought of his humiliation sickened me. I hoped I would have the opportunity to tell him that I loved him and that I was not angry with him for ending my life.

I dozed off. I woke up to find Ralph on top of me. I struggled, but it was all over in a very short time. He went back to his charpoy and fell asleep in seconds.

I curled up and stayed awake for a little while, then drifted off too. My married life had begun. My husband had not discovered my secret. Married sex was something I now knew I could cope with. I was alive. I didn't have to commit suicide, and my father's honour was safe. I felt a faint stirring of hope for the future.

Chapter Nine

Husband versus Father

Our marriage was doomed to failure, but not because it was arranged. Arranged marriages can and do work in cultures where it is the norm. In the beginning I had no reason to think our marriage would not work. Knowing my secret was safe provided a kind of euphoria of its own. Ralph did not handle stress well, as I would come to understand, but he was not by nature unkind and our early months of marriage passed without any omens of future strife.

It was only as time wore on that our troubles began. I can see that if I had married a Punjabi man, as my father would have preferred, life might have been simpler for me. In that scenario it would have been understood that I would have little or no further contact with my family. My family would see me when my in-laws decided it was appropriate, such as at family weddings or other celebrations, and even then they could choose not to invite my family. In a Punjabi marriage I would belong to the in-laws and there would be no question of where my loyalty lay. If Ralph were Punjabi, he would have been my new Lord and Master, and my father would never have dared to treat him with disrespect.

But our situation was not normal. I was now a woman, not a girl, but unlike most Indian brides, I didn't make a clean break with my family. Ralph and I slept in our apartment, but the rest of the time our lives and fortunes were entwined with those of my parents. We would breakfast with them, then spend the day at the school where Ralph taught and I cleaned and looked after children. After the school day, we had dinner at my parents' home and only got back to our apartment late at night. It seemed normal to me, but in retrospect I can see that my ill-defined status was not the best foundation for a healthy or mutually supportive relationship.

I found myself torn between a powerful man I had loved unconditionally all my life, whatever his faults, and a stranger I happened to be living with, whose languid temperament and westernized family background I quickly prejudged as manhood and character deficits. I was as dutiful a wife as I could be under the circumstances, but in my heart, lacklustre Ralph never really stood a chance against my charismatic father.

My father was a man of limited education, but high ambitions and, thanks to strong family ties and the adulation lavished on him as an oldest son, a man of supreme self-confidence. He had married a poor woman whose family made no demands on him, a woman utterly dependent on his good will, and therefore reliably supportive of all his initiatives and decisions.

Ralph's family ties were rather weak, so Papa assumed Ralph would emulate him. It was Papa's idea that he would mould Ralph into a younger version of himself. But Ralph lacked Papa's dynamism and entrepreneurial spirit. Instead of deferring to him, he felt humiliated by Papa's crude attacks on his personality, family and cultural background.

Papa would say things like, "The Anglo-Indians are the 'leftovers' of the British" – but the word for 'leftovers' in Punjabi can also imply 'feces.' When introducing Ralph to someone, Papa might say, "We are Punjabi from Jullandhar," but of course Ralph wasn't Punjabi, and he understandably resented Papa's obvious message to others that his son-in-law's provenance was so embarrassing it had to be covered up with a lie.

They were as different as day from night. If Ralph went into a store to buy a shirt and the salesman said it cost 25 rupees, Ralph would say, "Oh, I only have 20 rupees. I will come back when I have 25 rupees. I really like that shirt," and the shopkeeper would give it to him for 20 rupees and they would both be happy. My father would say, "What? 25 rupees? Is it embroidered with gold to ask such an outrageous price? If I had the time to look around, I could find it for five rupees. You think you can rob everyone who walks though the door, but I am not that stupid." He said this with a smile, so instead of kicking him out, the inwardly seething shopkeeper would have to haggle. In the end Papa would pay 18 rupees and consider Ralph a wimp and himself a manly fellow.

Papa's nephews and cousins were just like him, and he would joke to them in front of Ralph, "One of you should take Ralph out and train him. He has a lot to learn about being a man." But he wasn't joking, and Ralph knew it, and like the shopkeeper, seethed inwardly, but unlike the shopkeeper, was too proud to haggle.

I should have been sympathetic to Ralph when he complained of these humiliations. But the truth is, I adored my father's wit and loved his stories of success, so when Ralph complained, I usually took my father's side. "What harm is there in learning to save money?" I would reason. "Why not learn from him, since he is now your father as much as mine?" But a father-son relationship between Papa and Ralph was never going to happen. Papa would probably not have had much respect for any man who was not a full-blooded Punjabi like himself, and especially not people who had almost completely lost touch with their Indian roots, a fact I confirmed for myself during a visit to Ralph's family shortly after we married.

The family lived in the big central city of Nagpur. Their large but rather shabby home was situated in a gracious, leafy neighbourhood that had seen better days during the Raj. It had once belonged to a British engineer involved in the development of the area's coalmines.

Ralph's stepfather was a bookkeeper for the coalmines. His mother was fair-complexioned, with light brown hair and blue eye. She dressed in a western style and was often taken for British. Ralph's older sister went to clubs, dated men freely and even brought them home. She ended up marrying the younger brother of his stepfather. Yet they all loved each other and tolerated behaviour that was unthinkable in my home. But instead of envying the informality and democracy of this *laisser-faire* household, I was appalled by it.

The household language was English, and fortunately the conversational level was simple enough for me to understand. Once his mother called out to Ralph's nineteen year-old brother and asked him to make her some tea, and he yelled back, "Put down your romance novel, get up and make your own cup of tea. Shake a leg!" Everyone laughed. I was shocked. Surely she would be furious at him. But then on his way out, he bent down and kissed her good-bye, saying he would be late and not to wait up. She yelled at him, "Have fun, and don't get anybody pregnant." They all laughed again.

Once, sitting with all of us in the living room, Ralph's sister started to shave her legs, up to her knees. I was mortified by this coarse and immodest behaviour. The youngest of the brothers started to yell at her for using his last blade. The mother gave him money to buy new ones. My cheeks burned. These people said and did anything they wanted. They were unaccountable to anyone but themselves. I hated it. I thought they were the most shameful people I'd ever met, and I rather foolishly said so later to my parents, which I am sure only poured oil on the flames of my father's contempt for Ralph.

Raised in this socially amorphous household, Ralph had no role models or inner guidelines for heading his own. His father had left the family financially secure, but his stepfather had frittered away his and his siblings' inheritance. Embittered, Ralph preferred life at boarding school and vacations working at school or visiting friends' homes to life in the same house with his stepfather.

So between the two of us – me brainwashed into hero worship of a cavalier and insensitive father, he without inner certainties about what a real Indian husband should be – we were ill equipped to resist my father's domination of our lives. Sometimes Ralph would buy into my mother's soothing scenario: "Father sees you as a son, Ralph. He loves your obedience and respect. He pushes you so hard because he wants you to be successful. Your success is his success." Other times he could not contain his anger and would come home in a rage that frightened me.

If I agreed with him to bolster his ego, he would urge me to go and make his case to my father, which I could not do. If I defended my father, Ralph would sometimes lash out at me physically. Afterward he felt terrible and I accepted his apologies. Ralph was not a chronic abuser. He wasn't the kind of man who enjoys controlling women or exercising violence against them for its own sake. A pattern emerged in his episodic violence against me. It happened when he was frustrated by a situation he could not control or when he felt humiliated by someone higher than himself in our rigid cultural pecking order. Or, as I would discover, when I cast aspersions on his manhood. I understood why it was happening, but with the first blow, my brief hope that I might find a protector in marriage died.

A few months into our marriage, during a day following a particularly tense episode between Papa and Ralph, one of my sisters brought me the message that I was to get dressed nicely. My parents were taking Ralph and me out for an evening meal and, I was told, they were going to buy me a new outfit too. I was delighted. I told Ralph that it was Papa's way of making up to us for his rough treatment of him.

We travelled by rickshaw, the only necessary means of transportation in such a small place. Ma Ji and I were in one rickshaw, Papa and Ralph following in another. I remember being excited and very chatty because this was our first social outing as two adult couples. My mother seemed strangely sulky and unresponsive, but nothing could dampen my high spirits, and I continued babbling on about clothes and what we would have for dinner, until finally my mother snapped, "Shut up. Shut up. I have something to tell you."

Startled, I complied, wondering how I could possibly have offended her this time. Ma Ji said, "We are not going for dinner. We are not going to buy clothes. We are going to see a woman. She will help you drop it."

Drop it? *It*? What did she mean? But before I could frame a question, Ma Ji had plunged into what was obviously a prepared speech. "She will open your legs, and with a metal stick she will pull it out and then everything will be fine. It hurts, but not too much. You just have to grin and bear it. There will be one or two other women helpers there to hold your legs open. I have done this several times and I know what I'm talking about. Just be quiet. We are almost there."

I realized she was describing an abortion, but why? Now Ma Ji began crying as she saw the bewilderment on my face. "You don't even know you are carrying a child. You don't even know you are going to be a mother. You are so young and naïve. You know nothing about being a woman. But now you are going to learn."

It came out that after only a few months of marriage, I had casually mentioned to a church "auntie" that my periods had stopped, and she had passed this information on to my mother. I had no idea why they had stopped and didn't consider it worthy of concern. I couldn't be blamed for failing to connect the absence of periods with pregnancy, because nobody had ever taught me the basic facts of reproduction. Even when I started having morning sickness, I didn't comprehend what was happening inside me.

As the light of understanding dawned, my mother clutched my arm, saying, "We decided this was best for you because you are too young and immature for so much responsibility." So much *responsibility*? I had changed the diapers, fed, bathed, soothed and kept every one of my siblings safe from snakes since I was a child myself. I knew as much about childcare as any woman on the planet. Ma Ji then added as a casual afterthought what was clearly the real reason: "We need you to help out at the school. Father cannot afford to hire a cleaner."

For a second I wondered if Ralph was in on this plan, if this was his revenge for my disloyalty to him. (Years later, I found out he was as clueless as I was.) The rickshaw slowed down to turn a corner. Without thinking, I jumped out and started to run. The element of surprise gave me a good head start. I ran through back alleys, shop-filled streets and finally into farmland, not knowing or caring where I ended up. I ran out of steam in a field of ripe green beans. There was a tree in the middle of it. Trees had always been a symbol of pleasure and refuge for me, and instinctively I climbed into it.

I hid in the branches for the better part of the evening and considered my situation. It began to grow dark. First I worried about snakes, then about the farmer finding me, then about men who kidnap women and sell them into slavery. I considered the child growing inside me. Suddenly, unbidden, an image of my unborn child overwhelmed my mind and my emotions. It was a baby girl. I was sure it was a girl. But this baby was not going to be aborted. This baby girl was not going to be unloved. This baby girl was never going to be thrown on a heap of garbage, or threatened with drowning in a well, This baby girl was never going to be called an unworthy creature. At least not by her mother. I crouched in the tree and prayed that I would be strong enough and live long enough to protect my daughter from harm. Running away and hiding was not a very good beginning to my plan, though. I wasn't hungry yet, but eventually I would have to eat. I had no other options, so I got down from the tree and trudged back to the town lights.

I found my way home, and without a word to Ralph took a shower and went to bed. I felt anger, but I had nowhere to direct it. I could not allow myself to be angry at my parents. After all, everything they did was motivated by concern for my well being. And if Ralph were complicit, I could therefore not be angry at him either. I slept it off. It took forty-eight hours of near-continuous oblivion, but I wasn't angry any more when I woke up. Ralph and I never discussed it then, but the episode nudged us into an unspoken alliance, and the recognition that if we were to live together as a couple, we needed to put distance between us and my father.

Chapter Ten

Somebody at last

We had been married less than four months when Ralph and I left for Amritsar, where Ralph's application for the job of pastor at a SDA church and administrator of a small school had been accepted. My parents offered no resistance. By then my father was curious to see if Ralph could make it on his own.

The next six months were the happiest of my life. With a full heart I gave my undivided attention to my husband, who finally felt like a real man with a biddable wife. He stopped taking out his frustrations in abuse. At the same time my pregnancy offered justifiable freedom from sexual obligations. I slept unmolested. I had leisure to cook, which I loved, and which pleased Ralph.

And for the first time in my life I went to see films in air-conditioned theatres, a longstanding pleasure of my husband and a welcome respite from the oppressive heat of our apartment. At first I felt guilty about eating this forbidden SDA fruit, but as it was my husband's wish, I persuaded myself I was only doing my wifely duty in accompanying him. I adored all the Indian films, of course. But how I loved *Gone with the Wind,* and I cried and cried during *Doctor Zhivago.*

The city of Amritsar is the seat of the Golden Temple, the most holy site for Sikh people, who constitute a majority of Amritsar's population. Its beauty and historic importance summoned particular ambition in the hearts of Christian missionaries. However, they had little luck with the middle and upper classes of Amritsar, the most prosperous inhabitants of the already disproportionately well-off Punjab. Most of those who converted were Untouchables and lower caste people who had left their villages to seek jobs in the big city. They had a habit of changing religions for opportunistic reasons. Once they integrated into their respective communities, the majority of the new converts reverted to what they had been before, the adoption of a new faith having been a temporary distraction during their settlement phase.

On the other hand, people of all religions wanted their children to learn English. This made the Church school very desirable.

As I had hoped, my baby was a girl, born March 18, 1969. We named her Romina, although from the beginning we called her only by her nickname, Mina. I was thrilled by the unexpected intensity of my father's joy. This female child's purity and marriageability would not be his burden. Free of the heavy cultural anxieties attached to sex, he could rejoice in his new status as, at only 41 years of age, the youngest grandfather on the head office campus. He would walk around holding the baby, exquisitely outfitted in one of Naani Ji's expertly crocheted dresses, showing her off to everyone. "Look at her! She looks just like me. I am the youngest Nana ever."

But I was thrilled with everything. For the first time in my life I was treated by my family as an adult. I was fussed over by my mother, who cooked me foods I craved, and gave me her undivided attention. Papa booked me into a private maternity clinic rather than a hospital, which must have cost him quite a lot of money. I was attended by a female doctor and two nurses, and afterward my mother and two aunts were allowed to stay with me. I was the wife of a man with an auspicious career before him. I had given birth to a beautiful, healthy child, even if it was a girl. My parents were proud of me. Everyone was kind to me. I was Somebody at last. It was bliss.

Chapter Eleven

"Stand up for yourself"

We were posted to Jullandhar in July, 1969, where Ralph took up his duties as Church Pastor of the SDA North Indian headquarters, a career coup for him. Ralph was pleased with his job, which involved a diversity of routine functions, none very onerous. He especially enjoyed entertaining officials from the national head office or showing off the city to visiting American SDA people. Everyone treated him with respect, and life was very agreeable for him.

My experience of Jullandhar life was rather different. Our SDA-owned flat was located in a pleasant middle-class neighbourhood, but it was quite far from the SDA campus, at least 45 minutes by rickshaw, which meant I had no opportunity to mingle with SDA community members. I had become pregnant again when Mina was only six months old. So I felt especially vulnerable and socially isolated, an unusual situation for a young Indian mother, especially someone like me, who had spent most of my life up to then constantly in the company of sisters and aunties and friends.

On the floor above us lived distant relatives by marriage on my father's side – the Gilberts – but there was a kind of cold war in progress between them and my parents, so that was a social opportunity lost. Our next-door neighbours were high caste Hindus, but they might as well have lived ten miles away. Even if there had been a houseful of young mothers living there with a whole nursery full of babies, I would never have dreamed of initiating any social contact of any kind with them.

So I was lonely, restless and slightly anxious. Then too, my first pregnancy had been easy, so I was surprised at how physically miserable I was during this one. I seemed to have very little energy, and struggled to care for Mina and manage our little household by myself. I depended on Ralph to bring us groceries. Without a refrigerator I could only cook for one day at a time, so when Ralph was delayed I would go hungry until he got home. Most nights Ralph came home late after a convivial evening with some local or national big shot.

The heat was oppressive. I would sometimes block the shower drain, fill the shower floor with cold water to the top of the six-inch overflow wall, and sit in it with the baby to prevent heat stroke, a very common cause of death in India. Our ground floor quarters were spacious and comfortable enough, except when it rained. Then the flat could flood without warning. I never knew what would float in – snakes, insects and all manner of filth from the streets.

I coped pretty well for a while, but as the pregnancy progressed, I often felt depleted, sometimes even ill, and it became harder to give Mina her due attention. There were now occasions when Ralph was away on three or four-day trips, and I grew uneasy about our vulnerability. Ralph explained that these trips were necessary for his career advancement, but I felt a disproportionate sense of abandonment when I was left with little or no money, and meagre handfuls of staples like flour and oil and rice. When I had to shop by myself in a rickshaw for the fresh vegetables I craved, my growing bulk made it awkward and uncomfortable managing the bags of food with a baby in my arms.

One day the region was struck by a monsoon. At first I wasn't too worried. Monsoons were no novelty to me. I had plenty of clean water and enough food for a few days. If things got bad, well, Ralph was in town. He knew our situation – that we were really alone, the incommunicative Gilberts having gone home to their village – and would find a way to get to us.

The second night was very bad. Ralph had not come home, and the thunder and lightning didn't let up. Cataracts of rain fell incessantly. I dozed fitfully, but when I got up to go to the bathroom, I stepped into water up to my ankles. Water with *things* in it that made me shudder with dread. I quickly amassed as much food as I had in the flat for myself – fortunately I was still nursing the baby – as well as boiled water in a *matka*, the clay pot that kept our water cool, and as many clean diapers as I had. Then I settled in with the baby on my charpoy.

The solitude was terrible. I was desperate to hear a human voice, see another human face. But even if I had overcome my reflexive social taboo against initiating contact with them, I could not have attracted my Hindu neighbours' attention. The windows were closed, and the inundations had reduced visibility to zero, giving me the impression that my flat was an island, completely cut off from the rest of the world and not just my neighbours, but all humanity. Even if the windows had been open, the roar of the rains would have drowned out my cries for help. I was utterly alone.

I prayed to God to find my father or Ralph to come and get us. I imagined our eventual death. Would we drown or would the snakes get us first, I wondered. I reminded myself of how often I had dealt with unpleasant situations, and tried to convince myself I would survive this one too.

As time wore on, and nobody came, I thought about my pledge to Mina in my womb, how I had vowed to protect her from harm. I couldn't do that alone. I made deals with God. I reminded Him of how dutiful I had been, and if that wasn't a good enough argument, He should consider how faultless my baby was. But I didn't really believe He would respond to that argument either. I couldn't help thinking of the newborn baby girl on the garbage heap and Kiran burning in Delhi when I was a teenager, and everyone standing around doing nothing to help her. Where had God been then? God did not seem to care very much about the deaths of girls and women. Maybe if Mina had been a boy, God would have listened to me. The irony didn't escape me that if I had done as my parents wished and had an abortion, I wouldn't be in this perilous fix.

At a certain point my terror dissipated and I began to accept the fact that we were going to die in this fetid trap. Strangely, instead of making me sad, the thought of Ralph and my father finding our dead bodies evoked a little thrill of satisfaction. That my father would be with Ralph for the discovery was an irrational thought, because Papa was so far away, but in my altered state it seemed logical. I found myself grimly cheered by the anguish they would feel when they realized it was their fault I was dead. These were treacherous fantasies. I had never suppressed my doubts about Ralph, but now I had finally to admit to myself that my doglike love for my father was not as unconditional as I had always believed it to be.

And once I was in a truth-telling mode, I also admitted to myself that our deaths would not really affect Papa and Ralph all that much, or for all that long. The only one who would truly react with any emotion would be Naani Ji. She wouldn't mourn my dying so much as be angry at me for letting it happen. I pictured her scolding me for wasting time on self-pity and blaming others. I pictured her telling me that she would have found a way to survive and save her daughter, and I should too.

It rained for two nights and three days. I ran out of food and water after the second day on the charpoy. Ralph managed to get home twenty-four hours later. By that time the water in the apartment had receded, leaving a stinking mud-based slurry on the floor and lower walls. I was parched, starving, filthy, and exhausted. Ralph said he had wanted to get home, but the flooding was too bad, and the roads were all washed out. He explained that a staff member had invited him to stay at his home until the rains let up, and he had accepted. He said he had no way of getting in touch with me.

Realistically, he hadn't had much choice. But in my hysterical state I was convinced he did, and chose to keep himself dry and cozy instead of somehow making his way to us. When I found out that he had not even left the campus – hadn't even tried to make his way to us through the flooded streets…

Images of Simla rushed in on me. My mother, near-catatonic on the bed, nursing Baby in that frigid apartment. Me roaming the neighbourhood stealing food and money. My hungry siblings wailing. Of course I felt a disproportionate sense of abandonment. I was reliving my mother's experience in Simla. I saw my father, walking in after six weeks of well-fed glad-handing and busywork, cheerful, full of himself, oblivious to our helplessness and Ma Ji's derangement. Now I understood in my gut something of what had happened to her. I too had been temporarily crazed with fear, but I wasn't mad like she was. Perhaps the next time I would be, though. Or the next. I had no confidence that there wouldn't be a next time.

I vowed that I was not going to go mad waiting to be rescued by my husband or any other man. I recalled kindly Master Singh, who ran the small school I attended where I was the only Christian student, who had said something to me once that puzzled me, because it was a concept I had never come across before. When he saw that the other girls were mocking me, he told me first of all to stop singing the "bad" songs from the films because I was not being complimented in being asked to sing them. Then he added, "You must learn to stand up for yourself." Stand up for myself? Such an idea would never have entered my head. Then. Now I understood what Master Singh had meant. From that day forward, I was going to depend on myself for my survival. I was going to be like my Naani Ji. I was going to *stand up for myself.*

A cold draught blew through my heart. In its depths the flickering candle of hope for our marriage was extinguished once and for all. All I could think of was my husband, my supposed pillar of strength and protection, eating three meals a day, sleeping in a clean, dry bed, playing cards by lamplight in convivial company, while I …while I …

I looked at Ralph, and felt nothing but revulsion. I said, "My father was right about you. You are not a man, just a lizard. You are a lazy good-for-nothing, leaving your wife and child to die." Ralph grabbed the baby from me and threw her onto the other charpoy. Then he began smacking me. I didn't care. The more he hit me, the harsher grew the invectives that flew from my mouth.

The family with whom Ralph had spent those four days had sent food for us. He threw the bag on the bed and walked out. After comforting the baby and devouring the bag's contents – milk, rice, lentils, bananas, rotis – I rested. By nightfall the electricity was on and the water was running. While the baby slept, I cleaned myself and the apartment. I washed and bathed the baby. I made a little bed for her with dry towels from one of our big metal boxes. Sometime that night Ralph came back and I found him sleeping on the charpoy next to mine.

My anger subsided like the monsoon waters, but it left behind a slurry of contempt for my husband. Before that night I had found sex with Ralph distasteful. From then on I was disgusted at the very thought of his hands on my body.

For a few weeks after the monsoon, Ralph came home on time every night, and always with decent food as well. From time to time he brought luxuries like oranges. He said he was sorry for hitting me. But it was too late for that.

From then on I spoke only the words that were absolutely necessary. If Ralph asked, "Have you forgiven me?" I would reply "Yes." Then he would ask, "Do you care about me?" And I would reply "No." That would be the end of our conversation, and he would blow up, saying as he stormed out, "Well, you and your father can go to hell. I don't care. I don't have to come home, and maybe I won't come home."

One day Mina was very agitated and crampy, and no matter what I did she would not sleep. I felt very weak and ill myself, but I began to rub her stomach and sing to her. As the night wore on, I kept singing, hoping she would doze off, unaware that I was crying as I sang.

The windows were open, and I was overheard by the Duttas, the Hindu family living next door. Mohinder Sen Dutta was a young barrister, living with his sixty-something mother. That summer they had been joined by Mohinder's older sister Anita and her three daughters from South Africa. Another sister and her family lived in England. There was a high wall between our buildings, but their ground floor was six steps higher than ours, and they could look down from their living room and see into our apartment. When our windows were open, they would easily have heard my screams when Ralph was beating me.

The next day there was a knock at the door, and I opened it to find three girls – two teenagers and a seven-year old – standing there with baskets. They explained they were Mohinder Dutta's nieces. They said their mother thought perhaps I was unwell and unable to cook, so they had brought me some food.

I was dumbfounded that high-caste Hindus would even think of crossing my threshold, let alone treat me with such kindness. It was my good fortune that these people were highly educated and progressive in their thinking, and that their experiences in South Africa and England had distanced them from the caste system. The girls offered to babysit for Mina at their home, and I gratefully handed the baby to them, then lay down to rest. Soon after that the girls' mother appeared at the door. Her daughters had reported that I seemed ill, and after one look at me, she announced she was taking me to the local hospital.

I protested that the SDA campus had its own hospital, and my husband would take me there, but Anita, whom I would soon be calling *Behan Ji* – older sister – just said, "Good. I will call the Ruby Nelson Hospital and give them your name and tell them we are on the way there in a rickshaw." I didn't protest. I felt awful. At the hospital, I was examined and told I was extremely depleted, sleep-deprived and malnourished. I was given prescriptions to fill, with admonitions to rest, an impossibility I politely agreed to.

Anita Behan Ji and I were gone for three hours. When I got home, the apartment, which usually stank of baby urine, smelled like disinfectant. The Duttas's servant had cleaned the whole apartment. The threadbare bedding had been replaced with fresh linens. I found four unfamiliar towels – not new, but soft and clean – and other things too: boxes of biscuits, a jar of Horlicks, toothpaste, face cream, bath soap, and four saris with blouses large enough to fit my growing belly.

Next morning Behan Ji had my vitamin prescription filled. She brought me a bag of diapers – that is, machine-finished rectangles of thick, white cotton actually intended as diapers, rather than the thin and porous squares cut from bed sheets my mother used – and four pairs of plastic panties to cover them with, a fascinating novelty to me, as well as a plastic sheet to protect the bed.

When he returned that night, Ralph was shocked at the transformation of the apartment and demanded an explanation. I told him about the kind family next door, which didn't satisfy him at all. He went upstairs and asked the Gilberts about the Dutta family. He was told the occupants were an old woman and her bachelor son. Ralph came down in a fury and started hitting me as I cowered with the baby in a corner, accusing me of carrying on an affair with a man I had never even met.

As in a theatrical farce, Anita Behan Ji saw Ralph beating me through the open window and immediately came over to confront him. She said her brother was a lawyer and she could arrange for Ralph to spend a few days in jail, where he would undoubtedly learn what it felt like to be beaten himself.

This intervention was a serious affair. Mrs. Gilbert, who could also bear witness to the beating, was an illiterate village nobody, and could be easily intimidated by Ralph. But Anita Behan Ji was a high caste Hindu of Kashmiri royal lineage. She could not be intimidated or challenged, and Ralph didn't even try. Mrs.

Gilbert volunteered to inform my father and the SDA people about what had happened. By the next day everyone at SDA headquarters knew everything.

The following day the SDA president and his wife came by to see how I was, and to ask if there was anything they could do. They left me an envelope with 200 rupees in it and urged me to come and see them if ever I needed their help. Within days, I had passed from a state of morbid isolation to being surrounded by a warm and caring circle of generous friends in high places. The more care my new adoptive family lavished on me, the more Ralph absented himself from our home. That suited me just fine.

Chapter Twelve

Friends in need

Relations between me and Ralph did not improve. We barely spoke to each other, and Ralph found many and varied excuses to be away from home. But our estrangement was in its own way a blessing. The monsoon nightmare had convinced me that my social isolation was dangerous, so I was now alert and receptive to any opportunity to meet other women in the neighbourhood.

The Duttas found me two little children to tutor. Their parents wanted them to become familiar with English before starting English elementary school. This was a simple job, involving no literacy skills. I taught the children basic words like 'water,' 'bathroom,' 'please' and 'thank you.' I sang them nursery rhymes I'd learned from the missionaries, tunes I sang to my own child. I earned a bit of money and enjoyed the socializing the arrangements entailed.

Another unexpected but welcome consequence to the public exposure of our dirty domestic laundry was that I no longer strove to believe in my marriage as a work in progress. I once again settled into my role of dutiful wife, but my new emotional detachment from Ralph shielded a small niche of mental autonomy that he could not touch.

Everyone in the church community was gossiping about us, and to my surprise the majority opinion was sympathetic to me. Now, if I needed money, I would take the babies – Rubina, whom we never called anything but Bina, was born at the SDA's Ruby Nelson hospital in June, 1970 – in a rickshaw to the SDA accounts office and just collect small amounts on my husband's tab.

I became friendly with the Dutta children's grandmother, whom everyone called *bardi Mama* – '*bardi*' means 'older' – and she would invite me for tea, which often ran into supper. Bardi Mama would tell me stories of her past, especially the terrible events she witnessed during the turbulence around India's Independence, when Hindus were fleeing Muslims in the newly created state of Pakistan and Muslims were fleeing from Hindus in India.

One day she said to me, "You are now a teacher, a good teacher. You have to think and act like a person who is respected." I confessed to bardi Mama that I could barely read and write, so I could hardly call myself a real teacher. She waved away my doubts. The children were learning English. Their parents were very happy with what I was teaching them. So I was a good teacher, as far as she was concerned. Bardi Mama was a generous woman, working patiently and systematically to build up my self-esteem, a novel and exhilarating experience for me. When she praised me, I felt as though a locked door in my soul were creaking open to reveal a vista of previously unimagined possibilities.

Bardi Mama further astonished me when she told me that she had made a deal with her future sons-in-law before she handed over her daughters in marriage, that they would support their wives' wish to go on to university. Marriage, she said, should never stand in the way of an education. I couldn't stop thinking about that. A seed of hope lodged deep within me. Was there still a chance that I could get the education I longed for?

The seed took nourishment from the tentative friendship that had sprung up between me and Mrs. Gilbert after she bore witness to Ralph's bad treatment of me. I cultivated a positive relationship with her with an eye to an upstairs refuge in future monsoons. I would cook a little something for her, or buy some candies for her children, and little by little she warmed to me.

Mrs. Gilbert was happy to have a receptive audience for her complaints about my aunts who were married to her brothers, and I nodded polite assent to everything she said. Much more interesting were her stories about an older brother living in California, who was married to "Liz," an American woman who worked as a nurse. The brother was a high school principal and wealthy by our standards. He had sent his family in India money to build a larger home in their village. Mrs. Gilbert showed me photographs of him and his family, and letters, which she kept in an old cookie tin. One day – I don't know why, it was a sudden impulse – I reached into the tin when Mrs. Gilbert was distracted, and snatched one of the letters from America, even though I had no idea why I wanted it.

Weeks passed. I forgot about the stolen letter. But all my conversations with bardi Mama about women going to university and her continual prodding to get an education were making me restless. I finally mentioned to her that it was too bad I didn't know Mrs. Gilbert's brother in California. I told her about the letter, and between us a scheme was born.

Together we wrote a letter to Mrs. Gilbert's sister-in-law. I introduced myself to Aunt Liz and told her we were related by marriage. I explained my life situation and confided my wish to go to school. We had the letter translated into English and sent it off. And waited.

In September 1970, three months after Bina's birth, I received a letter, written in English, from Spicer Memorial College in Pune, the SDA's flagship centre for higher education in India. I rushed next door with it to have it translated. Bardi Mama's son revealed its contents, while I took in his words with stupefaction. Spicer College had received funds toward two years' worth of tuition and board, and they were writing to say I could start classes immediately. There was no time to waste if I intended to enrol even as a late-starting student.

In my naiveté, I accepted Aunt Liz's generosity as the hand of God reaching down to me. Of course in reality it was not quite the bolt from the blue it appeared to be. Years later I met Aunt Liz in Michigan, and I asked her why she had given such a beautiful gift to someone she had never even met. She explained to me that she was angry at the Indian side of her family, who didn't care about her for herself, but constantly pressed her for money to buy houses and cars. She said she knew about my situation through Mrs. Gilbert and was touched by my request for money to get an education, a means to a better life rather than an end in itself. It was her way of giving the finger to her more materialistic relatives.

Bardi Mama was all practicality. "You will need suitcases. You can't manage babies and metal trunks." It took a few minutes to understand what Bardi Mama was suggesting. She was telling me I should travel almost 2,000 kilometres with a toddler and an infant by myself. I hadn't thought about the logistics of such a trip, because I had never believed my fantasy would come true. Now the idea seemed terrifying, but also exciting.

Ralph was on tour. I had no way of discussing the situation with him, but I took that as a sign from God as well. I decided that my only hope was to present the situation to him as a *fait accompli*. If I could only get myself and the children to Pune, he might bluster, but since it would cost him nothing, he would accept it. He must. I had often prayed to God for a miracle that would allow me to continue my education. Bardi Mama believed I could do it. Aunt Liz in California believed I could do it. She'd even given me the money to do it. The heady, unfamiliar gift of other people's moral and material support for my dream was a miracle I would be both stupid and wrong to turn down. I had to believe Ralph's cooperation would be part of that miracle to have the courage to go, so I chose to believe it.

Everything happened very swiftly. In a matter of days I had sold my brass pots and pans, a few lamps and dinner plates and sewing machine. When I was ready to depart, Bardi Mama gave me a suitcase and a bag full of food. I was touched by this gesture. She had often shared her food with me, but I had never cooked for her, and now, considering the difference she had made in my life, I regretted that I had not been able to repay her generosity in kind. It wasn't because I was selfish. She was progressive in her thinking, and as proof had opened her door to a low caste woman like me, but as a high caste Hindu, she would never eat any food my hands had touched. We both knew our boundaries.

I packed only what was absolutely essential for myself and the babies. I did the laundry, cleaned the apartment and said my farewells to the few people I cared about. Saying goodbye to the Dutta family was difficult. I loved them and trusted them. They had helped me through a terrible time of my life, and to this day I never think of them without a pang of gratitude and wonder at my good fortune in attracting their patronage when I needed it most.

❈

Pune is in southern India. Delhi, where my parents lived at the time, was on the way. I intended to visit them, surprise them with the news of the gift, and enlist their support for my plan. But I arrived at their home to find Ralph there with them. They had summoned him, because Spicer College had informed them of the news as soon as the money arrived there. The miracle had been nothing but a brief illusion that I had some control over my fate. My father and Ralph had already double-crossed me. They had informed Spicer College that it wasn't me, but Ralph who would be finishing a two-year degree. They even gave the college administrators to understand that the California benefactor was Papa's relative.

I was devastated. All my dreams were like a dazzling sun suddenly eclipsed by a cold moon. Perhaps in my heart I knew all along that my dreams would be no match against my family's entrenched attitudes. And since there was no choice, I had to accept the situation. Well, I had always been a practical sort of person, and adaptive to situations I had no hope of changing. So I swallowed my disappointment and my rage against Ralph for his duplicity. But I avoided even thinking about my father's collusion with my husband. Conscious resentment of my father for any reason at all was still forbidden territory. So I told myself that being on the campus of a college was better than nothing, and perhaps I would find a way, once I was on the campus, to pick up bits of education here and there.

I was soon distracted from Papa's bombshell about my lost opportunity by news of their own. My parents informed us that they were leaving for Canada in a few months. The plan was that they would settle in and then set the bureaucratic wheels in motion for the rest of us to follow. They would be taking with them the three younger children, Paul, Pamela and Heather. Jessica and Dorothy would stay with me and Ralph. Mary would board at Spicer, which had a high school as well, so that we could all be together in their absence. Although their announcement was unexpected, it wasn't a complete surprise. Two of my uncles had already left for Canada the year before, and we knew many other SDA families who were planning to leave India or had already emigrated.

Ralph and I arrived at Spicer College two months after classes had begun. Neither Ralph nor I nor my father had thought to inform the college of our plans for such a late arrival. If we had, the college would have reserved student housing for us. Now we found they had given it away, and we had nobody but ourselves to blame. There was no affordable lodging in town. We were told that until proper housing could be found, temporary accommodation had been arranged for us in the college's *goodam* – the storage area.

The goodam was a vast industrial structure the size of a football field, subdivided into sections with tin walls. The south end housed the college's tractors, lawn mower and other maintenance machinery. The west side was filled with drums of seeds for the planting season, as well as enormous canisters of wheat, rice, flour and lentils for the cafeteria.

The east and the north sides were divided into smaller units, supposedly temporary overflow dwellings for us and four other families in need of student housing. We were placed in a two-room unit and told we would only be there overnight. We lived there for two years.

We settled into a routine. Ralph went to classes and I looked after the children and the house, such as it was. I would have been gloomy if I had been alone, but having my sisters with me made a big difference to my spirits. Mary boarded at the school, but Jessica and Dorothy stayed with us. My parents assured us they would send money for expenses once they were settled in Canada.

The plan was for Ralph to attend classes and for me to find work. A month before Ralph's family arrived, I had found a part-time job in the college bakery for the morning hours before Ralph left for classes. I would arrive at five a.m. when the bread had already been baked. I filled orders in the back as they came in and brought them to the cashier in front. Then I would rush home so Ralph could leave for class. I would have been happy to work longer hours for the welcome extra income, but we couldn't afford to engage a servant.

Not more than a month into our Pune adventure, I was on my way to work, and as usual on the lookout for the small but deadly water snakes that abounded in this area. I noticed a woman sitting under a tree beside a stream. That was a strange sight at such an early hour. From her stillness and vacant stare, I had the feeling she had been there all night. I asked her if she was not afraid of the snakes. She responded that she was waiting for the snake god to come and bless her.

Indians harbour an ambivalence toward snakes. There is the fear, of course, but also a kind of respect and admiration for them too. Certain Hindus leave milk out for them. If they see a snake slithering away, they think the snake came to bless them. But in this woman's case it turned out that by "bless," she meant she was waiting for the snake god to come to her and kill her.

The woman told me her name – Shanta Bai – and something of her history. Shanta had been married for twenty-three years, but she had not been able to give her husband children. He took a second wife, who threw her out of the house. Shanta Bai was in her late thirties, but looked twenty years older. She had nothing to her name but the clothes she was wearing and nowhere to go, so she was calmly waiting for death to claim her.

Something about Shanta's dignity in her dispossession spoke to me. Impulsively I told her I too had on occasion prayed for death to deliver me from hopelessness, but that if the snake god really wanted to find her, he could do so just as well if she were in a warm bed as under a tree. I invited her to come with me, adding that maybe we could be of use to each other.

At first Shanta was reluctant to abandon her fatalistic plan, but eventually she yielded to my determined urging. Shanta was taller than me – about five foot nine – and muscular, obviously a woman used to hard work. An idea was already taking shape in my mind. I took her to the bakery and gave her bread and the awful soya "tea" Adventists drink. While I attended to my chores, I told her something of my own history and how I had come to be in Pune. Then I told her that I had two young daughters, and that I could not work and look after them at the same time. Her listless eyes brightened as she saw where the conversation was going.

I told Shanta I would find a charpoy for her. I could not pay her anything, but she would eat what my daughters and I ate, and she would have a roof over her head. All I asked was that she keep my girls clean and safe, and I would work more hours to help feed us all properly. Shanta Bai lit up at the prospect. She came home with me after my shift.

Shanta became an active contributor to our household from her first day with us. The girls fell in love with Shanta at once. She sang to them, told them stories and took them everywhere with her. Not a minute of her day was aimless or without material purpose. As they walked around the neighbourhood, her sharp eyes were on the lookout for bottles to take to the recycling centre. Every cent she got went toward food for the house.

I trusted Shanta completely. I would give her my household allowance for a month and tell her she was responsible for feeding us all, five adults and two children, as well as friends Ralph or my sisters brought home. Magically she managed. She had an arrangement with the milkman, helping him deliver milk to certain homes morning and night in exchange for a few jugs for us. She let the girls drink all they wanted and set out the rest to make yogourt. Nothing was wasted, and we were never without food for dinner, cooked in the outdoor chulah and eaten as we sat on upturned milk pails under a tree.

I noticed that Shanta Bai went barefoot all the time, and I worried about her being snakebitten while out with the girls. So I insisted on buying her shoes – a pair of sneakers and a pair of flip flops – and felt rather proud of myself. Never having owned a pair of shoes in her life, Shanta found them to be a strange and rather hilarious encumbrance. A few days later our paths crossed while she was out with the girls, as usual one on her shoulder, one on her hip – and hanging from her waist by a string both pairs of shoes. I gave up and decided not to worry any more.

For two years Shanta Bai loved and protected my daughters. She was always happy. You could hear her laughing with the girls as she fed and bathed and played with them. Seeing how carefree my girls were, I was filled with gratitude, and never took Shanta for granted. I wouldn't begin eating until she was sitting beside me, and I made sure her meal was exactly the same as mine. When she went to the wedding of a distant kinsman, she wore one of my saris and had with her enough money that she would not feel humiliated before her relatives. She was our mother and our household manager, and we happily did as we were told.

During the winter of our first year, Ralph informed me that he had sent some money to his family so they could come and spend their holidays with us. We would be feeding and sheltering his mother, stepfather and two teenage half-brothers. My sisters would stay in the college dorm for the duration of their visit. When I asked him where he had found the money for such expansive hospitality, he replied off-handedly that he had withdrawn it from my college fund. He added that we shouldn't have to worry about money any more, since the person who had created this fund would send more if necessary. And anyway, he concluded triumphantly, as if this were an irrefutable justification for his free spending, my parents were *in Canada*. He seemed to believe the streets of Canada were paved with gold.

A few days later Ralph's family arrived. Ralph must have spun fantasies of sudden wealth for them, because from the first day they acted like tourists, taking taxis wherever they wanted and eating in restaurants and going to movies. In the evenings I would listen to Ralph, as he sat outside with them, talking about all the money that would soon be coming from Canada. "There are only good times ahead!" he would brag to his family and, foolishly, to anyone else in the vicinity. "We are feeding his daughters, so my father-in-law is beholden to us. He better send us truckloads of money." Word of Ralph's bluster got back to my father, who learned that all the money they were sending us was being spent on showing Ralph's family a good time.

My father had always been contemptuous of Ralph, and here was further validation of his assessment. But there wasn't much he could do about it. Their working lives in the tightly-knit SDA community were bound up together and Ralph was right, my siblings were living under Ralph's protection. So they had to rub along together as best they could. As the son-in-law, Ralph had the upper hand in the relationship. He could blackmail my father at any time by threatening to leave me. I had come to him without a dowry, which gave him additional moral authority, and without my father's intimidating presence as a counterweight, Ralph was revelling in his power.

Shanta Bai was aware of my unhappiness around Ralph's family's visit and the money he was lavishing on them. When I grumbled, she would gently remind me that I must consider the importance of winning my mother-in-law's good opinion so that she would be kind to me.

Well into their visit, when the family arrived back from a day's outing, Shanta Bai announced she had made some special treat for dinner. Ralph's brother said not to bother as he and the rest of the family had just eaten at a restaurant. As calmly as I could manage, I asked Ralph how we were to afford all this, reminding him that we also had to provide all his family with bus fare home, and where was that going to come from? To this he angrily shouted, "They are staying put until I say they go. You can get your lawyer boyfriend or your boyfriend in America who sends you money to send some more – or you can write to your damn father, the King of Canada, who sold us a bill of goods…"

A bolt of white-hot rage shot through me. How dared he say the word "boyfriend" to me? A real Punjabi man would have killed me if he thought I was sleeping with another man. That Ralph could believe I had sexually betrayed him and do nothing about it to redeem his honour proved he wasn't a real man in my eyes. I snarled, "You are the damn loser. And you call yourself a man. Telling your wife to beg money from her boyfriends. Only an Anglo-Indian man would say something so vile." These words sound far more poisonous in Hindustani than in English. Everyone was stunned into silence.

As a rule Shanta did the cooking outside the unit in a chulah similar to the one Dadi Ji had in Chukwal, but instead of cow dung, she used painstakingly collected wood. Ralph strode to the woodpile, snatched a cudgel-size piece, and with it struck a hard blow to my shoulder that sent me flying into the dirt. He threw it aside and turned to reassure his mother that everything was fine. His nervous family suggested he sit down and cool off. He slumped down onto his charpoy, near our baby, Bina. She had witnessed all this and was frightened by it. She began to scream. Ralph picked her up by one arm and flung her to the ground. Shanta, hovering over the baby as always, lunged at her and managed to break her fall.

I gasped in shock at Bina's narrow escape from injury. I lost it. I could have coped with him beating me, but not my child. I picked up the same piece of wood and attacked Ralph. I hit him in the head first and blood spurted out. Then I hit him on his shoulder and then his head again. I was clubbing him with all my strength and if his brothers had not grabbed me, I would have kept at it until I killed him.

After the brothers wrestled the wood away from me, I turned to Ralph's mother. Shanta grabbed me, fearful I would now attack my mother-in-law, but I was calm and in control of myself. I hissed at Ralph's family to pack up and get out. They were gone in ten minutes.

Ralph left too. I did not see him for weeks. I brought Jessica and Dorothy home from the dorm, and told them what had happened, warning them to be careful, not to walk around alone. I could not be sure Ralph wouldn't take revenge on me through my sisters.

Of course the story of my violent assault on Ralph raced like wildfire through the SDA community, and it wasn't long before my father was informed of it. I was called to the registrar's office to take a telephone call from Papa, the first time I had ever spoken to him or anyone else through this apparatus

Papa said he had heard the whole story from witnesses he trusted, and that he did not blame me. But he asked me to consider the big picture before burning my bridges with Ralph. He explained that the only way we could come to Canada was as a family unit. That Ralph had the power to prevent me and our daughters from leaving India. That I had to put aside my anger and think about our future.

Papa quickly made arrangements for Mary, Jessica and Dorothy to travel to Canada, and they were soon gone. For Ralph and me mediation and prayer sessions were arranged, and there was a great deal of talk about forgetting and forgiving. But it wasn't prayer and spiritual strength that brought me to an accommodation with Ralph. In August of 1972 we received a letter from Papa telling us that he had made arrangements for us to come to Canada in October. Excitement at the thought of leaving India overwhelmed my domestic misery.

Emigration was in the air amongst Adventists in India. We were all infected with the virus. Indian nationalism was gaining strength. Many Hindus were chanting slogans like "Hindustan for Hindus." Everyone knew that the white missionaries were being forced out of their posts in Christian institutions and urged to leave the country. Amongst the native SDA leaders there was increasing political infighting. The SDA culture no longer seemed very healthy for the long term, and we were swept up in a general exodus to the West.

My father's younger brother, Chacha Sadiq, had been in Canada for three years. He had gained entry at the invitation of a missionary, who gave him a letter of employment once he arrived. At that time, if they had relatives to sponsor them and an offer of employment, foreigners could come on a visit to Canada and then apply for residency from within the country. But after 1970 that changed, and you had to apply from outside the country.

My father wrote buoyant accounts of Canada as a land where success came quickly. He told us his younger brother, my Chacha Sadiq, had a beautiful home and a big car. I was particularly enchanted by my father's description of a magical small card my uncle owned with his name on it, which had salespeople running around to please him as soon as they saw it. These accounts confirmed what I had taken in from the missionaries, who also described Canada in glowing terms as a land where success and wealth came easily to God-fearing Christians. In the proselytizing films I saw, Christians were clean and good looking, with beautiful teeth and happy smiles. Converting to Christianity was always associated with better food and houses for the formerly poor and godless.

Besides, I had known hundreds of white missionaries in India. They told us they had made sacrifices to come to India and to teach the heathen and the uncivilized. But they all had exquisitely furnished homes, two or three cars and many servants. If that was what a life of sacrifice was for westerners, I imagined Canada must be the wealthiest nation on earth, and I was eager to get my share of it. But mostly I couldn't wait to be a member of the majority at last, no longer a despised minority. In short my image of Canada was that it was paradise on earth. My parents and sisters might have nuanced this fairy tale vision, but Papa only communicated with Ralph about practical matters, and I was still too illiterate to exchange letters with my sisters.

I had no regrets about leaving, and nobody to whom I was particularly attached. Except Shanta. Parting with Shanta was painful. I helped her to find a place to live before we left and gave her everything we had in that little tin hut. She sold several of the charpoys and other things that did not fit into her new one-room home. From the time we arrived in Canada, I sent her money every month until she died of cancer in 1978.

Chapter Thirteen

A rude welcome to Canada

We kept secret the news of our imminent departure for Canada. Indians leaving for the West at that time did not make a show of their good fortune. Inside I was bubbling over with anticipation. I wanted to jump up and down and shout, "I am going to Canada!" But I remembered my father's warnings. He had told me that amongst the very people who smiled and warmly congratulated me, there could well be someone so filled with envy and resentment, he might go and lodge a false complaint for the malicious pleasure of scuttling my plans. So I bottled up my excitement, and concentrated on the obstacle course that had to be negotiated in order to leave India even when nobody was trying to stop you.

There was no getting around the fact that civil servants had to be bribed. In India it is useless to take the view that since your claims are legitimate, bribery is unethical. There is nothing to be gained by refusing to take part in this established charade – unless, of course, you don't mind when your official documents get processed, if ever.

Preparing for the bribery process, Papa had sent money to the Delhi SDA head office, with clear instructions that the money should be delivered to me, not Ralph. We stayed in Delhi with *Taaya* Lall, one of my father's cousins. (If he were young I would have called him Chacha, but he was older, so he was Taaya Lall to me.) Taaya Lall and Ralph were to plod through the bureaucratic labyrinth together, while I looked after the girls. Everything – getting the airline tickets, assembling birth, education certificates and other documentation, the medical examinations – was time-consuming. Our inefficiency was directly linked to our – or rather to Ralph and Taaya Lall's – clumsiness in negotiating the bribery system.

The way it worked was to ramp each bribe up or down according to the functionary's place in the civil service hierarchy. We had to give enough to win favour for our petition, but not go over our budget. The officials usually assumed we could give more if we wanted. It became clear to me, watching them operate, that Ralph and Tayya Lall were acting too arrogantly in their dealings with the functionaries and adding insult to injury by under-bribing them. So I began to accompany them with the children in tow to add pathos to the appeal. I broke down crying more than once, begging the officials not to take away the only opportunity we might ever have to emigrate.

Three weeks went by. We had everything else, but we still didn't have our visas. Finally there were only two days left before the flight. The tension was unbearable. This time all three of us got up at the crack of dawn and took the girls. The office was mobbed, every transaction agonizingly slow and the waiting interminable. Taaya Lall was not feeling very well. I told him to sit on the lawn with Ralph, and I stayed in line with the girls, who were getting crankier by the minute. Just as I got within sight of the window, the clerk announced he was closing up for lunch and would be back in an hour. That meant the window would open in one hour, and the clerk might be back in two if we were lucky.

There were several men ahead of me, but I pushed myself to the front and leaned into the window just as he was about to close it. With a coquettish air I inquired, "I am from Pune and I don't know where to eat lunch. Where do you normally go?" The balding, middle-aged clerk smiled knowingly at me and said, "There are many places to eat. I have no special favourite." "Well," I purred, "If you could show me a good place to eat my lunch, it would be a wonderful memory to take with me to Canada," and as I spoke, I discreetly tossed an envelope containing our applications and 1,000 rupees to the counter on his side of the window. Without betraying a flicker of interest in the envelope, the clerk smoothly replied, "I will find the address of a good place for you to eat and write down the directions to get there." Then he deftly scooped up the envelope, went to the back and a little while later returned with directions to a restaurant – and our visas.

By the age of twenty-one, I had covered thousands of kilometres in trains, buses and rickshaws, but I had never travelled in an airplane before. Motion sickness was a novelty to me. From the moment we took off, I began to feel queasy. The plane was almost entirely full of Sikh men who were leaving their Punjabi villages to work on farms in British Columbia. Free alcohol was an astonishing novelty for them. The men got drunk within a few hours, danced boisterously and wouldn't sit down. The girls couldn't sleep. A stewardess felt sorry for them and moved us up to the near-empty First Class. The girls fell asleep, but I couldn't stop throwing up. The lemony smell of the bathroom made it worse. But I didn't bother the stewardess with it, because I assumed I was pregnant. In between periods of fitful doziness, I wondered how one got an abortion in Canada.

After fourteen hours in the air, the stewardess touched my shoulder and told me to buckle up for our landing in Paris. We were supposed to connect there for our flight to Montreal, a cheaper ticket than Toronto. But when we landed, we found that something was wrong with the Montreal-bound plane. The long trip became eighteen hours longer as we waited for a new airplane. After a tense and restless night in an airport hotel, afraid to sleep and miss our flight, we were finally in the air, and now our anxieties focused on the possible problems awaiting us upon entry to Canada.

My father's letter from Canada regarding our clearance for entry in Montreal had provided us with very precise instructions. We were to tell the immigration officers that we were visiting relatives and that our family members were waiting outside. We were instructed not to attempt to give them information, only to say that my father who was waiting outside would answer their questions. Most important, we were told this letter of instructions must not be found on our person. In his last phone call to us, Papa sternly emphasized the care we must take not to indicate we had any plans to apply for residence from within the country. Even though the law said we could do exactly that, Papa told us the law was in the process of changing, and some of the more proactive immigration officers were already sending visitors back if they suspected their motive was to remain in Canada. Just the thought of being interviewed by a Canadian immigration officer turned my stomach.

During the flight I had repeatedly asked Ralph if he had all the papers and passports, and had he destroyed Papa's instructional letter? He responded irritably, "For the millionth time, I am not stupid. I destroyed it before we got on the plane." Ralph was just as afraid of the authorities as I was.

After disembarking at Montreal's Dorval airport, me holding the children, and Ralph struggling with all our carry-on luggage, we followed the crowd into an open area and shuffled into one of the queues. The lines were very long, and our tired and hungry girls began to fuss. People standing in line started watching us as a distraction from their boredom. Ralph was mortified. He snarled in a low voice, "Why can't you keep the children quiet? Do something to shut them up, or I'll leave you all right here." It was an empty, unhelpful threat – where exactly did he think he could go? – but it heightened the tension between us.

At that point an immigration officer came over to us and said to me, "Miss, you and your party follow me. This way please." I brightened, assuming he had taken pity on us, like the stewardess, and had singled us out for the processing equivalent of First Class. I looked forward to seeing my parents, and pictured their happy faces when they saw us walking towards them in the waiting area. It never occurred to me that my family, having waited so long with no information about the delay, would have given up on us.

We followed the immigration officer through a door and down a long hallway, whose floor was covered by a most beautiful royal blue carpet, into another open area, where people were busy at desks. On the right side of this room was a wall of glass and on the left doors with signs that Ralph told me said "Holding" and "Interview." We were taken into the one that said "Holding," which was also covered with the blue carpeting. There was no furniture in this room, but to my relief there was a bathroom. We took turns. It felt good to wash my face and make myself presentable.

It was pleasant to find ourselves alone in this spacious, quiet room after so many hours of confinement amongst throngs of people. A smiling woman came into the room and gave me a box of crackers, a small slab of cheese and three apples. She apologized for having nothing more substantial to offer. The girls didn't like the taste of the cheese, which they had never eaten before, so they only ate the crackers and apples. I didn't mind, as long as their tummies were filled. I was enjoying the luxury of our private waiting area, which, I assured Ralph, had doubtless been arranged by my father for our convenience and comfort.

Time crawled by. Nothing happened. Suddenly a uniformed immigration officer burst into the room and ordered us to the interview room. He joined two other officers, a man and a woman. These were the first white people I had met besides the SDA missionaries. Just like some of the missionaries, their eyes were stern, the tone of their voices harsh and judgmental. I felt a familiar flutter of panic in my bowels as I scrambled to comprehend what crime it was that I had committed, even though I couldn't think of a single thing I had done or said to earn their apparent contempt.

The inquisition began. The younger of the men and the woman alternated with rapidfire questions. The older, red-haired man sat quietly and just stared at us. When he did speak, his voice was gentle and he thanked us for our responses.

At first I said very little. I was fully occupied with keeping the girls quiet, and anyway, that was a man's job. They wanted to know how long we planned to stay in Canada; how many relatives we had here; what did they do for a living; what did Ralph do for a living in India; did I have any schooling; how did my relatives get to Canada; who was paying for this so-called vacation.

Ralph attempted to answer, but so much of what they demanded to know was not included in my father's coaching that he became confused and then so stressed he was blurting out the first thing that came into his head. I was sick with fear that they would send me back and let Ralph stay. At one point, when the youngest of the officers started shouting at Ralph, I jumped in to defend him, saying he was very tired. The officer's gaze then fell on me, and he said, "So you can talk too." Then he started asking me questions. I just kept saying, "My husband already answered that." Finally, obviously disgusted, he stood up, kicked his chair and said, "Well, I am going to make sure you go back home. Someone will come and get you for the first plane to India."

We were sent back to the holding room. Ralph was exhausted and only wanted to curl up on the floor and sleep. I couldn't let that happen. I started yelling at him. He had to resist the urge to give up. He yelled back at me to leave him alone. We attracted the attention of the immigration officials, and the same woman who had brought the food came in and said, "Please calm down. We are working as hard as we can. As soon as we can, we'll arrange your passage home to India."

I wanted to scream, but not at her. I was filled with rage at Ralph, that *naa mara'ud* – that "unmanly man" as Papa always called him. My mind was racing. I had to do something. I had nothing to lose, so I got up and strode to the door, ignoring Ralph's frightened command to sit down and not make things worse for us. I turned the knob, expecting it to be locked, but to my surprise it opened. I saw the crackers and cheese lady and ran to her. I grabbed her arm and pleaded with her in my clumsy English. "You don't understand. You cannot send us back. My husband will kill my daughters. I did not give him a son. To send us back will surely be death to us. Please," I begged, "Do not send us back."

(This wasn't true, of course. Ralph loved our daughters. As an Anglo-Indian, Ralph was not caught up in the greater cultural obsession with sons. He treated his male and female family members with equal affection and respect. But over time, seeing how important it was to my family, he came to find my failure to produce a son a useful instrument for psychological punishment in moments of stress.)

The crackers and cheese woman tried hard to free herself from my grip. But the more she struggled, the more desperately I clung to her. She kept saying, "I am sorry, I can't do anything. I am not the boss. I don't make the rules. I am sorry." I wouldn't let her go. Finally she pointed at a tall man across the room. By his height and red hair I recognized him at once as the quiet, polite member of the interrogation trio. She whispered, "Go talk to him, he is the boss."

He had just turned to walk away. I ran after him. I fell at his feet and grabbed his leg and started screaming hysterically. "Please do not send me back, and please do not send my daughters back. My husband will kill me and my girls. He wants boys and I only have girls. Please do not send us back. I don't want my daughters to die."

I babbled on. I told this immigration boss that my father had promised to wait at the airport. He and my uncles were coming to pick up us. Wouldn't he please allow me to find my father? My father would explain everything to him. "My father is a Pastor in the Church. He will tell you the truth." Such was my ignorance of western ways that I would have offered him money if I had any. Fortunately for me, I didn't, for that would surely have sealed our fate on the spot. Instead, I kept scrabbling through my little change purse of English vocabulary to find the precious gold coins, the heart-touching story that would purchase a Canadian official's favour.

My captive looked terrified as I held fast to his leg and poured out my heart. He must have been intensely embarrassed looking out at the circle of fascinated faces watching this melodramatic tableau. He tried to pull away, but I hung on like a crazed monkey. At one point he reached down and his big hand hovered around my arm, but he pulled it back. I knew he did not want to touch me and I didn't blame him. I remembered what my mother looked like when she attacked my father in Simla, and I suppose I must have presented a comparably grotesque picture as I kept screaming over and over, "I am a Christian! I am in a Christian country! You must let me stay!"

Now the man was shouting too. I could not understand a word he was saying, and didn't care. I had no plan except to carry on with my emoting and begging until they got tired of my histrionics and let me stay. I had decided that if I was going to go to jail, then I would rather go to jail in Canada than go back to India. If Ralph and I were sent to jail, my parents would have to take my daughters, and they would get their chance at a better life.

Then the crackers and cheese lady was sitting on the floor with me. I had pulled my hair back into a ponytail for travelling, but many strands had by now worked their way free of the elastic. She brushed all the loose hair back from my face and soothed me, telling me softly to let go of the man's leg. She said, "You have permission to go and look for your father. Now let go of his leg. Let go, dear, let go."

I stopped screaming. She pried my fingers one by one off the man's legs and helped me stand up. Then I saw dozens of people standing around. They looked shocked. All I could say was, "I am sorry, I am really sorry, my father will tell you I am telling the truth."

The boss man pointed a long finger at me and decreed, "These two men will go out with you to look for your father. You have twenty minutes to find him. If he is not there, they will bring you back. You are not to leave their side." With that each of the men grabbed one arm and led me out of the holding area.

They brought me to an unfamiliar area, not the first room I remembered us queuing up in. I panicked. The place was swarming with people. I pulled myself away from the immigration officers and started dashing madly around the room, screaming "Papa, Papa, where are you?" Tears coursed down my face as I zigzagged through the crowd. The two men behind me couldn't predict my course, so they kept bumping into people. I ran and ran, now and then stopping and randomly pleading to bewildered and frightened strangers, "Oh God, please help me find my father."

Miraculously, one woman I stopped knew who I was looking for, because she had actually spoken with my parents as they waited for me. She said in heavily accented English, "Your family was here, but now they gone. They was here long long time, now is gone, gone." I screamed at her. "No, No! They can't go!" The woman said that my family had been waiting for hours and they had been asking all the passengers from every flight that disembarked if a family with two little girls had been on the plane. But they had left, just a little while before I appeared. I howled an agonized, drawn-out *"No!"*

As I would learn later, my father and uncles had already crossed the street on their way to the parking lot, but my mother wanted to have one more look through the glass. She stepped over the flowerbeds and pushed the bushes out of her way, and stepped up to the window, shielding her eyes with her hands so that she could have a better look. Papa called out to her. He said there was no point in waiting any longer. The best thing to do was to track us through the travel agent. But she couldn't bear to leave, and hung on just a few minutes more.

And then she saw me running around the hall screaming, immigration officers at my heels. She started to pound on the pane as if her object was to shatter it, screaming all the while, "There she is! The men are chasing her. Two men are dragging her, come quick, they have got her, now they are dragging her." The sound of her fists beating on the glass alerted people sitting in the waiting area. They started to point at the window. A crowd formed around me. People kept trying to tell the officers that the family was here. They were swept up in the drama. They became my advocates. Some of them were berating the officers, others were telling me not to worry. All the tumult took just enough time for Papa and my uncles to run back. I flung my arms around my father and broke down in sobs. He was crying too. Some of the onlookers started wiping their eyes as well.

Just as I was being taken away, my mother arrived. I broke away from the officer and hugged her. Other immigration officers were now arriving on the scene, and I screamed to my mother in Urdu, "Ma Ji, *do something*! They are going to send me and my girls back. Do something!"

The woman with the accent charged at the men, pulling me away, crying to them, "What is *wrong* with you? You want her, you have her anytime! So anyway, let her hold her mother once. What is *wrong* with you?" As she yelled at the men, I clung to my mother and told her that Ralph had told the immigration officers the truth and that we were going to be sent back.

Now the red-headed immigration boss waded into the commotion. His eyes flicked from one disapproving face to the next in the gathered crowd. You could almost see the wheels in his brain assessing the optics of this scene and considering the possible consequences for his department. His face was a bit red too as he demanded, "Who is the Papa?" When Papa stepped forward, he said, "You come with me." Then he pointed that long finger at me and growled, "And you go inside with these officers. No screaming. No grabbing. You will be very quiet. Do you understand?" I nodded meekly.

As I was about to leave with the officers, my mother asked me in a worried voice, "What are you wearing? Did the immigration people make you wear this?" She was grimacing with distaste at my clothes. For the first time in weeks I felt like laughing. I was wearing what was considered the height of western fashion at the time, a "maxi" dress that fell to my mid-calf. I would have worn my best sari so my parents would feel proud of my appearance when they saw me, but one of the church "aunties" who coveted that sari insisted that I should show up in the West wearing western attire. She presented me with the maxi dress in exchange for the sari. The dress was too tight in the bosom and the rest of it hung on me like a tent. I looked ridiculous, but I didn't want to hurt her feelings, so I wore it. I hastily murmured to my mother I would explain everything later and went off with the officials.

The boss then turned to my father and said, "You follow me." At the door to the holding area, Papa hesitated. Mr. Redhead held the door open and yelled, "Are you coming or not?" Papa replied, "Sir, I am very emotional and I am not able to think properly. You will have a lot of questions to ask, and I would like to give you the correct answers. I would like your permission to bring my brothers with me. I could use their support, because I am emotional right now." The boss impatiently agreed. All three men walked into the room.

Ma Ji told me years later that during the time she was left alone, the woman with the accent held her hand and patted her back, and said over and over, "OK.

OK. It will be OK." This was a great comfort to her and encouraged us in our belief that Canadians were very kind people.

Whatever Papa and his brothers said to the immigration boss, it worked. We were allowed to leave with a $5,000 bond and a promise to appear before the immigration officer when we were notified to do so. Which we duly did. We were allowed to apply for residence, as we had come into the country mere days before the law changed. We were the luckiest people in the world.

Chapter Fourteen

Winter and its discontents

We were taken to my Chacha Sadiq's home in Toronto's edge city of Oshawa, Ontario, a journey of five hours from Montreal's airport, by my Chacha Manzoor and my cousin Adil. My father sat up front, and I was with Ralph, my mother and my daughters in the back seat. I didn't get to see much of my new country's scenery because we left late in the darkening autumnal afternoon. But the straight, endless ribbon of Highway 401 mesmerized me. It reminded me of pictures posted by the missionaries in the children's Bible study room in our church at home. One featured a long, straight road with Christ at the end of it, his arms open wide to welcome his children to Heaven.

Tears streamed down my cheeks. My mother patted my hand, and commiserated with me for all the stress of the last few days, which she assumed was the source of my weepiness. But that wasn't it at all. I was flooded with emotion because I was finally in a Christian country, my real home, and I was overcome by joy. Now that we were in His country, and now that God could really see us, He would single us out for His blessings. At the end of this highway was opportunity – I wasn't clear about what form it would take – and safety. My heart swelled with renewed faith in the Creator, and I determined to be the best Christian I could possibly be.

*

Chacha Sadiq lived in a lovely house that his wife, Chachi Saroj, kept spotlessly clean. I remember being amazed by the extraordinary desserts his eleven-year old daughter could turn out almost instantly, as if by magic: Jello, which could be cut up into any wiggly shape one wanted, and that was hard to keep on a spoon, chocolate chip cookies and pound cake. I was enchanted to find out that all the ingredients for these delicious treats came out of a box, and could be produced with no effort whatsoever. I was also surprised to see my cousins eating their food with a fork. We had always eaten with a dinner spoon.

Too soon we had to be on our way. Now my father had to take the wheel of the car, and we could see that he was terrified of driving on the heavily trafficked highway that connected all the cities of southern Ontario. He warned us that nobody was to speak while he drove or we might all be killed. Before boarding, we stood around the car and prayed to God to care for us and for those we left behind. My stomach was in knots the whole two and a half hours it took to get to my parents' home. It was a harbinger of things to come. I would soon find that my glowing image of Canada as a seamless paradise, a land of milk and honey and easy living, had been a complete fantasy. Heavily trafficked highways were to be the least of our worries.

My parents lived in Kitchener, Ontario, home to a SDA church. Papa was employed by the Church to sell Bibles and Christian bedtime stories. He knew when he started that Canadians were not as receptive to door-to-door salespeople as Indians were, since two of his brothers and several cousins in Canada were barely making a living at it. In his sales training he was encouraged to leave sample storybooks in doctors' waiting rooms with self-addressed postcards tucked into little pockets on the back cover. But this only worked occasionally.

We lived with my parents in a small house they had rented the summer before our October 1972 arrival, in an area mainly populated by German immigrants who had come after World War Two. Everyone kept to themselves mostly. We bought our milk and sundries from a corner store at the end of the street run by the gossipy Mr Shoemaker – that was how I spelled it in my head, but it was probably Mr. Schumacher – who was a fountain of knowledge about everyone in the neighbourhood. I wouldn't have understood much of what he was saying, but my younger siblings were by now perfectly at home in English. Mr. Schumacher would engage them in conversation with questions about our family, and why we had come to Canada, information that doubtless found its way to other customers. During these exchanges I marvelled at the fluency of my siblings' English, as well as their confident air in an environment where I felt disadvantaged and shy.

Paul was now fourteen, Heather was twelve and Pam/Pinky was ten. After only two years in Canada, they were comfortably assimilated into Canadian life. English was their language of communication amongst themselves. We were now divided by more than language, though. They looked people in the eye, as was the custom in the West, a behaviour I found rude and challenging, insolence for which we would have been punished in India, but which they had learned was a sign of respect and civility. They had learned that it was good to persist in asking questions if they didn't understand something, but to me their probing questions seemed disrespectful. They were absorbing their new culture and its values with ease, but I was too old, and too bound up in my domestic responsibilities to even think about throwing off the customs I had grown up with.

I became aware of a shift in the balance of power between us. As the eldest child, I had always bossed them around, but now I was the ignorant student in this unfamiliar culture and they were my teachers. At times I found that disturbing. Revelling in their power, they leaped at every opportunity to correct my mistakes. If I told little Mina to use a "tissue" to wipe her nose, Heather promptly said, "No, no, here we say 'Kleenex.'" Once when Pinky said she was hungry for breakfast, I volunteered to make her some rotis. She crisply informed me, "In Canada we eat cereal." When I told Paul to take a bath, he retorted, "In Canada people take showers." And in these showers, I was informed, one didn't wash one's hair with soap, but with shampoo.

I began to feel stupid and clumsy, like a country bumpkin amongst urban sophisticates. It soon became a kind of game amongst them to see who could be the first to expose me to ridicule when I made a mistake. In the car one day Paul said to Papa, who was driving over the speed limit, "Papa, if you don't watch it, you'll have the fuzz on your tail." I scolded him for being so rude and mouthy, but the other children shrieked with laughter. Then they crowed that the "fuzz" were the police and "on your tail" meant they were chasing you, and not, as I assumed, hair on a bum. I cried from embarrassment and, I suppose, from the realization that being the oldest child was no longer any guarantee of special status or authority.

My younger siblings had become very Canadianized in their food preferences as well, and through them we learned what Canadian children liked to eat. At home they continued to eat rotis and lentils and vegetables, but they didn't want to take curry to school because its strong smell would draw attention to their difference. They wanted sandwiches made with white bread like the other kids. They loved macaroni and cheese, and since it was only fifteen cents a box, we grew to like it too and ate a lot of it.

The girls did not want to buy their school clothes at K-Mart, where you could get three pants for the price of one pair at Sears. If they were driven to K-Mart, the girls would weep and plead for Sears. While my sisters appealed for understanding about how important it was to look like the other girls – they were the only dark-skinned kids in the class – Paul would cunningly appeal to Papa's obsession with status and family honour. "Do you want the other girls to think we can't afford to get them decent clothes and laugh at them?" This did the trick, and even though it was an extravagance my father could ill afford, they got their jeans at Sears.

I remember being annoyed at this outcome. I felt Papa should have taken a belt to them for resisting him. It was pure spite on my part. It would never have occurred to me to even ask for special entitlements at their age, because I would have been punished, yet my Canadianized siblings had no fear of negotiating for privileges – respectfully, to be sure – and my parents, unsure about local mores and inclined to trust the children's familiarity with Canadian culture, were now receptive to their pleas. It didn't seem fair, ironically enough a concept I would never have entertained before coming to the West.

Snow began to fall in early November. It got colder and colder. The windows iced over. The house didn't grow warm, even though we put the thermostat up as high as it would go. None of us knew anything about furnaces or insulation. Even though this was my parents' third winter in Canada, it was the first time they had been responsible for the care of a house. The first winter they had stayed with Chacha Sadiq in Oshawa. As the older brother, Papa had not been expected to bother his head with domestic details. The second winter they had passed in a rented apartment. So they were quite ignorant about home maintenance. It didn't occur to them to complain to the owner or inquire about remedies. We simply compensated for the house's frigidity by wearing long underwear and coats in the three-bedroom, one-bathroom house that had to accommodate all ten of us.

Papa bought a portable heater from Canadian Tire. He kept it on all the time. My mother opened the oven door, and we stuffed towels around the windows to block the draughts, but we were still shivering. We were all in low spirits, but Papa especially so, because his books weren't selling. With Christmas almost upon us, money was so tight he had been forced to borrow from his brother, who could ill afford such largesse.

On the night before Christmas Eve, something happened that shook me to the core of my being. I was passing the entrance to my parents' bedroom, and the door was half-ajar. My father was on his knees by his bed, his head buried in the blankets, sobbing and praying. He was pleading, "Dear God, I don't know what to do. How will I feed these children? I have made a mistake bringing them to Canada, and now we can't go home. I have made such a horrible mistake. Please help me to get my family back to India."

I froze in the doorway. Go back to India? Was my invincible father really giving up on Canada already? I had never before seen my father so discouraged. I was assailed by a tumbling mixture of treacherous emotions – anger, disdain, pity – that disturbed and frightened me. Mostly I was furious that here we were in God's country and he was giving up on God. How could he let me down like this after so many years of convincing me that he was God's deputy here on earth?

All my life I had seen my father as immovably confident. He was the oldest brother, the pillar of the family, the man his relatives went to when problems needed sorting out. Yes, he was arrogant, but a monarch is allowed a touch of self-importance, and Papa's haughty manner had always seemed perfectly justified to me. But a king showing evidence of failed nerves makes even his most loyal subjects anxious.

Papa's sense of defeat was doubtless linked to the house and its vulnerability to the weather. Ironically, Papa had always perceived himself as something of an aristocrat in India, no matter how modest our accommodations were. Now he lived in quite luxurious surroundings compared to our Indian homes, and felt like a beggar. In India we were always outside. Heat can be punishing, but if one has shade and water, there is no need to be afraid. Implacable cold is frightening. Now we were mostly indoors and miserable, looking to him for expertise he didn't have. He didn't know how to make the house do his bidding, and I think he felt, as we all shivered in the cold air, that our unhappy eyes were accusing him.

Winter was a bane to him in other ways. He didn't feel confident when he was driving even in good weather, not only on highways but on city streets. Snowy conditions downright scared him. He would pray loudly all the time he was at the wheel. Nor would he drive alone if he could help it. He wanted someone with him, even one of the children, to navigate the route and show him where to park.

The most startling proof of the change in him was the reversal of roles between him and my mother. One day while the family was performing Morning Prayer, I opened my eyes and saw my mother spread her palm over Papa's folded hands. I almost gasped aloud. I had never before seen any physical contact between my parents. Ma Ji had always been the caregiver and disciplinarian for us children, but with Papa she had been submissive, a conduit for his decisions and wishes.

Our altered situation was having a domino effect on all of us, it seemed. The daunting challenges of a new culture and intimidating climate that aroused insecurity in Papa had triggered some latent self-possession and pioneer mettle in my mother. With no intention of usurping his masculine role – on the contrary, she was shoring it up – Ma Ji had simply risen to the occasion of his demoralization. As I watched her interact with him, I realized she was pouring her own strength and determination into him, willing him not to give up. It dawned on me that bolstering Papa's ego had become almost a fulltime occupation for her. She was always talking to him, flattering him, encouraging him. She went with him to sell his books. She would go into the homes of the farmers, speak with the wives in her broken English, show them photos of her grandchildren, admire their produce, and bring home baskets of tomatoes they pressed upon her. She was constantly telling Papa that they were in this struggle together. His English was very good and hers was poor, but she was more realistic and therefore stronger than he was in the resettlement process.

So when I heard Papa asking God to help him go back to India, I ran down to my mother. I told her what I had heard, and she hastened to him.

I didn't want my sisters and Paul to see him in that state. Everyone was gloomy enough already. I took Mary and Jessica aside and told them about Papa, and that we had to get the other kids out of the house for a while. I gathered everyone and said, "I know Christmas is celebrated differently here, but it is freezing in the house anyway and we won't be any colder outside, so let's go carol singing." I tried not to show my trepidation at this bold idea of mine. We were the only non-white family in our neighbourhood. Our neighbours stared at us all the time. When my younger siblings went to school, Ma Ji always told them, "If anyone stares at you, don't stare back. Just mind your own business, stay together and hold hands." These warnings of course only served to make us feel more uncertain and nervous.

But now I didn't care about what the neighbours thought. I was doing this for us. One thing our family could do well was sing. Thanks to the missionaries, we had been taught all kinds of English carols, sung in harmony. Mary and Jessica and Paul sang alto, the rest of us soprano. All seven of us and my little daughters went across the street and knocked on a neighbour's door. As the door opened, we launched into "Joy to the World." The lady of the house stared at us, unmoving, as though in shock. Then, tearing up a little, she invited us inside for cookies and cake. We were a bit hesitant at first, but she seemed so needy, and urged us in such a warm and welcoming way, our fears dissipated, and we sang and sang for her: "O Little Town of Bethlehem" and "Silent Night" and all the other old favourites. Our hostess was delighted. She said we must go to all her friends' houses too, and began telephoning everyone to prepare them for our visit.

We went from one house to the next. Everyone gave us something delicious – hot chocolate, fancy Christmas cookies, candies – until we were stuffed and couldn't eat another thing. We finished the row of houses on the side of the street opposite ours, and then we noticed doors opening on the other side, old people framed in the doorway with sweaters clutched around their shoulders, looking out to see when we would come to them.

We were happy to keep singing, but we couldn't eat any more. So the people started to pack food for us to bring home. This worried me. If Papa saw us come home with all this food, he might think we had been begging. We tried to refuse the gifts, but they wouldn't hear of it. Some of the older people grew weepy when we sang to them. They told us that we had brought back memories of the old country, before the war, when they were young. We noticed that several of the people who invited us in were alone in their homes. Some of them said their children had moved away and would not be there for Christmas.

There still remained houses on the street we hadn't been to, but the children were tired. We told our neighbours that we would return the next night, on Christmas Eve.

The next night we were in high spirits after a potluck dinner at church and the enactment of the Christmas story, and better prepared for our adventure. We left the babies at home. Our neighbours were waiting for us. We sang our hearts out. This time we explained to everyone that we could not take food home with us, as our parents would be embarrassed by charity of this kind. Then people started shoving dollar bills in our pockets, and this alarmed me even more.

On the way home we discussed the situation, wondering if we had offended our neighbours by refusing the food. We all took out the money people had given us. Pooled, it came to $175.00! I told everyone not to say a word to our parents. I said that when the time was right, I would give it to Ma Ji and she would know what to do with it. We had by then been out for hours, and were all exhausted. I went to bed very happy with my first Christmas Eve in Canada.

On Christmas Day, mid-morning, there was a loud knocking on the door. We had all slept in and when nobody responded right away, the knocking turned to pounding. My first thought was that someone must have reported us to the police for taking the money. I was terrified that our carol singing had got our family into trouble.

When Papa opened the door, he saw four men and three women standing outside. They yelled "Merry Christmas! Merry Christmas!" as they pushed their way into the house. One was carrying a big turkey, another a ham, a third a pot of stew. We stood there in shock, not knowing what to do. One of the men told Papa, "The children have brought back Christmas, they have brought back joy."

Still half asleep and unaccustomed to their strong German accents, Papa was having difficulty understanding them. One of my sisters translated, and he began to weep. But he was upset about the ham, and kept shouting above the din of voices, "Thank you, but no no no pig, please. We do not eat pig!" Everyone laughed, and the neighbour who brought the ham took it away.

A few hours later, one of the neighbours came back with a pump. He took Papa to the basement. It was flooded with water. We had never gone down to this dungeon, so it was a surprise to us. The neighbour told us that he knew all about this house. The owner lived in Toronto. He was aware of its many problems, but never fixed them. He just kept renting it out to unsuspecting greenhorns like us every year. Our neighbour told Papa that he should report the owner, as it was against the law to keep a rental property in such a condition, but Papa was too afraid we would be kicked into the street if he made trouble.

Christmas was a bright spot in an otherwise difficult winter. Our neighbour's magic pump caused the house to warm up enough to make the cold weather an irritant rather than an existential misery. But there was no pump magical enough to dissipate the chill we felt from relatives who had distanced themselves from us because of Papa's continuing requests for money. So we felt socially isolated in a way nobody ever feels in India.

People from the Church helped us, though. Their volunteers stopped by on a regular basis to see if we were okay, and often brought us food and supplies, charity we made sure to hide from Papa. One of their most useful contributions was to introduce us to the blessings of the Salvation Army Store. My sisters and I got our winter coats there. Mine was a fur coat that had seen better days, but it was warm. We all got what we needed there, dirt cheap and in fine condition. It was a marvel to us that such a cornucopia of life's necessities was made available to poor people at such a pittance, and with so much good will and efficiency.

All of us were focused on making sure we were not a burden to Papa. The post-Christmas season was a dead time for religious-book sales. The Church made an arrangement with Papa. They would lend him money for monthly household expenses, and he would pay them back when sales picked up. Papa found this arrangement humiliating, but had to accept it in order to save face with his relatives.

One January day there was a very heavy snowfall after Papa left for work. We sat by the window, anxiously watching the blizzard of fat flakes settling upon each other and pillowing up in our front yard. We worried about Papa. He had never driven a car in India. Since arriving in Canada, he had had many minor car accidents. I went out to clear the driveway, but the snow fell so thickly it wasn't long before I had to clear it again.

I considered the difficulty Papa always had in squeezing his car into our small garage, even in good weather. The three interior walls of the garage already bore evidence of Papa's difficulties in calculating distances from behind the wheel. Time wore on, and I could see that the driveway needed a third cleaning. I was tired by this time, but nobody wanted to help me. Paul and Heather had gone skating with friends, and the others weren't interested.

I noticed the garden hose looped over a hook at the side of the house. It occurred to me that I could easily disperse all the snow from the sloped drive merely by washing it away with hot water. I imagined how pleased Papa would be to see a clean driveway on his return from a hard day's work. So I connected the hose to the kitchen tap and, walking backward from the sidewalk, sprayed hot water over the short, car-length driveway. Sure enough, the heat of the water melted the snow away.

Within minutes the driveway was a sheet of ice. On both sides of our driveway, the neighbours had created a white wall of snow cleared from their own driveways. This gave ours a tunnel effect. When he came home, Papa was greatly puzzled to find his wheels spinning impotently at the entrance to the driveway. Finally he parked at the curb and started to walk to the house. He immediately slipped and fell headlong, smacking his face on the mirror-like surface I had created. We all looked on in horror as he got up and, bellowing with frustration, fell again and again.

My mother rushed out to help him. I was the only one who knew why he kept falling, but I was not about to admit to a thing. I ran upstairs and pulled all the sheets off our beds and tied them into a rope. At one end I attached a leather boot and threw it to Papa. By this means we pulled him slowly up the driveway and onto the steps of the house. With bated breath we waited for him to vent his fury, wondering who would take the brunt of it. All he said was, "Could you not find something else to tie the sheets to? What if someone had seen me hanging on to a boot to save my life in my own driveway?" It wasn't recognized as a comic moment at the time, but in years to come it became a stock narrative of family lore, guaranteed to evoke hoots of laughter from everyone, and eventually even from Papa himself.

One of our German neighbours had witnessed the whole tableau. He arrived at our house bearing a bag of salt, elucidating its properties in connection with ice, and one more piece of our Canadian jigsaw puzzle clicked into place. He also told Papa not to leave his car in the driveway after a snowfall, explaining it prevented the snow removal men from doing their job. Papa asked where we could buy the ice-melting kind of salt, and we were directed to a store called Dutch Boy, a short distance away.

Papa and I went to Dutch Boy while Ma Ji stayed home with the children. Papa asked a cashier where we would find salt, and she told us where to go. We filled our cart with boxes and boxes of Sifto salt. At the checkout counter, the clerk smiled at Papa and asked if he was going to do some pickling. Papa smiled back and explained to her that he needed the salt for his driveway. The clerk suddenly turned her back to us, and in perplexity we watched her shoulders heaving. When she was able to contain her soundless laughter, she picked up the phone and called somebody, and a few minutes later a man brought us two big bags of driveway salt.

Neither of us commented on our mistake on the way home. It was one of many such trial-and-error learning experiences that salted the slippery terrain of our assimilation into Canadian culture. Slowly we gained the upper hand in our annual battle with winter. Its discontents gradually taught us to stand more and more confidently on our own two feet, and all thoughts of going back to India were banished.

❃

Once Papa was introduced into the Mennonite community that flourished in the Kitchener-Waterloo corridor, the sales territory assigned to him, his bookselling career took off. Papa discovered there were two kinds of Mennonites: the fundamentalists who dressed in black and lived on farms, and others who dressed in ordinary clothes and held down jobs like everyone else. Papa felt a kinship with the fundamentalists. Those Mennonites liked the SDA health books, and they also liked the didactic tales of a prolific evangelical moralist called Arthur S. Maxwell, known affectionately to Adventists as "Uncle Arthur."

Whenever he went to their farms, Papa dressed in black himself. He would take Ma Ji with him and made sure to carry photos of all his children and grandchildren to build up a rapport with these family-oriented people. The Mennonites paid in cash, and Papa got fifty percent of the price of the books, more than he would have received if they had chosen the monthly instalment plan. Papa referred to the Mennonites as his "gold mine." Some months he sold $12,000 worth of books, very good money for the time. Towards the end of 1973 Father was able to buy a three-bedroom bungalow for $23,000. He was also able to afford to buy an only lightly-used car.

The next ten years were Papa's golden years. He made a name for himself in the Church, and was often written up in the church news bulletins. He won the "Literature Evangelists" trophy, a highly coveted motivational prize amongst the salesmen, for highest book sales five times in a row. Papa swaggered and threw parties, bigger every year, and his ego expanded to match the size of his bank balance. Christian humility had never been his strong suit. It was particularly absent in the palmy days of Papa's material success. He saw himself edging slowly but surely toward his dream of becoming the Punjabi Billy Graham.

Now that he could afford to do something about his loss of control over his children, and increasingly worried that they would adopt the sexually promiscuous mores of the West, Papa arranged for four of them to attend Kingsway College, a SDA boarding school in Oshawa. But if they were later to attend Andrews University, the flagship SDA centre of higher education in Michigan, as he intended they should to find husbands within the SDA

120

community, he would have to make a lot more money. Andrews is a private university with no government subsidy. As a Church employee, Papa would get only a twenty percent discount on fees.

So Papa petitioned the Church for a fulltime job at SDA headquarters in Oshawa as a trainer of new salesmen, a position they could hardly refuse their top salesman. He became the first Punjabi man to hold the title of "Associate Publishing Secretary," an honour that puffed him up enormously.

Throughout these years Ralph had never found job satisfaction. In the beginning he had no work permit. Then, when he got it, he could only find factory work, which he hated. But while we were living with my parents, he could not compete with Papa selling books. So in 1974 we moved to Toronto and began living on our own. Ralph took up bookselling, but he wasn't a natural salesman and had little success at it. I was pregnant with our third child, a boy, James, who was born in June of that year.

I had now been in Canada for three years, but I cannot say I had at this point any very clear notion of what ordinary Canadians were like, or what constituted a specifically Canadian culture. My world was a cocoon bounded by family and the SDA church. All my parents' close associations were Adventists. In Toronto I did not wander far from the house on my own. Our outings, such as they were, comprised shopping trips to Sears or Honest Ed's for clothes, to Knob Hill market for fresh produce and to Gerrard St. in the east end, known as "Little India," to buy familiar food. Until James was born, I worked in the kitchen at Branson Hospital, yet another SDA institution, which was attached to our church. Working there did nothing to integrate me into Canadian life. It provided only income and some superficial socialization with other immigrants, who mainly spoke Portuguese amongst themselves.

I think that my most common reaction to western "culture" at this point was disapproval. I watched TV, but seeing half-naked women in compromising sexual situations mortified me. Big Macs shocked me with their size; you had to open your mouth as wide as a tiger to take a bite of them. One Coca Cola was enough for four people. People licking ice cream cones like dogs disgusted me; I made my children eat ice cream with a spoon. I wondered why children all had to have their own bedrooms. For years longer than I should have, I remained almost completely ignorant about the history, and the positive character and values of my adopted country.

Chapter Fifteen

Embattled in Battle Creek

Papa felt Ralph's prospects in the Church would be much improved if he held a Pastor's degree from Andrews. There wasn't a great deal of discussion about it. Ralph had no alternative plan to offer that would advance his prospects in the Church, and it had not yet occurred to any of us that in this caste-free land of opportunity, where immigrants were making their way into every and all lines of decently-paid jobs, he might look for some kind of secure work that had nothing to do with the Church.

And so it was that in 1976 we moved to Michigan, where we were to remain until 1980. A year later Mary, Paul, Dorothy and Heather followed to begin their university studies. Some months after that, Jessica and her new husband Harili, a boy she had known since Roorkee days, arrived. Only Pinky stayed behind at Kingsway.

The original plan was for Ralph to go alone, while the children and I stayed with my parents. I convinced my mother that without me there, Ralph would be vulnerable to the charms of other women, and so won her support for us going as a family. Of course nobody had suggested that I take the opportunity to study as well. My job in Michigan was to continue attending to the care and comfort of my husband and children, with the additional mission of scouting out appropriate Punjabi fellows for my sisters to meet and marry. But I had not given up my dreams of becoming properly educated. Once on the Andrews campus for a projected four-year stay, I believed I would find a way to attend classes. And I did.

Andrews University, in Berrien Springs, Michigan, was founded in 1874 as Battle Creek College, the SDA's first institution of higher learning. Andrews functions primarily as a seminary to prepare ministers for the SDA Church. In its début year, there were only twelve students, amongst them John Harvey Kellogg, the future breakfast cereal king.

Here we were to pass a rather strange interlude. We weren't in Canada, but we could hardly be said to have familiarised ourselves with the United States, as Andrews is a self-sufficient environment governed entirely by its SDA faith, and we almost never left the campus. Theoretically it should have been a positive experience for us. We lived in decent student dorms on a lovely campus that encompassed farmlands as beautiful and vigorously productive as in the Punjab, and whose cheap bounty ensured nourishing and delicious meals. We were away from my father, free from the constant comparisons of his success with Ralph's inertia. We were surrounded by hundreds of other young people from all over the world, many with children as well, all committed to the same religion and values. Our children attended an excellent pre-school on campus. All kinds of entertaining and enriching cultural activities were available to us at no cost.

But something in this recipe for wholesome maturation was missing or went sour. At least for Ralph. The religion was the same as in India, but the culture was western. The sexes mingled freely and sociability was governed by mutual respect. The hierarchy at Michigan was based on achievement and talent. Traditional values permeated social and domestic relationships, but the rigid, caste-like pecking order of India, where everyone knew his or her place, was nowhere in evidence. Something like the changes in my parents' relationship happened to us here. Since it worked to empower me, I took to the new environment with pleasure and enthusiasm. Ralph found it threatening and retreated into an old-world paradigm of sexual possessiveness and patriarchal arrogance.

We were housed in a two-bedroom student apartment, sparsely furnished with much-used furniture and broken appliances, but it was better than our housing, in India and I didn't think to complain to anyone about our useless refrigerator and worn-out sofa bed.

Every now and then a truck laden with slightly damaged fruits and vegetables would park in the student housing lot. We could have as much as we wanted for free. The first time I took a small amount and stepped back. The driver, a friendly young man called Tim, urged me to take more, but I told him I didn't have a working fridge. He came up to see it and called for a repairman. While

124

waiting, we chatted. I told Tim I would love to find work, but didn't have a U.S. work permit. No problem, he said. Andrews was a private institution. The student office had a special arrangement with the government, because they had students from all over the world. He told me they always needed farm labour, even if it didn't pay a lot.

Tim made another call and told the repairman to bring a freezer with him. I had never seen one before, and when it was installed, gazed at the twenty-eight square feet of space inside in awe. I thought excitedly of all the food I could cook and store in it. But when Ralph saw it, he reflexively accused me of having an affair with the appliance guy. I explained the sequence of events, but there was no convincing him. He was jealous of every man I spoke to. Just as my father stopped physically abusing us in Canada, Ralph had for the most part stopped hitting me as well. But his verbal abuse still had the power to evoke fear. I tried hard to avoid angering him.

Excited at the prospect of filling up the freezer, I applied for a job picking fruits and vegetables the next day and was hired within a week. Because we were on student visas, I could not work more than twenty hours a week. So I would work from five to eight in the morning, come home and prepare the older children for school. Later, if they had work for me in the afternoon, I would take James to the orchards, where he played with the migrants' children while I worked. I made money and filled the freezer with ready-to-cook produce.

After the harvest season I went to work in the university's market store bakery, where I learned to make all kinds of bread. I was allowed to take home imperfectly shaped loaves, and soon my freezer had lots of bread in it too.

Jessica and her husband rented an apartment across from us. Mary, Dorothy, Heather and Paul stayed in the residences. With so many children enrolled, Andrews offered Papa a substantial discount, and each of my siblings received student loans. Papa's finances didn't extend to subsidizing Ralph and me, though, so I needed to work as many hours as I could to keep us solvent.

In SDA institutions everything shuts down on Friday afternoon in preparation for the Sabbath, which Adventists celebrate on Saturday. The only thing open in the area was a private retirement home run by an Adventist, and they always needed staff to look after the seniors on weekends. I made an arrangement with my sisters. I would provide their meals for the weekend if they would look after my children while I worked at the nursing home. They were happy to have home-cooked meals and my children were thrilled to go out and about with their aunties. Working twelve hours both Saturday and Sunday, I made $200 a weekend. My fifteen hours Monday to Friday in the bakery earned me $120.

Determined not to be cast down by Ralph's poor attitude, I enjoyed this first year. I liked our apartment and I liked working hard. I attended whatever events were on offer. I remember one Saturday night the U.S. Navy Band came to give a concert. There were talent shows I thought better than anything on television. Politicians and renowned scholars visited the campus and gave talks. The environment hummed with energetic purpose.

Best of all, everyone was SDA, so in spite of our cultural differences, there was a strong bond uniting us all. Most of the community members were white North Americans, but there were also many black families, and some brown ones like us. I fell into a sorority of campus wives, and from them I learned a great deal about budgeting, banking, paying bills, and cooking healthy meals cheaply. Without realizing it, I was becoming more managerial in our household affairs, and this did not sit well with Ralph.

Ralph was shocked to learn that I had opened a bank account for my earnings, and demanded access to it. I tried to explain to him in a very gentle, non-assertive way that some of the pastors' wives had told me I was not obligated to do that, and that it was good for women to have some financial independence. Ralph was not at all placated by my citation of the pastors' wives, as I had hoped. The thought of me having my own bank account activated his instinct for control. He started to pick fights with me, and cross-examine me about where and with whom I was spending my time. He warned me about getting stupid ideas from my friends.

What Ralph considered "stupid ideas" were of course from my perspective quite smart ideas that advanced my independence. On the advice of friends I learned to drive by tooling around the campus, and managed to get a licence. The freedom to get into a car and go where I wanted when I wanted, with or without the children, was probably the single most liberating development on my journey to personhood.

My girlfriends also encouraged me to take classes. Because I was still registered as living at my parents' Ontario address, I was eligible for student loans, and with my father's help I applied and received money, nominally meant for application to studies in Ontario, a technicality my father sidestepped with help from the SDA network by registering me at Kingsway rather than Andrews – and this time tucked safely into my account and out of Ralph's reach.

The only program that didn't require proficiency in English writing was Home Economics. My advisor urged me to take it, as it was very popular amongst women in the mission field. Home Economics was conceived as a scientific training in the details that every good Christian wife should know. In Home Ec I was to learn how to take measurements, sew clothes, cook healthy casseroles and create a "peaceful home environment." With my advisor's further guidance I also registered for what I was assured were three easy courses: "The Church in the Middle Ages," "The Development of the SDA Lifestyle" and "Christian Parenting."

The tests were of the true and false variety, and in the introductory courses I was taking, one only had to submit one five-page essay and one class presentation. We were assigned presentation partners. Mine was Matthew, a nineteen year-old farm boy from Tennessee. Our topic was the creation of a Christian home environment in the modern day. We both thought the other had a funny accent, and we teased each other a lot while we worked on our presentation.

One day Ralph saw us laughing together in the library. He charged over and accused me of having an affair with the boy. Poor Matthew was so scared he ran away, leaving his books behind him, and subsequently asked the professor for a change of partner.

I am sure Ralph and I were not the first couple at Andrews to be trapped in an unhealthy dynamic, but I doubt any other domineering husband was so care-less as Ralph was in making it public knowledge. The walls between the apart-ments in our student housing were thin. One day my apartment neighbours to the left and right of us – Gloria, a black woman from Alabama, and Julie, a white woman from Texas – knocked on my door, and asked if we could have a little chat about my marital situation They told me that Ralph's many loud harangues had been a frequent topic of discussion in their households, both agreeing that ours could not be called a Christian home environment.

I was informed that I was living in an abusive situation, and that if it didn't stop, they would report it to the administration. They said they felt that any man who spoke to his wife in such tones should not be allowed to be a pastor. Pastors were supposed to be role models for their members. They were supposed to treat their wives as equals.

This was my first foray into the realm of "women's rights." It was a gentle introduction. My friends at Andrews were devout Adventists and their idea of "equality" would have been hooted down by a real feminist of the era. What they propounded was an equality of human value, but a separation of functions. They were more like the original suffragettes, who wanted the vote, but still cherished their natural roles as wives and mothers. They were comfortable following their husbands and acting chiefly as handmaidens to their husbands' ambitions, a traditional approach that accorded with my understanding of domestic relations, but they had high standards for respectful behaviour between the sexes. These women watered the seed that master Singh had planted in me when he told me I must stand up for myself.

But I could not allow that seed to blossom quite yet. My horror at the thought of shaming my father was far stronger than my wish to get out from under Ralph's thumb. Somehow I knew, not consciously at the time, that if I allowed my thoughts to proceed along these lines of "equality" too far, I would inevitably arrive at the conclusion that I should leave Ralph. But even if such an idea were admissible, even if I thought I could muster the courage to stand up to my father and shame him publicly, I would suppress it, because such a move would put an end to my education. I would have done anything, anything at all for Ralph, as long as it allowed me to keep going to school. So I had to come to an accommodation with him, even if it meant appeasement and submission.

I tried to explain all this to my friends. I told them that my father would be very angry if Ralph were to get into trouble, and that I would be blamed for it anyway. I tried to make them understand what Indian culture was like for women, but I could see they were sceptical. The more I tried to mitigate their concern, the angrier they got. I found myself defending Ralph, telling them it was my fault that I hadn't learned to respect and obey my husband's wishes. My sole concern was to make sure Ralph didn't get expelled from the seminary, as I knew what the fallout would be for me.

I can see that I must have been in denial about Ralph's inability to adjust to our environment, and the depth of the vessel – sexual jealousy – into which he had poured it. One morning a neighbour from the apartment building opposite us knocked on the door. I found out that sometime in the night Ralph had written terrible things on pieces of cardboard: "My wife is sleeping with every fellow in town" and "Knock on this door if you want to meet a whore" and "I am Aruna, I will sleep with anyone who wants me." He had stuck them on the outside wall of our apartment, so that anyone in the parking lot and beyond could read them. The neighbour and his wife and I pulled them down. They wanted to report the incident, but I begged them not to. I explained that if Ralph were expelled, my education would be over too, and I was only one year away from a degree in Home Economics. They understood and agreed not to go to the administration.

A few days later, while Ralph still slumbered, I woke up to find that all my blouses and other tops had been cut up into thin strips and neatly laid out on the kitchen table. Adrenalin flooded my body. I would have preferred any kind of physical abuse to this terrifying symbol of Ralph's rage. I dashed to the children's room in a sudden panic, but they were unharmed and sleeping soundly. I had to put on one of Ralph's shirts to go to Gloria's apartment and borrow some clothes. She came over to see the vandalism for herself, and was aghast at the intensity of feeling it represented. The meticulous way in which Ralph had arranged the strips of cloth made her shudder. She felt the act was charged with pathology. "This man was walking around all night with scissors in his hand. He could have stabbed you. He could have killed you."

Gloria reported Ralph to the authorities. It was decided that we could not remain with Ralph. The children and I (and the freezer) were moved to another apartment in a high-security building. My parents were informed. They came for a weekend visit and spent most of the time talking to other people. Two hours before they were scheduled to leave, they finally visited me in my new apartment.

For the first time Papa openly acknowledged that Ralph was abusive. But old habits die hard, and he still held me responsible for other people knowing about it. I can vividly remember the diatribe he poured out, almost word for word: "You have been a curse to your mother and me from the day you were born. We have done the best we possibly could have done for a cursed child. If you had not produced those three children, also three curses as far as I am concerned, I would have suggested that you take some rat poison and kill yourself. In fact I would happily drive you to the hardware store to buy it. But if you do that, then we would be stuck with those children and that is out of the question. We would have to give them up for adoption."

I wept hysterically at these words, but he went on. "We have spent hours speaking with people who helped you move. We have spoken with the authorities. They have all been fooled by you. All this is your fault, because if you had not insisted on starting to attend classes and if you had not wanted to compete with your husband, none of this would have happened. Ralph is a weak man. Weak mentally and physically, but you and your mother wanted this marriage, and now I have been humiliated again. Your stupid brain cannot understand the seriousness of the humiliation you have brought on me. People from all over the world come to this place. Now everyone will know my name, not as the Billy Graham of India, but as the disgraced and dishonoured father of a daughter he could not control."

I had no heart for defending myself, no will to remind Papa that he had approved my studies and that I was paying for Ralph's education. I was no longer a grown woman, a mother, a student, a reliable worker, the confident manager of my household, a Christian. I was once again an unworthy creature, a Punjabi girl who had brought shame to her family. Every single ounce of confidence I had built up over the last three years by my achievements and my healthy relationships with strong women of high self-esteem was nullified. Papa was right. It was all my fault.

As my parents were leaving, Papa turned to me and said, "If you return to my house, you will come with your husband or you are dead to me. You are on your own. You brought this on yourself." With that they were gone. Ma Ji had said nothing at all during the forty-five minutes they were in my apartment.

I stayed away from Ralph for about three months, and we both had individual counselling. Eventually Ralph offered an apology, and my parents pressured me to accept it and go back, so I did. My counsellor was after all an Adventist, with strong beliefs in the biblical hierarchy of man and wife. So we agreed that I should accept part of the blame for our difficulties. I started to wear looser-fitting clothes, I worked only in places that Ralph approved of and I handed my paycheque over to him instead of putting it into my own bank account, a habit that, with brief interludes of assertiveness on my part, persisted for many years.

After three years in Michigan, I had only three terms left before I would actually have a B.A. degree. By then I had taken many independent research courses. But my success in these courses was completely bogus. Working in the dorm had allowed me to borrow books, reports and term papers from other students, which I simply recycled. I was cheating, out-and-out plagiarizing work in a big way. My reading skills were so rudimentary that I memorized words by the way they looked and hoped to recognize them when I saw them again. Utterly primitive. When I was stressed, the words on a page would appear to float. When this happened I wondered if I had something of the mental illness that my mother had displayed in its most acute form at Simla, but that occasionally surfaced in irrational acts like throwing objects across the kitchen and substituting salt for sugar in Papa's tea. I set aside my scruples. All I could think of was the joy I would feel when I got my degree and proved to Papa that I wasn't stupid.

By 1979 we were going to run out of money for Ralph's tuition. We had depleted all our student loans and could expect no more money from the Canadian government. It seemed unfair when we were both so close to completion of our goals. We hoped Papa could bail us out, but it turned out his own situation was now precarious. His tenure at the salaried job in Oshawa training religious-book salesmen, representing the prestigious status he had lobbied so hard for and been so proud to receive, was not going well. His students had been reporting to his superiors that Papa pressured potential clients on limited incomes to buy the books on the monthly instalment plan, even though they really couldn't afford them at all. There were other complaints about his methodology. Most serious was the allegation of blatant racism. He would make inappropriate comments about blacks and Jews that came from such ingrained prejudices he even repeated them to a black man he was training. Now his job was on the line.

If I was to continue with classes, I needed to make enough money for Ralph to complete his studies. So with my sisters' help I started a kind of catering business. I cooked up masses of Indian food – rice, curried vegetables I got from the farm, and chicken. I would take the cooked food and park within reach of the cafeteria, but closer to the road, so if an official came by, I could drive away. I would ask students on their way to the cafeteria if they wanted to buy an Indian meal for five dollars. I couldn't be seen doing this on the Sabbath, but as soon as the sun set Saturday night, and throughout Sunday I would be there, and pretty soon the students were looking for my station wagon. I cooked vegetarian meals, and chicken curries for those who were sick of vegetarianism.

The first weekend I made $200. When I got the hang of it, and knew the quantities I could expect to sell, I started to earn about $700 and sometimes $800 a weekend. Before word reached the administration and I was called in for an investigation, I had earned the $5,000 Ralph needed for his tuition. And more – enough for me to finish my degree.

As long as Ralph stayed out of my way and didn't insist on me handing over all my money, I didn't mind supporting him. But he could not contain his anger or his jealousy, the fights started over, and we ended up in counselling again. Yet again, I was told that I needed to be a better, more supportive wife. While the word "obey" was not used, I was told that I should listen to my husband and "heed his counsel." The Lord had ordained that Ralph was to be the head of our household, and it was the Lord's wish that he become a pastor, because nothing happens without the Lord's guidance. I needed to be humble, study the Bible and spend more time in meditation with the Lord. I outwardly agreed with every word that was being preached to me, but all the while I wanted to say, "While I am studying the Bible and meditating with the Lord, can Ralph be cooking the curry for me and selling it? Because the only way this man is going to become a pastor is if we find some money really quick." But I did not say anything and agreed to do as I was told. I now had one term to finish and was loath to rock that boat.

In April of 1980 I received my BA in Home Economics. By then we were out of money and Ralph had failed too many courses to get a Pastor's degree, so it was time to leave. It was also better to leave on our own before we were asked to go by the administration. They had had their fill of us. I left first to work and amass enough money for us to settle down with in Toronto, and Ralph came a few months later with the children. I am sure the entire administration breathed a great sigh of relief when they saw his loaded station wagon rolling away from the Andrews University campus.

Chapter Sixteen

Intellectual awakening – and Jews

It was agreed that I would come back from Michigan first, and live with my parents until I had found a job and an apartment. I found work as a short order cook at York University. My shift began at five a.m. and ended at noon. I found a second job, from four p.m. to eleven p.m., as an attendant in York's women's locker room. Within two months I had saved enough money for first and last months' rent and some furniture. I started looking for an apartment within walking distance of my work.

York University in Toronto is located at the heart of the Jane and Finch area – Jane-Finch, as it is known – a northern city enclave notorious for its high crime rate. Jane-Finch was originally developed as a model high-rise suburb in the 1960s. Between 1961 and 1971, the population exploded from 1,300 to 33,000. The area has housed diverse immigrant groups: Jewish, Italian, South Asian, Russian, and now Caribbean families. I arrived during the South Asian wave. Jane-Finch was to be my new neighbourhood and the sociological petri-dish for my future career.

I went to see an apartment that turned out to be a condominium. The owner was under pressure to get to his new job in the U.S. His wife and children had already moved. As we talked and he sensed my desperation, he suggested he take my two months' rent money and call it a down payment on a sale. I was ignorant in these matters, and brought my father back with me that night. They came to an agreement – it was an unusually good deal for us – and we ended up owning a condo. Ralph and the children came home and we settled in.

❊

While Ralph and I were in Michigan, Papa had begun a church for Indian Christians who spoke Hindi, Urdu and Punjabi. He had been successful in establishing new congregations in India, and assumed he would do equally well in Toronto. Better, he felt, because his plan was to convert Indians who were already Christian. How hard could it be to convince them to change denominations and become SDA? He'd seen the process evolve smoothly in the Chinese, Korean and Caribbean communities. When he had converted a critical mass, he reckoned, he could become their official salaried Pastor and he could give up selling books. His idea was to employ Ralph as his Assistant Pastor, and then they would both be doing what they liked best.

(It might seem strange to westerners that my father would wish to work with a man he detested. But in patriarchal societies like ours, relatives have to work together and appear on good terms no matter how they feel privately. Nobody outside our family knew that my father disliked Ralph. Since Papa had himself arranged the marriage, admitting his disdain for his son-in-law would be an acknowledgment that he had chosen unwisely. His name and his honour were inextricably tied up with Ralph. Our marriage was an extension of him, and so to outsiders we were obliged to show a united front.)

My father's Indian church was not a success. The Indian Christians in Toronto were more diverse than the other immigrant communities. They were from all kinds of denominations and educational backgrounds, and some were third or fourth generation Christians. They had their reasons for coming to Papa's church – they were homesick, they enjoyed speaking their native languages, they felt comfortable in the cultural and social environment and it was a good place to meet friends – but they were not keen on changing their denominations. It soon became clear that Ralph was not going to become an assistant Pastor. He would have to set his sights a little lower.

But before he could find work, Ralph was knocked flat by a serious case of pneumonia, whose effects lingered for months. It was nearly two years after leaving the seminary before Ralph finally landed a secure job as a bus driver for the Toronto Transit Commission. This made a tremendous difference to our security and allowed us to save money. Eighteen months later we were even able to buy a four-bedroom house in the area.

Financially we were now much better off, but as Papa's criticisms fell away, and Ralph's confidence in himself grew, so too did his jealousy and controlling tactics. He once again started tightening the psychological screws in our relationship, and my spirits plunged into an all-too-familiar trough.

I had nobody to confide my depression to but my journal. I had taken up journaling as a way to keep my compartmentalized life at Andrews organized, and I never stopped. Gradually it became less about schedules and more about my feelings and observations about life.

One day I was writing in it while sitting at the counter in the women's locker room. A pretty, petite white woman in her early forties, with a shy smile and bright, intelligent eyes, stopped and gently asked me what I was writing that was making me cry.

I was alarmed. I thought perhaps she was a supervisor, or would report me for bringing my children to the gym with me. I had no childcare for them after school, so they would come with me, sometimes take a swim, eat in the cafeteria and then go home. When they didn't come with me, I was constantly on the phone with them, nagging them to get their projects done, mediating conflicts and warning them about taking safety risks. Like many other immigrant women, I was running my children's lives from work.

The woman introduced herself as Elspeth Hayworth. She came to swim at the York pool three times a week. She'd been born in India, she told me, and was interested in connecting with me to chat. Although I didn't know it at the time, Elspeth happened to be the community "outreach" liaison with the university. She was very careful not to probe, but let me know in a nuanced way that if I was in need of help or support, she was available.

Elspeth asked what language I was writing in. I told her Hindi. We talked and got to know each other a bit. Elspeth told me she had been trying to establish contact with South Asian women in the Jane-Finch area, but had so far been unsuccessful. She said that she was concerned about what police had told her – that there was a great deal of domestic violence in this community. The police felt stymied, she said, because when they were called out, the women being abused would not cooperate with them, and refused to press charges. Social service agencies wanted to help these women, but had no entry to them and were also frustrated.

She asked if I would be willing to share my knowledge and views with her. I had no idea what "outreach" meant, but I said I was happy to help if I could. Elspeth began to come an hour early for her swim. She would sit in the locker room and talk to me about her own work, what the social service agencies did, and all the barriers they faced.

Elspeth fascinated me, with her confident air and novel ideas, articulated with a posh British accent that made me think of the Royal family. Meeting her was a watershed moment in my intellectual awakening. Up to now, I had lived in a cocoon of family, church and ideologically homogeneous classrooms. I had never before spoken to an "outsider" about personal subjects like my goals and ambitions and problems, let alone established a close relationship with one.

It was Elspeth who opened up the new and sometimes frightening world of ideological feminism to me. I had made friends with other women from different cultural backgrounds in the seminary, but we shared the same Adventist beliefs and the same conservative and somewhat passive outlook on relations between the sexes. We had all been taught since childhood that our lives on earth are but a way station, and we but pilgrims readying ourselves for our real life on the new earth that Christ had gone before us to prepare.

Elspeth was Protestant, Anglican as I recall, but also clearly someone who thought life here on earth was just as important as the world to come, if she thought about that at all. We bonded as mothers before I became her intellectual protegé. She had three children about the same ages as mine. Elspeth loved being a mother, and she often spoke to me about how important it was to put the needs of one's children above all else. I too had always put my children's needs first, but mostly their physical needs. What Elspeth meant was that she put her children's psychological needs before her own.

I remember how surprised I was when Elspeth told me her greatest pleasure as a mother was to hear her children arguing with her, and challenging her with their own ideas and perspectives. Elspeth explained to me that when children's minds are developing, they must be allowed to make their own mistakes. I considered the implications of such a parent-child relationship. It was very high-minded, but only practical for people with a lot of time and energy to lavish on their children. My mother had not had such a luxury, nor had I. We were too caught up in the struggle for survival. For women in our situation, life was simpler when children simply did as they were told without any assumption that they had the right to question our authority.

I learned new words and phrases from Elspeth. Words like "outreach," "government programs," "settlement," "English as a Second Language," and "community development." I agreed to Elspeth's suggestion that I start reading the newspaper and listening to the radio while I worked to inform myself about national and local news.

I was happy to talk with Elspeth about everything except my own domestic situation. I wasn't sure how to go about sharing private information with someone who wasn't family or an Adventist. She might think badly of me if she knew how inept I was at solving my marital problems, and I didn't want to lose her friendship.

Elspeth told me that as a fulltime employee at York, I was entitled to free tuition. This was exciting. I had my Andrews transcript sent to York. But I was thunderstruck to find that Andrews was not recognized by York as an accredited university, and that my credits there were worthless. This was a terrible blow.

How could such an established, big, beautiful and venerated institution like Andrews, so central to my faith, and charged with turning out our spiritual leaders, have no standing in the eyes of this secular university? It was as if God were playing a cruel trick on me. Was it a test of my faith? Or a punishment because I had passed my courses at Andrews under false pretences? So much of the received wisdom my life was built around was crumbling, I again felt that terrible sense of isolation I had experienced during the monsoon.

There was no use dwelling in self-pity, though. I was going to have to start from scratch in realizing my dream of an accredited education. I learned that I couldn't take any classes at all until I had passed an English equivalence test. I took it. The test indicated my written English was slightly better than Fourth Grade. I was informed I couldn't register for any courses before passing an English as a Second Language, course.

And so once again I found myself surrounded by a banquet of knowledge I was not allowed to partake of. I began seriously to consider that it was my *kismet*, my fate, never to achieve my educational goals. But I kept hearing the voices of the missionaries, telling us "Canada is blessed, because people there are Christian. They are hard-working people and God has blessed them. People in the heathen countries have to repent and accept Christ in their lives to be able to receive his blessings." Well, I was from a heathen country, but I wasn't a heathen, I was a Christian. Why wasn't I getting the blessings I was promised? I decided to press on until Christ remembered I was in Canada.

I had told Elspeth I was planning to leave my kitchen job. She suggested that I work with her to develop an outreach plan in the South Asian community. I could attend language classes, and work with her two days a week. She also offered to have a student tutor me in English.

Elspeth had a list of South Asian women she had met. The police had been called to their homes and the husbands had been arrested. Because I could speak all the languages these women spoke – Urdu, Hindi and Punjabi – she asked me to phone them to see how they were managing, and ask if there was anything we could do for them. So that was "outreach." Outreach, it seemed, was actually a very simple thing.

I was to make these calls from Elspeth's office. If I needed any information, she would be there to help me. I would be paid by the hour. All I had to do was to initiate a conversation and let the women know they were not alone, that help was available if they wanted it. This was my first job as a *de facto* social worker.

From the list we were aware of the husband's employment status and hours, so we were able to estimate the optimal time to call. If a man answered, I would hang up. As I got used to the work, we decided I would be fine making the calls from home or the locker room, in the evenings when Ralph was on shift work or on the weekends. That way I could devote more time to it and augment my income without Ralph knowing.

Now that Ralph had a job he liked, he informed me that the children and I would be spending less time with my parents. That was fine with me, and it helped Ralph feel I had chosen loyalty to him over my father. I registered the children in extra-curricular activities, so I had more time to establish a support group for women experiencing abuse. Elspeth continued to mentor me. She would encourage me to attend specific workshops or listen to speakers to further my education on the subject of domestic violence.

Eventually I passed my English equivalence test and I was permitted to register for the undergraduate program in sociology, on the condition that I continue with advanced ESL classes. I chose sociology because that department was next door to the locker room.

Neither Ralph nor my parents had any idea I was taking courses. Home life was finally calm. Ralph and I had come to an understanding. I would hand over all my paycheques and he would pay the bills. He would give me a food allowance, and I would make sure all the household chores were done. Stability, a good enough substitute for happiness after all we had been through, reigned for a while.

Elspeth started to invite me to meetings where she introduced me to other women working in the non-profit sector. I was very impressed by how smart these women were. They discussed ideas that were new to me, and I found their articulate presentations quite brilliant. These women were not shy in the least about speaking in large groups. They didn't seem to care if their ideas were rebutted. On the contrary, they seemed to relish the cut and thrust of debate. They defended their ideas with vigour. They weren't the least bit apologetic about attacking another woman's assertions, and they laughed when their own ideas got shot down.

They were also quite loud, which I found disconcerting. The women in the seminary had also discussed many ideas. But they were always ladylike, soft-spoken, gentle and sensitive to the feelings of others when they disagreed. I was conscious of these York women being "them," "white," and "not Adventists." Their ways were not "our" ways. We Adventists were soft and feminine, not brash and bold like men. We spoke in tones as humble as birdsong. We glided gracefully like deer. We didn't laugh like hyenas and clomp about like horses. I was judgmental of these women. I felt they needed lessons in humility, especially when I watched them challenging men and acting as though there were no difference at all in their status. And yet they called themselves social workers! How could social workers be so rude, with nobody calling them on it? I disapproved, but a little wistfully, because they were obviously enjoying themselves hugely.

Over lunch one day with Elspeth, I confided my misgivings about one woman in particular I had seen in action at a meeting we had both attended. I said the woman was neither ladylike nor adequately humble. She was opinionated and argumentative, and furthermore dressed like a hippie. What did Elspeth think of her? I wondered aloud. Elspeth just grinned and said, "Oh, Terry comes by her nature quite honestly. She is Jewish, with some Irish in her and maybe a few other cultures too. But she is well-respected. And as for being ladylike" – Elspeth laughed merrily – "Terry would find such a description most insulting."

I was stunned. "What do you mean, she is Jewish?" Elspeth seemed equally stunned by the animus behind my question. To my surprise, I learned from her there were many Jews in Canada and had been for generations. "Does the government know about this?" I inquired sternly. Elspeth struggled to contain her amazement at my ignorance, and her alarm at what looked like anti-Semitism.

Nobody had told me there were Jews in Canada, let alone at York University. The missionaries had said Canada was a Christian country, and that was why it was blessed. I thought that all the Jews had been sent to live in the Middle East.

But here this Terry was: A flesh and blood Jew, and talking so loudly and arrogantly, as if she had every right to consider herself our equal. I was thrown into mental turmoil. To compound my discomfort, I thought she was smart and I had admired her boldness just a little. I had even laughed with everyone else as she made fun of herself in her argument. She seemed so "jolly."

While we were at Andrews University, I had attended many a workshop and lectures and taken classes where I came away with the impression that Jews were a problematic nation to Christians. Jews were not referred to as people, just as a nation. The "issue of the Jews" was causing a lot of debate in the Church. We women did not concern ourselves with it. It was a problem the men would contemplate and discuss, and then they would tell us what we in the SDA now believed. But I knew that within the SDA Church, depending on their origins, people were divided on the Jewish question.

The British Adventists and missionaries from countries under British influence believed that the Jews must return to Israel prior to the second coming of Christ. The Jews were considered to still be God's "beloved nation." Of course the Jews had made terrible mistakes in rejecting God time and time again, but they had been punished for their mistakes. And God's promise to them was a promise he must keep. So now that they had their own country, Jews from around the world had started to "go home." Which meant that Christ would come soon, and we, the SDA, had to be ready. On the day the last Jew entered the Promised Land, Christ would come. Since we can't know it in advance, we must be ready every day. This thought is preached in SDA churches even today.

I had found the American Adventists' view on the Jewish question more palatable. They believed that the Jews would have to be returned to their ancient land, but first they would first have to be converted to Christianity. The rationale was that the Jewish nation had rejected God's son, thus forfeiting their claim to remain the "beloved nation," and therefore, there was no promise to keep. These views still prevail amongst American Adventists.

In India the majority of the SDA missionaries were American, and many of them had attended Andrews University in Michigan. It was their job to train the native Pastors on church doctrine. It often happened that when natives were asked to translate or interpret what they heard, their enthusiasm would lead them to add or embellish. I don't know if the missionaries ever said that Adventists don't like Jews because they killed Christ, but I certainly remember the translators saying that, and emphasizing God's disappointment in the "Jewish nation." A foreign graft on the tree of Indian culture, Jews became Untouchables, and we did not want to have anything to do with them. We, the SDA, were the "Lord's Army," and His new "Beloved Nation," His new "Chosen."

Questions assailed me. How could I be sitting in the same room with these women? How come they looked normal? How come they were smart? How come they were not ashamed of themselves for what they did to Our Lord?

My greater fear was that my father or Ralph would find out, or that someone from the church might see me and report that I had been associating with Jews. I told Elspeth I needed more time for my class work, and stopped attending the meetings. However, I kept attending the support group for the South Asian women and finding comfort with those who were like me. Even though they were not SDA, at least they were Indian.

Soon enough I learned that York University was full of Jews, and I began to scrutinize every face I saw for signs of Jewishness, so I would know who I should avoid. I felt very conflicted about this. Finally I confided my prejudices to Elspeth. She said that the important thing was that I was struggling with my thoughts and feelings about what was right and what was wrong. She reassured me that I would learn to judge people for who they are, and as I developed a "moral compass," I would know what was right. She of course had to explain to me what a moral compass was.

One of my Jewish teachers was a short blonde woman, Dr. Nancy Mandel, who was known as the doyenne of feminism in Canada. Her ideas only served to deepen my anxieties. She taught in a department called Women's Studies, which I assumed would be very like the Home Economics program I had taken at Andrews, a course where I could shine without effort. I was soon disabused of any such notion. In her course I heard words and ideas that were new to me: "empowerment," "gay rights," "Marxism," "sexual exploitation," and "human rights." I did not understand her jargon, or the point she was trying to make. I had the impression she hated men, so was surprised to learn she was married and the mother of sons.

The SDA gender paradigm of the man as head of the household with the woman as the angel of the hearth had made perfect sense to me before I started getting an education. Now everything seemed upside down. I respected my church and my family. At the same time I was working with women from my culture who were being abused by their husbands, and who refused to testify against them, and even wanted them to come back home. That would have seemed very normal to me before I started taking these courses, and now I didn't know what to think.

Elspeth was sympathetic to my inner turmoil, but felt it was the price I had to pay to raise my consciousness. She began introducing me to books she was reading and thought I would benefit from. The first one was *In a Different Voice: Psychological Theory and Women's Development* by a feminist called Carol Gilligan. Given my life experiences, I could relate to much of what she was saying – that women are society's moral teachers and are passive victims of the patriarchy; that men are oppressive by nature and have therefore created oppressive institutions that they police. Then I read *The Feminine Mystique* by Betty Friedan, but I didn't like it. It just seemed to me like a lot of whining by a woman who had a good education and an enviable life of comfort and material security. I would have been the happiest woman on earth in her position. No American middle-class woman was living in any concentration camp, as Friedan seemed to imply. Quite the contrary.

Elspeth and I would discuss my reactions while we drove back and forth from meetings or while eating lunch on benches outside. She would ask me to read aloud paragraphs she had highlighted while she drove. Then, just as if I were her intellectual equal, she would ask, "What did you think of that? I found it disturbing." And because Elspeth found it disturbing, I readily agreed that I too had found it to be so. But Elspeth might then remind me that some weeks earlier I had expressed an opinion that contradicted this one. She didn't want my hero worship. She wanted me to think for myself. She told me it was okay to change my mind if I found evidence to persuade me that I had been wrong before. She said, "Changing your thoughts is not a bad thing as long as you know why you are doing it."

Eating outside became a habit. Elspeth would come to get me, hand me a bag, and with a twinkle say, "A sandwich and a book. Are we now content?" Some of these books were on my course syllabus in Women's Studies, and I would very cheekily rattle off Elspeth's commentaries as my own thoughts in class. When I confessed my naughtiness to her, she just laughed.

Chapter Seventeen

Burning bridges

The outreach program Elspeth and I had embarked on started to take shape. We recruited volunteers from the South Asian community. In 1982, only two years after I plunged into my education at York, I was asked to join the North York Community Relations Committee, which both thrilled and terrified me. Elspeth's constant support reassured me. She would say, "You don't have to say anything. Just pay attention to other people's views on issues that are important to the community. If they make sense to you, fine. If not, think about why they don't, and write down your own views."

Throughout these years, without putting a name to it, I was acquiring the technique of critical thinking. It was not good enough simply to hold views; I had to defend them with reason and logic. But at the same time, it was drilled into me, I had to make sure I didn't offend anyone with opposing views, even if I failed to grasp their logic. For example, there was a high crime rate amongst the Jamaicans who densely populated our area. I felt the Black community therefore had internal problems, but I instinctively knew I mustn't say so aloud.

It took me a while to understand the tremendous guilt that white Christians felt towards other ethnicities and religions, even Christians like heritage Canadians who had never themselves been imperialists or acted badly to other races. They were so ultra-sensitive to the sin of racism that tolerance for anything other races or religions, even behaviours they would have disapproved of in themselves or in other white people, was always their guiding principle. I had no such sensitivities. As an ethnically Indian Christian I had always been the butt of other races' and religions' intolerance, so I felt no guilt in lacing up the other shoe once it was on my foot. But I did learn to keep my mouth shut, because any criticism of people of colour was just a no-no and made everyone unhappy.

I was mentally tough on other ethnic groups, but soft on the South Asian women who were being abused. I wanted to find a way to reach them and help them. As I got to know the South Asian women, I began to see them less as individuals separated from other South Asian women by class, caste or social affiliations, than as a victimized collective, all of them in thrall to cultural codes of honour and shame they could not break away from. The attitudes, the abusive behaviours, the reactions to the behaviours – they were the same for all the women, whatever their religion or region of origin. What was happening to them was a mirror image of my whole life.

But not entirely. I had been ignorant, and I had lived in a social bubble bounded by monolithic cultural codes and Adventist perspectives. What shocked me in Toronto was that many of these abused women were highly educated and worldly. Many of them had even been professionals in their countries of origin and respected members of the higher social classes – women I would never have dreamed of socializing with in India. In Canada they seemed all the more pathetic, because they had known status and lost it, while I had been at the bottom of social life in India, and had nowhere to go but up.

Elspeth and the volunteers working with her decided that the outreach project should be incorporated. To incorporate we needed a board of directors and a salaried executive director. As Elspeth was filling out the forms, one of the volunteers pointed at me and said, "We'll put her down as executive director." And just like that, I was a professional director of an agency. Other positions were handed out just as casually.

The board of directors was assembled with more thoughtfulness. Elspeth said we needed people with experience in social services. She brought aboard responsible people she'd worked with, and as well three South Asian community members to round out the board's "diversity."

I had no idea what was involved in being an executive director. Elspeth drew up a job description, explaining that she would work with me until I got the hang of things, and then gradually hand over more responsibility, until I was eventually flying solo. The hardest part was writing the grant proposals. By now my spoken English and reading comprehension were good, but I still had great difficulty with written English, and I wasn't keen on exposing that particular deficit to others.

I continued taking undergraduate courses, supported by the student tutoring service, my classmates and my professors. My knowledge of history and the real world beyond my ethnic and religious borders was expanding by leaps and bounds. It was all intellectually exhilarating, but inside I felt continually conflicted between the values I was absorbing from my studies, and the ingrained cultural habits that refused to submit to reason.

One day Dr. Nancy Mandel said to me, "You know what would be fantastic? To conduct research on the status of the South Asian women in Jane-Finch. To document their experiences around immigration and settlement. You could study the nature of the domestic violence they suffer, and identify the needs of this community." Then she added, as if it were just a casual afterthought, "You could use part of this research for your master's thesis."

Master's thesis? I could not have been more stunned if she had said I could use the research to walk on water. I didn't know what to say. I squeaked, "What do you mean?" I was asking her to explain why she thought I would be capable of doing a master's thesis, but she interpreted my question as a query about the mechanics of such a project, and launched into an explanation of questionnaire methodology and passage of the topic through the university ethics committee and training volunteers and so forth. As she elaborated on these details and started writing notes to herself, I tried hard to follow what she was saying, but my mind kept replaying her words, *"You can use part of this research for your master's thesis,"* in an endless loop.

Dr. Mandel had opened a door into a room she imagined any ambitious woman student in her field would find inviting. I did and I didn't. I was excited, but also scared at the idea of walking across that threshold. At first all I could imagine waiting for me as I entered that room were the faces of my father and my husband. They would be angry at me for pushing this educational business too far – associating with people they could never approve of (I never did tell them that many of my professors and classmates were Jews), and learning ideas and attitudes that ran completely counter to the teachings of our church, not to mention insulting our cultural traditions.

In truth, I myself was often thrown into conflict and confusion by some of what I was learning. It seemed to me that the two most actively promoted orthodoxies at York University were instructing me to think in two opposed ways.

Feminism made me question my whole upbringing, encouraged me to be judgmental about the patriarchy, and challenged my loyalty to the men in my life. Feminism told me I had to be strong and forthright and autonomous.

But at the same time multiculturalism, an equally prominent philosophy that Prime Minister Pierre Elliot Trudeau had decreed would be Canada's guiding principle for a just society, seemed to be telling me that judging the behaviour of people from cultures other than western Christian ones was patronizing and elitist. Multiculturalism seemed to be telling me I should continue to live exactly as I always had, because inequality of value between men and women was part of my culture, and all cultures were deemed to be of equal value.

I remember seeking counsel about my difficulties in harmonizing feminist values with my personal situation from a trusted friend, a social worker of Irish provenance in North York. Ann, a soft-spoken woman with a quirky sense of humour, was an ardent multiculturalist. Ann would say things like, "Well, you see, there are so many ways one could look at this, it is usually contextual," or "People have different views of the world because they have had different life experiences, and so before we get judgmental, we must really try to learn their views."

Part of me found Ann's words very soothing. "Contextual" was a word now quite familiar to me. Since I had never in my life considered my upbringing from a critical perspective, I had come to realize that I had all along been "contextualizing" my life without knowing what that was.

What I took from Ann's musings was that because devaluing women was part of our culture, I could accept my father's and my husband's behaviour toward me as perfectly normal and acceptable. Thus Papa's contempt for me was not really his fault, and I was therefore absolved from the anguish of judging his behaviour as wrong.

What a paradox it all was. My recently-acquired education had given me the critical tools to compare my life with the lives of women from other cultures, evaluate the differences and pass judgment on my past experiences. So it seemed to me quite ironic that those more educated than I were telling me on the one hand to throw off the shackles of my past, and on the other to accept them with serenity and even pride.

If I only had myself to think of, I would have found Ann's relativism the answer to my conflicts. I could be a feminist and strong at York, and a submissive daughter and wife at home, and nobody would be "judgmental" of my duality. In fact, that is exactly what I did for far too long.

But I could not accept this solution for the abused South Asian women, whose plight weighed so heavily on my conscience. How could I tell them that their culture was more important than their right to live in dignity, the same right as my new Canadian women friends expected and demanded for themselves? So many times, as I listened to my friends talking so confidently about diversity and the value of multiculturalism, I felt they really knew very little about the women who lived so close to York. I would see them all the time – women my age, new immigrants from South Asia – in the streets and at the mall. Usually they were with their husbands. If I smiled at a woman or attempted to speak to her, even if I spoke in her language, the husband would always look at me suspiciously, and if she instinctively smiled back, the woman would then look anxiously at her husband, worried that even a smile to another woman might have offended him. I felt I knew what was going on in their homes and it cut me to the quick.

I had three weeks' vacation time from York. So, along with two volunteers from the South Asian community, I started our organized outreach program. Our methodology was simple, but effective. We went to apartment buildings in the neighbourhood, checked the names of the occupants in the foyer, and made a list of names that looked Indian or Pakistani. Then we knocked at those doors. During the three weeks, we knocked on 1800 doors. If a man answered, we would say we had made a mistake. If a woman answered, we would say that we were new to the area, didn't know very many people and wondered if the occupant would be interested in getting together with us for tea. We named a date and time and place. At the Driftwood Community Centre on the corner of Jane and Finch, we prepared tea for the thirty women we hoped might take the bait. More than 150 women showed up

Taken aback by the turnout, I felt overwhelmed. I stood in front of the women and offered effusive apologies for my insufficient hospitality. An impatient elderly Sikh woman interrupted me. "Never mind the tea. Everyone has tea in their homes if they want some. You know and I know that the women in our community are having a lot of problems. We don't know what to do about them. Do you have any suggestions for helping us?"

Well, so much for diplomacy. All our rehearsals in dealing with sensitive issues went out the window. The cat was out of the bag. This woman had just laid it out in the form of a challenge. She wanted to know if I was going to be a leader or a talker. I told her and everyone there the truth about my life and the obstacles I was still facing in harmonising cultural traditions with Canadian values. I told everyone how terrified I was about making the wrong decisions, and how I wondered if there was anyone else who was facing the same inner conflicts.

Then Elspeth and Ann spoke about the programs being offered in the community, and I translated what they were saying. My role reminded me of how my father used to translate the white missionaries' English sermons into Urdu or Punjabi for the lower-caste converts in our churches back home. He took great pride in this status-conferring task. I would have loved to tell him that I had now arrived at a similar level of achievement, and was performing a similar educational task, even if my task was to teach values diametrically opposed to the ones he taught. But there was no way I could tell him that we were effectively training women to challenge the cultural norms that held them back from full participation in Canadian life.

That first meeting lasted for four hours. The women agreed that they would like to take English classes. It was decided we would start classes in basic English, advanced English, resumé writing and job hunting. Health and childcare courses would be provided too. The Toronto Asian Community Centre was now open for business.

Classes were given on Saturday mornings. Our first speaker was a public nurse. All of us attended. The nurse spoke in English and I translated. The topics were chosen by the women. They ranged from personal hygiene to children's health to healthy eating to coping with the depressing effects of lack of sunshine. Then the women were divided into their respective groups.

I taught Basic English. I helped the women memorize sentences, such as, "Where is this bus going?" "How much does this cost?" or "I am lost. I need to go to Jane Street." We had assistance from York's English as a Second Language students doing practicums, and Elspeth pitched in too when she could. The women eagerly sponged up knowledge and showered me with their gratitude. I was finally a confident fish swimming easily in the waters of immigration and settlement. My self-confidence soared.

But my domestic life was a mess. I was an absentee mother at the worst possible time for my vulnerable adolescent daughters. Aged fifteen and fourteen, Mina and Bina attended the volatile C.W. Jefferys High School, where they were faced every day with a gamut of social hazards amongst tough, often aggressive boys. I was working two jobs and taking classes, and whatever free time I had, I lavished on the Community Centre.

In the eyes of the children I was more a dictator barking out orders than a mother. To keep the household running smoothly, I would delegate a list of chores I expected them to do. I didn't care that their obligations to clean, do laundry and babysit their brother meant they had no time to socialize with their friends as their peers did. If they didn't do the chores, I would turn nasty.

The unvarnished fact is that I had lost sight of my priorities. I was caught up in the heady rush of feeling useful to women I wanted to help, and approved of by women I wanted to impress. My work was uplifting, and my home life was depressing. So I gave my heart to my work rather than my home, and I basked in the addictive psychological warmth of mentoring and validation. On occasions when I was made aware of my neglect of my children, I tried to convince myself that staying away was actually helpful. I told myself that the kids didn't have to witness Ralph's abusiveness when I wasn't there, and that made up for my truancy.

But the reality was that my absence did not ensure peace in the house. Ralph was a loving father to our son, but he simply switched the focus of his grievances about me to the girls and browbeat them, which only added to their resentment against me. I was torn up with guilt, but paralyzed by indecision.

I was candid about my problems with the South Asian women in the group. They began to query my double standard. I was trying to help them absorb Canadian values of gender equality, and they quite rightly wanted to know why I was not doing something about my own marital malaise, and not providing a safe place for my daughters. Until then I had always looked at them as clients who needed help, and myself as the dispenser of help. Now I realized I was no different from them. "Physician, heal thyself" was the implied message I was hearing from within and without. My friends at York had been urging me to move to a women's shelter. Around this time another South Asian woman, along with her parents, had just been stabbed to death. She lived on the next street to mine. When Ralph made a menacing gesture to me with a kitchen knife one night, I finally acted.

I took the girls and left the house. I knew James would be safe with Ralph – Ralph doted on his only son, and James was always happy with Ralph – and I agreed to let Mina stay over with a friend. But I did not want to leave Bina in the house. She was the one who constantly challenged her father and was on the receiving end of his threats and abuse. So Bina came with me.

I drove to the police station to ask for directions to the nearest shelter. The officer told me that was not a nice place "for a lady like you." He said it was a place for prostitutes "and their likes." I told him that I could not go back home because I feared for my life, and he eventually gave me directions to a shelter.

As soon as I walked in, I knew I had made a big mistake. It was two in the morning, but there were a number of women sitting around the kitchen table smoking. The whole floor was blue with smoke. Bina began to cough and soon I was coughing too. The women, all scantily dressed, looked hostile. We were both terrified. I remembered what the officer had said. All the teachings of the Church and the warnings from my parents came flooding back. I felt sick at the thought of my daughter spending even one night amongst such lowlifes.

The staff members welcomed me politely. But they immediately ushered Bina away. They said she should make up our beds, while they did the intake with me in another room. She was visibly shaking, and I did not want to leave her alone. The staff person kept saying Bina was fine, and old enough to make the beds. She said if Bina needed help she would ask for it. During my interview I heard Bina crying piteously. I wanted to go to her, but the staff person interviewing me insisted someone else would attend to her. I'd had enough of being bossed around. Being bossed around was why I had come to that place. I pushed the interviewer out of my way and ran to Bina. As I held her, she sobbed, "Mum, we have reached the bottom of the pit, haven't we?" Her words pierced my heart. I said, "No, not by a long shot. Let's get out of here."

We left and ended up at a motel. I thought that it would give me time to think things through. We had never been in a motel. The front desk person did not turn on the heat, and knowing no better, we didn't ask for it. The two us huddled together in one bed, covered with all the bedding from both beds. Neither of us slept.

The next morning we went home. I was resigned to whatever fate awaited us. Ralph was calm and disengaged from me. He didn't ask where we had been and we did not say. I know that Bina was terribly shaken by the experience, but we have never talked about it to this day.

That episode should have been my cue for planning a realistic separation scenario we all could live with. Instead, I sank back into a state of denial. But I was physically and mentally exhausted. One night I came home close to midnight after my shift at the locker room, and Mina came running down the stairs. She began to scream at me. "Why do you keep coming back to this house? You are never here. You just make the money and pay the bills. Your parents were here all evening, and they told Papa to kick you with his boots, because that is the only language you understand. Don't you get it? You should not come home."

I stood there staring in wonder at my child, Mina, always the shy withdrawn one, now yelling and screaming at me and telling me to get out of the house. I said, "Mina, I have stayed in this house and in this marriage because I believe that children need both their parents. I thought that by working hard, I was giving you the money you need to buy nice clothes and shoes that you want. I have a second job to help buy these things. Why are you being so nasty?"

By now Ralph was standing behind her, and Mina knew it, but she looked me squarely in the eye and said calmly, "You should know you are going to be beaten tonight. And don't tell me you came back for us. You can't even protect yourself. How can you protect us? Tonight might be the end of you if you don't get out."

The warning in her eyes was enough. Something was not right. I just had enough time to get back into the car and lock the doors before Ralph reached it. He tried to stop me by banging on the hood of the car. I reversed and took off, not knowing where I was headed. Like a homing pigeon I returned to York and parked in one of the residence parking lots, where I spent a sleepless night.

I lived in the car for two weeks. Finally my supervisor at York, Sheila, a warm and caring woman from Barbados, asked me why I looked so rundown, and why I was taking showers in the locker room every morning. I told her the truth. She invited me to sleep on her couch until I could make up my mind about what to do. I gratefully accepted.

It was now the end of November and I had no place to take the children, even if I had had access to them. Night after night I sat at the end of the street in my car, fearful of going back into the house, but longing to check on the children. I wanted to be sure they were eating properly and warmly tucked in at bedtime, responsibilities I had managed to block out concern for before this crisis. I tried to get in once when I knew Ralph was at work, but he had changed the lock.

James was a Daddy's boy and always happy in Ralph's charge, and I knew Mina was happy I had left, but I worried about Bina. When I stopped her on her way to school, she was very angry and refused to speak with me. When I asked how she was doing, she refused to answer. I told her that I was sorry, and she shrugged, saying, "You're the one who left, so you deal with it." It was clear to me that Bina felt totally abandoned. I tried to explain to her that I felt my life was in danger, but she didn't want to hear about that. An icy curtain fell between us that sadly, because I am afraid of what I might hear, I have never really attempted to lift.

While all this was going on, my parents, unaware of my situation, left for Texas. Papa had finally been let go from his salesmen-training job, thanks to his lack of humility and stubborn failure to adapt to western norms in dealing with subordinates. Career-wise, he had hit a brick wall in terms of opportunities and good will in the Ontario SDA community. Mary and her family lived in Houston, home to a large community of Adventists where Papa had many contacts, and the move represented a potential fresh start for pastoring.

When his career spiralled downward in Canada, Papa had toyed with the idea of returning to India. But he was no longer a young man, and he knew the SDA glory days in India were over. So he was doomed to stay in the West, but he had not saved any money for a rainy day. It was more difficult than they expected to find decent lodging and remunerative work in Houston. I couldn't bring myself to tell them what had happened to Ralph and me. I knew I could expect neither material nor moral support from that corner, so there was no point in my adding to their worries, or opening the door to unhelpful scoldings.

It was about four or five weeks after I left Ralph before Paul, living in London, Ontario at the time, called my father and informed him of developments. Papa told everyone not to have contact with me, so none of my siblings called me or would take calls from me. Paul did have contact with Ralph, though. They all believed that I would come back, as I had before.

My parents leaving Canada just at this time was in a way a blessing, but it was also very frightening. There was less pressure on me to justify what I was doing, but I was now expected to make all my decisions by myself, and I would have to deal with the disastrous consequences if I chose the wrong route to independence. I did not want to share this information with Elspeth, or any of the other women in the centre. I felt I now had a certain professional status to maintain, which meant I had to lower a veil over my private life. I had never felt so lonely and so lost. Yet another psychological monsoon.

I found a bachelor apartment close to the house. My supervisor co-signed for me. I decided it was best to leave the children in the house, so that they could continue to attend their school and follow their usual routines. I told the girls I would hire a woman to clean the house and do the laundry. I told them they could come to the university after school, we could all have dinner together, and they could then go home and sleep in their own beds. At first they balked, but little by little they appreciated the practicality of my plan, especially since it meant they did not have to cook dinner.

I met with Ralph a few times to talk about the children. He asked if I would consider coming back. For the first time he declared himself willing to agree to any conditions I set down. He pointed out that we had a lot going for us: his secure job at the TTC and our comfortable home, which we had only recently re-carpeted and filled with new furniture. We had finally made it, he said, and this was not the time to break up the family.

I couldn't help but agree with his reasoning. I felt very sorry for Ralph as he begged me to come home. And I felt very guilty too. I had never loved this man and he knew it. I had tried to be a dutiful wife, but could not find any affection in my heart for him. He knew that his touch repelled me. That has to be a terrible thing for a man. I believe that if he had married a woman who loved him, or had it in her to grow to love him, he may well have been a good husband. It certainly hadn't helped that my father had bullied him for eighteen years. My heart went out to him in spite of our miserable history.

I didn't want to dash his hopes completely. I told him that I thought that he and the children should stay in the house for six months, and at the end of that time I would make up my mind as to what I wanted to do.

During this period Ralph was every inch the sober, respectful Canadian husband. We even went grocery shopping together a few times and attended church as a family. I dropped in and out of the house, making sure the children were taken care of, but always returning to my apartment to sleep. As time went on, I began to believe that Ralph had finally matured and set aside his penchant for violence once and for all.

But then one day at work, Security came by to say that they had found someone "lurking" around my car. When they described the man, I knew instantly it was Ralph. I had already had suspicions that I was being followed, and now I knew it wasn't just my imagination. When I confronted Ralph with Security's report, he admitted that he had been hanging around my car, but refused to explain why. I began to fear him once again, and stopped meeting him for our "talks."

There were times when the children would come by themselves to my apartment for a whole weekend. I had hoped to make these occasions for bonding. My idea was to keep it simple, cook homey meals, and create a normal family atmosphere. But they showed little interest in the cocooning scenario I envisaged. Like many other children of separated parents, they leveraged my bid for their love and forgiveness into the material payoff of restaurant meals and shopping trips at the mall. I was ashamed to be buying their affection, but I did it anyway. Not that it worked very well, as they continued to resent me.

Ralph found our reunions very threatening. He couldn't handle the possibility that I might live separately from him, and yet continue to get along well with the children. I discovered later he had been telling family and church members that we were officially back together, because I couldn't make it without him. He boasted that he would be the "man of the house" when I came home. He let it be known to all and sundry that he and my father had agreed there would be strict rules imposed on me when I returned. According to his version of the future, I would stop working and stop studying, and the family would live on his salary, while I tended the house and the children.

But meanwhile, in my presence Ralph was polite and deferential. He said that he had considered my suggestion of couple's counselling and concluded it was an excellent idea. I was somewhat buoyed up. One day I mentioned that I was coming to the house to pick up some books I needed. Ralph pleasantly agreed, but when I got to the house, he invited me out to see something in the backyard. I stepped outside and gasped. When I registered what I was looking at, my knees buckled and my stomach turned over.

Ralph had started a bonfire. Into its hungry flames he had already thrown many of my books. The rest were on the grass waiting their turn. I could see the still-unconsumed forms visible in the inferno. My books! My beloved books! Some were Elspeth's gifts to me and others I had discovered on my own: *I Know Why the Caged Bird Sings*, by Maya Angelou, that had roused in me such kindred emotion that I cried all the way through; Toni Morrison's *Beloved,* that made me feel the experience of slavery in my bones; Anita Desai's novels of her South Asian childhood that led me to the discovery of a whole literary canon, showcasing the experience and wisdom and courage of South Asian writers like Meena Shirwadkar and Fauzia Rafiq and Madhu Kishwas.

I was horrified, sick at heart. I couldn't think. I could only remember and feel. Suddenly I recalled with lurid clarity that night in Delhi when I was fourteen and I stood on our rooftop watching beautiful Kiran writhing inside her furnace. And at the memory I was smitten with profound shame. I had watched a human being burn to death and felt only fear and numbness. Now I was watching my books burn, and I felt the horror and the moral outrage I should have felt for her. Where had my rage been while Kiran, a human being, was burning?

The answer came to me. When I was young and was watching Kiran burn, I did not judge the people who burned her. I was "contextualized" then. Now I was educated. I knew that the same people who burn books are sometimes willing to burn people too. My books held the thoughts of gentle, civilized people for whom the fate of Kiran would be an obscenity. I was aligned with them now. So I watched my books burning, and I knew I could not share my life with someone capable of such brutality to the free mind at play.

I turned my gaze onto Ralph. I was further sickened to see him grinning. He was enjoying my suffering. I asked him how he could do something so vile. He just shrugged and said, "I am glad you have decided to stop all this foolishness. You are a mother and a wife. You will come on home and we will all be fine."

I was shaking as I backed away from the terrible sight before me, and ran to the car. That stupid man could have had me back, but in burning my beloved books, the symbol of everything good that had ever happened to me, he had forever burned all his bridges to my body and soul.

Chapter Eighteen

At long last, love

When a western woman leaves her husband, she leaves a man. When I left Ralph in 1985, I also walked away from my immediate and extended family, my Church and my cultural community. As soon as my parents learned of our separation, Papa told everyone I was to be treated like a "disease." And I may as well have been struck by leprosy, because nobody in my family would have anything to do with me.

Now that our marriage was well and truly over, I had ample time to reflect upon and regret the suffering our children had endured at both our hands. There was only so much blame I could lay at Ralph's door. I now had to confront my own failures and inadequacies. I could see that while I had loved my children passionately, I had never been a patient or affectionate mother. I took my parenting style from the way I had been parented. I used to yell at the kids and say cruel things. "If you don't wake up, I will come up and break your legs," I might shout upstairs. Or: "If you don't do the laundry by tonight, I will break your legs." I was channelling my own mother, of course, who had a fixation with broken legs ("Cover your legs," "hide your legs," "I will break your legs.")

One day when the children were still young, I received a summons from the children's elementary school principal. Alarmed, I rushed to the school. In his office I found four very stern-looking people: the principal, the vice-principal, the children's teacher and a Children's Aid worker. I was informed that it was a crime to hit children and threaten them with broken limbs. The principal said my children had recanted their complaints, but he was still obliged to investigate.

I admitted to smacking the children on occasion, and luckily was let off the hook with a warning. I stopped threatening the children with physical punishment. Instead, I would warn them that if they didn't do as I told them, I would call the Children's Aid Society and have them put in horrible foster homes. That worked. Until they reached adolescence, the children adopted a more acquiescent and respectful attitude. Of course, in the years to come, I would pay a terrible price in lost intimacy and trust for my insensitivity and cruelty.

Today all those memories haunt me. I am filled with remorse when I think of the things I said and did. But at the time I didn't feel guilty or recognize that my behaviour was unfair, or understand what kind of psychological impact it might have on my children. I did what was expedient for the moment, because I had no idea yet what constituted good parenting.

As the girls entered adolescence, I had less and less control over them. I was largely parenting them by telephone, and much of the time didn't know where they were. They began exploiting our situation to get what they wanted. They would threaten Ralph that if he didn't allow them the freedoms they wanted, they would move in with me. Then they would play on my guilt to extort material possessions. Other women going through a messy divorce have told me their children did the same thing. I was a knowing dupe. I wanted them to be happy at any cost, – not for their benefit, but so I could pursue my education and earn money without the hindrance of parenting obligations.

I have never felt more alone and fearful than I did after my definitive split from Ralph. Security at York had informed me my car had been tampered with, and asked me if I had any specific concerns. Even more frightening were phone calls at home from some of my father's friends, men I used trustingly to call "Uncle." They said things to me like, "Married women are used to certain services. I would be happy to provide them for you." At first I would just hang up in disgust. But then I started to get calls at work, and I reported these to my supervisor. Now I was angry. If I recognized the voice I would snarl at them, calling them bad names and suggesting they give their daughters to Ralph and see how they felt about that.

One day I was opening the trunk of my car to load groceries, when one of my father's friends suddenly appeared beside me. The last time I had seen him was in church where he and his family had listened to my father preaching the sermon. In a sleazy tone, he said in Hindustani, "Permit me to lift it for you. I can lift it up and I can put it down, whatever is your pleasure." I froze. By the time I recognized the real meaning of his words, he had driven off. I got into my car and cried. I felt dirty. I knew why these men were harassing me. They felt I should be taught a lesson. I was well aware that they were not speaking for themselves, but for my whole community.

Just as I was about to file my divorce papers, my uncle, Chacha Sadiq, who had been out of my life for years, called me and gently said, "I know you are going through a difficult time. How is it things are so bad between you and your husband, and I was not aware? I would have tried to help you. Will you not come to our house and speak with your aunt and me before you make irrevocable decisions?"

A dam broke inside me. A cataract of rage tumbled up and onto my tongue. I lashed out at my kind and blameless uncle. I snarled that he and my father, the patriarchs of the family, had ruined my life. I said if he wanted Ralph to remain a family member, why then, let one of his own daughters marry him, and see how happy she is when he beats her and accuses her of sleeping with every man in town.

Dearest Chacha Ji tried to stop me from shouting more invectives at him, words I would surely regret – and did regret – but I could not stop, so he finally hung up the phone. Years later his wife, Chachi Saroj, told me he had wept for hours afterward. She reminded me of the many times Chacha Sadiq had tried to save me from Papa's thrashings when I was a child. She told me he had felt guilty about not being there to save me as my marriage disintegrated, when I needed him most.

Dearest Chacha Sadiq

In the summer of 1958, in Jullandhar, my mother was expecting a baby – my brother, as it turned out – and I was seven years old. The year was marked by two exciting events. Chacha Sadiq was getting married, and Naani Ji would be coming all the way from Pakistan to attend the wedding.

At that time Chacha Sadiq was the treasurer for the SDA church in Jullandhar, and Papa was the Pastor. After the wedding, we all lived together in a two-storey house. Chacha Sadiq and his wife Chachi Saroj, a teacher at Roorkee, had their quarters upstairs, and our family downstairs, but we took our meals together.

I was very excited about this wedding. Chacha Sadiq had been a fixture in our lives ever since I could remember. When Papa was away on one of his many long selling trips, Chacha Sadiq looked out for us. When Papa was home, he often acted as a buffer between me and my parents. Chacha Sadiq was humble where Papa was arrogant, gentle where Papa was tough. If I did something wrong when he was in charge of me, he never punished me; he only said he was disappointed in me. Chacha Ji always tried to defend me from Papa's volatility – or as much as he could, considering the deference to an older brother's authority a younger brother was bound to pay.

The wedding took place at Roorkee. A large group of our relatives was to meet up with us in Jullandhar and travel there together as the *barat* – the "wedding party." Sadiq was the second brother to marry. My parents' wedding had been a rather hurried and simple affair, because of the recent war and partition of 1948. So in a way Sadiq's wedding was Papa's "coming out" as the head of the family. It was Papa who sought a suitable bride for Chacha Ji, young and handsome, college-educated, established in his career, a man that any woman would consider a good match. Papa could have negotiated a handsome dowry – 60,000 rupees, according to family gossip – but then Chacha Ji did the unthinkable and chose Chachi Saroj, a woman from a different caste with no dowry... for love!

My father was furious. From the day he met Chachi Saroj, Papa disliked her intensely. Chachi Saroj was not intimidated by Papa. She would not lower her eyes when speaking to him, and if he displeased her, would actually *glare* at him. Papa would deliberately never speak directly to her, only to his brother. But Chachi Saroj would respond if she felt like it, or add something to her husband's reply, just as though she were Papa's equal. And if Papa spoke disrespectfully to his brother, Chachi Saroj would actually chide him for it! I could almost feel the heat of Papa's royal umbrage in her presence.

One evening shortly after the wedding, while Naani Ji was still visiting, we all went out for a walk to humour her request to see a Hindu temple she fancied, one of a cluster of temples in the area. For a lark, and thinking I was unobserved, I slipped into one of them, prostrated myself before the gods, and scooped up the coins that Hindu worshippers had thrown down as offerings. But everyone saw. When I rejoined them, Naani and Chacha Sadiq smiled indulgently at my naughtiness, but my father, jumpy and irritable from the prolonged exposure to his two least favourite women, was livid. He dragged me home, threw me on my charpoy and laid into me with his leather belt.

I don't have a clear memory of the beating, because I passed out quickly. Naani Ji was disgusted, and cut short her visit. Chachi Saroj said she had never witnessed a child beaten so brutally over something so trivial. She told people about it, which didn't do my father any good with the community. That was also the final straw for their relationship with my parents. After the beating, Chachi Saroj and Chacha Sadiq withdrew socially from our lives. When they had children, Chachi Saroj made sure her three daughters had nothing more to do with us. Even though our two families lived fifteen minutes away from each other in Canada, we never celebrated holidays together. My cousins are nice people and have led successful lives, but I hardly know them.

Remembering all this, I know why I was so angry on the telephone with Chacha Ji when he wondered why I had not called him about my divorce. I blamed him for not having saved me from that beating. But in fairness, what could he have done? He was the younger brother. It was not his place to intervene.

✳

After my marriage dissolved in 1984, I was still working in York University's locker room, and active as the executive director of the South Asian Community Centre. Occasionally I filled in for a short-order cooking shift too. I was also attending classes.

The classroom was at least an oasis of calm and sanity. There I could lock out the world and lose myself in stories I had never heard before. It was in the classroom during this period that I discovered modern history, and for the first time learned about the Russian Revolution, Stalin, Hitler, Castro, and the Middle East. So many historical watersheds had taken place in my lifetime, and I had been entirely ignorant of them. I remember how sorry I felt for President Nixon. I related to him because he had clawed himself up from the wrong side of the tracks and overcome so many obstacles to achieve success. He reminded me of my father. I overlooked his faults.

For the first time in my life, even though I had an apartment and money in the bank, without any family around me, I felt homeless. I needed more money if I was going to buy a condo and prove to my father and Ralph that I could stand on my own two feet. My obsession with tangible evidence of my independence and success became a monkey on my back.

I picked up another job, this time with a health care agency. My job was to do light housekeeping and spend the night at the homes of seniors in the neighbourhood who had just come home from the hospital, and felt insecure being alone for the following week or two. It was easy work. Three nights a week and weekends I would arrive at my client's home and spend the night on a sofa near them. I was rarely disturbed and usually got a good night's sleep.

And that was how I came to meet David Papp, the man who redeemed my faith in men and who became my real husband – that is, a man I chose for myself because I loved him. He needed help caring for his elderly parents, and I was sent to his house by my agency. The work was undemanding and David and I had plenty of time to talk. I soon learned that David worked for an IT company, that he had married young and divorced years ago, and that he had one son, now university-bound, whom he adored. I immediately warmed to this big, quiet, attentive man who was so good to his parents. And I could see that he liked me too. In the evenings, after I had put his parents to bed, he would make me tea and ask me about my life. Little by little he coaxed out my life story.

After a few weeks it was clear to both of us that there something important was happening between us.

One day when I was off work, David invited me to lunch. I balked. I told David I had never sat down to eat alone with a white man in my life, and that I was married, and someone I knew would surely see us, and then my family would get me. David is a tall man – six foot four, fit and trim from his daily runs. He looked at me thoughtfully and then said very calmly and matter-of-factly, "Well, they would have to get through me before they could get to you, don't you think?"

They would have to get through me before they could get to you… I felt a peculiar, intoxicating rush to my brain. I never touched liquor, but suddenly understood what it was to be drunk. It was euphoria I was feeling. But why? Then it hit me. For the first time in my life I felt safe with an eligible, manly and protective man. *They would have to get through me before they could get to you…* Those were the most reverent words I have ever heard. David and I have never been separated since he uttered them.

Things moved quickly. It was a new and somewhat frightening experience to be loved so tenderly and completely, and to find that in spite of my history with men, I could give myself wholly and with delight to a man I loved. We were always together, either at his home or my apartment. David knew me through and through, and soon grasped the essence of my family dynamics. Although he never attempted to impose his will on me, even when he saw me making stupid decisions, his detached and objective observations were a godsend to me.

For example, one day I had a call from Texas. Mary told me my parents were in dire straits financially, and could I help? At the time I had saved $3,000 from all my jobs for a down payment on my long yearned-for condo. Impulsively I called my father and told him I would send him whatever I had. David noticed I looked rather miserable after I put down the phone and asked why. I told him I had pledged my condo money to my father. He said, "Why don't you take a day or two to think it through, and then if you still think it is the right thing to do, go ahead." That was his way from the beginning. He only ever suggested I think about what I was doing. He would never try to pressure me or scold me, even when we both knew I was acting out of old habit and against my own self-interest.

We talked a lot about my obsession with winning my father's approval. He would ask me plain, rational questions. This time he asked: "If the situation were reversed – if you were out of work and needed money, and your father had money he could afford to give you, would he?"

I thought for a moment. There was no simple answer to that question. I conceded that he wouldn't give me money if it were just a question of my own

160

needs, but he would give me money if it involved his honour, or if he would look bad in the eyes of the community for refusing. I realized that even though I didn't want to give my father money, and even though his behaviour to me didn't warrant it, and even though it was a true sacrifice to do so, I considered it dishonourable to refuse. That my refusal would prove shameful for my father. And then David asked, "Do you love your father or are you trying to buy his love?" And there was no simple answer to that question either. He made me think, but he never judged my actions.

In the end I withdrew my offer to Papa, a decision taken with agony, and received with predictable anger. I found out later that Naani Ji had come for a visit to Texas, but because I did not come through with the money, my parents' electricity was cut off, which ruined Naani Ji's trip and caused her early departure. This was of course intensely humiliating for my father.

I met David in 1985. Ralph and I divorced in 1986. I could not bear the idea of a protracted squabble over assets, so I took the course of least resistance. He demanded the house and I gave it to him. He wanted full custody of the children and child support. I agreed to that too. Eventually the children chose to live with David and me, but I kept sending Ralph the support cheque anyway to avoid a hassle.

But after I acquiesced to all his demands, and thought everything was settled, he wanted one more thing. He wanted me to stipulate that the reason for our divorce was adultery on my part. I knew this was more about saving face in the community than any personal need for such acknowledgement, but that was okay. I agreed to that too, since I had by then moved into David's home in Scarborough, and no longer cared what anyone in my family or community thought of me.

In 1987, when I was 36 years old, David and I decided that we were going to have a baby. It wasn't so much a baby that I wanted; it was a pregnancy embarked on with love, and one I could proudly celebrate. I had noticed that many young Canadian women wore form-hugging clothes over their growing bellies that all but shouted their pride in their sexuality. In India women wore loose clothing and were embarrassed to speak about their pregnancies, especially the first one. I felt that I had missed out on all that positive energy with my other children. I wanted to parade my love for David in the flesh.

I had had my tubes tied after James's birth, and untying them entailed a five-hour operation that would only give me a thirty percent chance of success in conceiving. But I had to try. I was thrilled when it worked. I hadn't minded "living in sin" before the pregnancy, but this was a new phase of life. David and I were driving on the highway one day. I looked down at my swelling stomach, turned to David and said, "I think it is time to get married." He said, "OK.

161

When?" I said, "Next week." He said, "OK." I called the pastor of a Presbyterian church. He was available. I called the local Holiday Inn. They said they could easily do a meal for thirty people. I wore a long, off-white dress that Sheilah, my supervisor at York and I made together in the locker room.

My parents were still in Texas, and wouldn't have attended anyway. But all my siblings were there – this was a period when we were all on speaking terms – and my three children as well, along with David's brother and sister-in-law and his son Gregory, plus a few friends from our respective jobs.

Meeting David was the best thing that ever happened to me. Christina's birth in November, 1987 was the icing on the cake. I had lived my fantasy of a healthy, glowing pregnancy, during which I was spoiled rotten, treated like a queen. The first of my four children to have her father in attendance at her delivery, and apparently in such a hurry to meet him, Christina was born after a labour of only twenty minutes.

Chapter Nineteen

Ideology and politics

The 1990s were an exciting time for me in every important way. Life at home was perfection. I was raising a child with a man I loved. David happened also to be a feminist's dream mate: manly, but sensitive and considerate, and unreservedly supportive of my ambitions in word and deed, he had also embraced fatherhood with hands-on enthusiasm.

Professionally I was in the right place at the right time, even though I was lucky for the worst possible reason. Only two years before my research on abuse of women in the South Asian community was published, an epic tragedy had become the public face of domestic violence against women.

On December 6, 1989, fourteen female students were gunned down by a misogynistic sociopath at a Montreal engineering school. The Montreal Massacre, as it came to be known, galvanized the nation. It was a singular event; objectively speaking, the massacre bore no relationship to the phenomenon of domestic violence. But the women's movement seized upon it as a symbol of all female victimhood at male hands, and the murderer, Marc Lepine, became an icon for the impulse to abuse women that some feminist activists believe is inherent in all men.

Urged on by women survivors of the massacre, within a few years Canada had implemented a (controversial) gun registry. Meanwhile a commemorative "white ribbon" campaign sprang up, its anti-abuse message percolating through the media, the family court system and all government services. Canadians took up the crusade against women abuse with a vengeance. I found myself at the vortex of the hottest social issue of the decade, when "second wave" radical feminists ruled the social policy roost, and made the most of it.

The same reformist wind that filled the feminists' sails brought a socialist government to power in Ontario. Progressive leader Bob Rae had surprised everyone by defeating a conservative government and leading the New Democrat Party to power. Multiculturalism and female empowerment were priorities for the NDP. Almost overnight, government agencies and not-for-profit organizations were scrambling to fill minority quotas. White leaders in the public sector were desperate to find people of colour to sit on their boards of governors or directors. As an immigrant woman of colour with an educational and budding career background in women's and immigrant settlement issues, I could write my own ticket for professional and civic advancement.

I received a slew of requests to join this organization or that. My ego was stroked by the invitations, but common sense held me back from accepting most of them. I had naively assumed that once I had my education and was able to apply it in my mission to help women in distress, I would find myself in the company of other high-minded women with the same disinterested ethic. It was an idyllic fantasy. It soon became clear to me that several of the organizations pursuing me were more about achieving politically correct representation than profiting from my expertise.

I could see that many of the token minority women on the boards and committees whose meetings I attended seemed out of their depth, and looked foolish when their lack of experience was revealed. I waited for offers that reflected my competence and interests, not my colour. I accepted two invitations, one to join the Board of Governors at Centennial College in Toronto, and the other the Board of Governors of Scarborough's Centenary Hospital. Both focused on education and serving immigrants, my twin passions.

I had been helping immigrant women who called me at home, and on the basis of the exponential growth in demand for my services, decided to start a new agency. At first, South Asian Family Support Services, which I incorporated in 1989, boasted a staff of one – me. I soon realized that I needed more shoulders to the wheel, as well as somewhere other than my living room to operate from. In a building right next to Centenary Hospital, I negotiated office space at a greatly reduced rent in exchange for interpretation services to the hospital emergency staff. Now I needed to find some warm bodies to assist me. I didn't have to look far or wide.

I never made appointments for my haircuts. I would just pop in to my local salon and take whoever was available. One day my cutter was a chatty young woman who wanted to know everything about me. Zarina Sherazee. My curiosity was piqued by Zarina's fluent, British-accented English. I learned that she had been trained as an English teacher in Iran, then made her way through refugee camps to the Philippines, where she taught English for a few years before coming to Canada. She was looking for that kind of work here, so far without luck. A single mom, having divorced her abusive husband, she was finding it difficult to make ends meet. I hired Zarina as my assistant.

The demands for the agency's help soon grew to the point where Zarina was overextended. I agreed to let her bring in a volunteer to answer the phones. So Jyoti joined us, a young mother of two daughters, married off in India as a teenager to an older, abusive husband. Working with us was a boost to her confidence. Within a few years Jyoti and Zarina both attended Centennial College and received counselling diplomas. Jyoti attended bookkeeping classes on her own time, and learned to use a computer, picking up whatever office skills she needed as necessity arose. When enough funding came through, we hired Jyoti as the office manager. In the next three years we would have seven staff members, all of them women who had left abusive marriages. Our office became a training ground in independence and self-confidence for them.

As Dr. Mandel had forecast, interviews with South Asian women formed the core of my master's thesis. Once I graduated, I shared my thesis with several social workers, who found it original and deserving of a wider audience. So in 1991 my report – "Wife Abuse in the South Asian Community living in Scarborough" – the first such research in Canada, was published. In order to capture media attention, a kind of marketing committee was formed, and advance copies of the report were distributed throughout the field.

Invitations to hear me speak on my research were sent out to media and social service professionals. I was thrilled when nearly 300 people showed up. At first I was nervous, but gradually warmed up and relaxed as I launched into my themes and anecdotes. The focus of my report was the inefficacy of western models of domestic violence counselling with South Asian victims of abuse. Not only were western models futile, I said, but they could prove dangerous to clients who followed western therapists' advice. When a Canadian woman walks out on her husband, I told them, she only has herself to think about. Her family will usually support her if the marriage has been abusive. A South Asian woman leaving her husband will be unlikely to have any support system at all. It is more likely that her family will side with her husband and direct their anger at her.

I received a round of warm applause at the end of my talk. I was enjoying myself hugely until, in the Question and Answer period, one of the therapists in the audience asked, "Do you think domestic violence in this community is a cultural pathology?"

I froze. I had no answer to his question. The word "pathology" stymied me. I couldn't remember what it meant. So I had no idea what he was talking about. I should simply have said something like, "That is not a perspective I have considered in my research," or "I would have to give your question further thought before drawing a conclusion," or anything that would mask my ignorance. But my instinct for self-preservation was overcome by my shame at all the gaps in my education, and my humiliation at being exposed as the academic imposter I really was. I felt naked before all these people.

Suddenly I became dizzy, and my stomach started turning over. I managed to blurt out, "I don't know." Then I rushed out of the room and made for the women's washroom, where I threw up, my head pounding with the refrain, "You are stupid, and everyone will soon find out what a phony you are. Stupid, stupid, stupid."

When I'd cleaned myself up and was adjusting my clothes and hair, I heard a soft voice from the corner. A white woman of patrician good looks, older, with piercing eyes and a messy thatch of grey hair that gave her something of a hippie air, was looking at me and smiling encouragement. "That's right, stand up straight and tall and pull your shoulders back. Now take a deep breath. Go on, breathe." She made me do this three or four times. Then she said, "Always remember this day. Today you have done something no one else in this country has ever done before. You opened up your life, and told everyone what is happening to immigrant women in this country. You are one of the bravest women I have ever met."

Her eyes darkened, and her expression became very grave. She said, "Your life is going to get very hard at times, but at the end of the day you must carry on and do what you believe is right." She handed me a card. "Here is my phone number. Call me any time if I can be of help." She patted my shoulder, saying, "Meanwhile, they are serving a really nice Indian lunch, and I don't think you should miss out on it."

I glanced at her card. June Callwood. The name meant nothing to me. She walked me out to where people were mingling, and soon a little group clustered around me, and asked me questions I was able to answer with confidence. The next time I looked around, June was gone.

A few weeks later, now informed of June Callwood's many accomplishments in countless charities and social justice causes, and the reverence her name evoked – people referred to her as "Saint June" – I called the number on the card she had given me to express gratitude for her kindness. June asked me what I thought was the best way to reach South Asian women in abusive family situations. I told her that many of them watched the ethnic channel Vision TV on Saturdays, and that would be a non-threatening way to get to them. It turned out June had had a hand in creating Vision TV.

June invited me to meet her at a "bistro." This was another word I didn't know. I quickly got myself up to speed on what a bistro was, what kind of food one ate there, and what one should wear to meet someone as famous as June Callwood. Gaining direct access to June's wisdom and experience was one of the memorable perks of my chosen career. June was a great help to me, but later, when I could have been of help to her, I am ashamed to say I chose discretion over valour.

❁

The media attention around my report did not go unheeded by the South Asian community. I was the first South Asian woman in Canada to bring honour-motivated abuse to public attention through stories of my own upbringing. This was very shaming to my community. There were now several men on my agency board. They were not happy that a woman was the media spokesperson, and they didn't like the things I was saying. If it had been left to them to represent the views of the agency, they would have blamed the government for our problems, or chanted the usual multicultural mantras to deflect criticism from the South Asian community.

The women on the board reflexively sought the men's approval, and deferred to their opinions. Board meetings turned into interrogation sessions. Staff were warned not to side with me. The focus of the agency's mandate changed from helping abused women to the controversy-free domain of settlement services. (Today, after twenty years in operation, with an annual budget of four million dollars, the patriarchs remain firmly in control.)

Board members started to drop into the office frequently, then daily. They noted the fact that Zarina did editing for me. They noted client wait times. They scrutinized my car mileage and gas claims. They grew bolder in meetings, often yelling at me. At such times I recalled the abuses of my childhood and I felt stressed and anxious.

Other stressors, some particularly distressing client episodes, accumulated during this period. One of our clients had gone to India with her three children. She gave power of attorney to her husband in her absence. On her return she found he had sold their home, cleared out their possessions and disappeared. She was taken to a shelter and her children were put in foster care. She had a nervous breakdown. Another client whose husband had threatened her with violence was encouraged to take refuge in a shelter. She left the house, but after a few days returned home to retrieve her child's security blanket to keep him from crying at night. Her husband killed her on the spot.

One day I was called to the emergency ward of Centenary Hospital. As I walked in, I heard a woman screaming and other people shouting. I saw that the centre of the hubbub was a woman, her clothing identifying her as Somalian. She was trying to pull a little girl of about eight off a gurney. A doctor and two nurses were restraining her. I wrapped my arms around the woman, and tried to comfort her. She pushed me away.

A nurse approached me, wanting to know if I spoke the Somalian woman's language. I said no, but asked what was the problem. The nurse beckoned me to the gurney and lifted the sheet from the girl's lower body. I gasped. The girl's genital area was monstrously swollen from infection to the size of a baby's head, and thickly coated in pus. We all knew exactly what had happened. The girl had undergone a clandestine cliterectomy with an unsterilized knife. I could see that the doctor and nurses were badly agitated and deeply disgusted.

Someone said something about calling the police. "Police" was one English word the woman understood. It set off a fresh round of screaming and more strenuous attempts to pull the child away from the staff. It was a horrible day.

It seemed to me that women were being mutilated and falling dead all around me, and all my board was concerned about was finding an excuse to fire me. They instructed me to stop advocating for abused women, and instead to prepare funding applications directed at settlement issues only. But there was no way to stop the flow of women seeking relief from the violence in their homes.

Zarina came up with a solution. She would attend the English as a Second Language courses the women were taking and turn them into informal support groups. If one of the women wanted private time with her, she would take her into an adjoining room. It worked, but it angered me that we were forced to fulfil our moral obligation by stealth, as if helping women in distress were something to be ashamed of.

In the world outside the offices of the South Asian Family Support Services, a much larger storm was brewing. The women's movement was experiencing turmoil within its political ranks. I witnessed many examples of the turmoil at first hand when, representing the South Asian community, I sat on committees run by organizations such as the United Way, the National Action for Women and the NDP Women's caucus. As political factionalism divided friend from friend, colleague from colleague, supposed leaders of the movement publicly trashed one another; invectives filled the air with accusations of betrayal and abuse of power.

The clearest division could be seen in the line drawn between black and white feminists. The black feminists saw themselves as double victims, oppressed by males and by whites in general. Even though it was clear to me that white feminists bent over backwards to support and encourage women of colour – who should know this better than I? – the black feminists accused white feminists of deliberately attempting to disempower them. I was late coming into the women's movement, and I found all this political infighting distasteful.

But it was unavoidable. For months, no matter what the agenda was ostensibly covering at the committee meetings I attended, the issues of power and colour kept arising. It became apparent to me that the same few women of colour made it a point to attend every meeting, just so they could pick on somebody and bring these two points forward. As soon as they hijacked the meeting, the white women would simply retreat into a corner and wait it out. I was astonished and rather contemptuous of their timidity. Many times I had the urge to jump up and yell back at the troublemakers, "Get over what happened 150 years ago. There are women being killed right now in this community, in our neighbourhoods. Can you please put your grandparents' fights aside and discuss what needs to be done now?" But I would not dare to say a word and always made sure I had the seat closest to the door. I hated arguing and fighting. Any thought of confrontation with angry, irrational people brought back fears I thought I had left behind.

It was depressing to watch these performances by women of colour, whose sole objective seemed to be humiliating white women. Their tactics worked. Half the time the white women ended up in tears, partly because they didn't get a chance to defend themselves, but also because they were steeped in guilt about their "white privilege."

Out of curiosity I did attend a few of the meetings held by the "Coloured Women's Caucus." I found dealing with them to be almost as frightening as life in my father's or husband's house. The women used warrior terminology in their declarations. They would say, "We intend to wrest power from white women," and "We refuse to be raped by white women" and "We will do away with the hierarchy of oppression." Then in the same breath, as if all women were seamlessly united, they would sanctimoniously speak of "the goals of our sisterhood." The backstabbing, the personal gossip, the energy and the time that went into the strategic planning of attacks on white feminists troubled me.

From my vantage point on the sidelines, I considered these black feminists hypocrites. They were only too ready to blame men, society, the patriarchy and white people for every problem, but they refused to look critically at their own abusive behaviours to their peers. I began to notice that before every meeting, one of the black feminists would lightly grill me to find out where I stood on particular issues. I soon caught on that this was a recruitment strategy. They assumed I could be enlisted on their side because I wasn't white. In fact, I was sympathetic to the white women, but was not about to martyr myself for them. Refusing to be drawn either way, I played the dim-witted innocent with both groups. The truth was, my knowledge of feminist ideology was flimsy at best, and even on the dogmas I understood, I was never in more than tepid agreement. The one thing I did know was that I was no revolutionary. I did not want to be identified with women who were planning to march to the gates of Parliament and bang on the door.

I quietly bowed out, not least because one of their strategies was to court constant media attention, and I did not want my father or anyone else to know about the people I was hanging around with.

Discouraged, frightened and unsure of what the future held, I would go home to David and tell him everything I had witnessed and conclude, "I know for sure I will never be a feminist." Laughing, he hugged me, and said, "I am glad you learned that as well. Now I feel much safer."

Our home became a refuge for me, the one place where safety, if not complete serenity, reigned. We were in the thick of things here as well, renovating an old home, raising a child together and worrying about our older children. My plate was full.

One day my plate cracked. I got a phone call at work. Elspeth, while vacationing in India, had been killed in a ferry accident. I was stunned. We had teased each other from time to time with fantasies about travelling to India together. But on my part these conversations were more about bonding with Elspeth than any wish to see India again. My family was now all in North America, and I was in no hurry to revisit scenes that held so few happy memories for me.

My grief at her loss was compounded by guilt over the infrequency of our contact in the period prior to this trip of hers. Elspeth had moved to downtown Toronto to be near her work as executive director of Dixon Hall, a social services agency; between work and family life, life was too hectic for her to socialize with friends. So for a few months before she had left, we had not been in touch. She had left a phone message: "This time I am going alone, next time let's plan on going together."

Now she was not coming back. For a long while I just sat, motionless as a stone, looking out the window, while Zarina and other staff hovered solicitously. Jyoti brought a glass of water and put it on my desk, saying softly in Hindi, "You have been sitting here for a very long time. Say something. Do something. You are frightening us, and we don't know what to do for you."

At this I leaped out of my chair. For a second I thought I was going to hit her. She scurried away as I dropped to my knees on the floor. I howled like a wounded animal. Jyoti phoned the hospital next door; someone came and gave me a needle. Jyoti drove me home and I stayed in bed for days. I felt like all the life force had been drained out of me.

There were several memorials for Elspeth. I did not attend any. I was very angry. Not at anybody or anything in particular. It just didn't seem fair. Some time later another agency in North York started up, named for Elspeth. I did not attend the opening, and even though I knew many of the individuals who worked there, I refused to attend their fundraiser, workshop or any other event. I did not want to hear the name Elspeth. I felt that any tangible reminder of her would be unbearable.

My South Asian Services board kept arguing amongst themselves. They had all been friends, but now, courtesy of Bob Rae's socialist government, large sums of government money were pouring into the agency. Fighting for control of the agency escalated into ugliness amongst the board members. On one particular evening, as the battle turned vicious, I decided I had had enough. I stood up and picked up my files. The chairman held up a silencing hand, and looked up at me inquiringly. Very calmly, I said, "I quit." He looked puzzled. The other fourteen people around the table just stared at me. When I turned to leave the room, Zarina, who was attending the meeting that night in her role as program manager, jumped up and cried, "You can't quit, Aruna, you can't quit. What about us?" I picked up my purse and went home.

I could afford to walk out, because I knew I would not be unemployed for long. I was building up an impressive *curriculum vitae*. In 1991 I won the YWCA Woman of Distinction Award for my agency initiatives and my original research. But instead of giving my prepared speech, I poured out my heart to my unreceptive and embarrassed father, the only person in the Toronto Convention Centre to remain sitting while the rest of the room gave me a standing ovation. That evening should have been a high point of my life. Instead, it had cast me down. I felt I had received an award for something I had failed to do. Yes, I had started two agencies and many women had been helped by our services. But I knew the women we helped were a drop in the bucket of overflowing needs that weren't being addressed. Immigrants were pouring into Canada in huge waves, the majority of them from South Asia. For every woman we helped, another hundred were living lives of quiet desperation and virtual imprisonment. I felt like a fraud. I never attended any of the subsequent YWCA banquets.

After the women of distinction award, more South Asian women started to come out to inquire about the services we were providing at South Family Services. We found that many of them would come for one or two visits and then not return. I thought that one of the ways to encourage them to seek counselling was to write some stories of women like themselves. Women could read them in the privacy of their homes.

I called my little self-published book, *Seven of Us Survived*. The seven stories were amalgams of the many client narratives I had heard over the years. Each served to illustrate how family members could not break out as individuals; how they were constrained to their roles: as mother, father, brother, mother-in-law, husband. Each portrayed the domino effect that occurs when a girl or woman steps out of her prescribed role. Each demonstrated how troubles cascade from an initial shaming aberration, and there seems to be no way to stop the multiplier effect. I hoped the book might find its way to social workers and teachers as well, so they would recognize in their South Asian charges the patterns I described in the book's stories. Recognition, I hoped, might lead to intervention before a situation got out of hand.

I started the book with my own story, because I wanted them to know that there is life after leaving their abusive relationship. What made this project particularly special for me was the fact that after many years of estrangement, I had reconciled with my family. My sister Heather typed these stories and did the art work for the cover. She did the editing as well. For me, the time we spent together was precious. I felt we got to know each other better.

Like little girls we took our project to our father. He told us how proud he was of the work we had done, but then pointed out that we had spelled Heather's middle name wrong. The family had a good laugh, because by then both Heather and I had earned masters degree, and here was our father, a self-educated man, who was better at English spelling then we were. My parents also participated in a training video I produced on heart health for the Heart and Stroke Foundation. It was my way of helping my parents financially as well as bringing the family closer after what we had gone through.

I received more awards: the Commemorative Medal for the 125th anniversary of Canada, a Women on the Move award and a few others. I had a "name" in the field. I considered my options. I knew I did not want a fulltime job with any organization. The same nonsense pervaded all agencies in the social services realm, and I was not going to "carry water" for anyone toeing the feminist party line.

Along the way I had joined the NDP party and had started to attend some workshops. Around this time, I received a call from a black woman I had long admired from a distance, Jean Augustine, the Chair of Metro Housing.

If you had asked me as a child what I wanted to be when I grew up, my answer would have looked a lot like Jean Augustine. From humble beginnings Jean had scaled educational heights and become an educator herself. She carried herself like a queen. She exuded the self-confidence that comes from having accomplished much through her own intelligence, and from being recognized for who she was, not for her skin colour. Whenever she spoke in public I wanted to hear her. I emulated her carriage and her gracious way of addressing people.

So when she called me in the summer of 1992 and asked if I was free to meet with her, I leaped at the chance. She wanted me to go around to see the young single mothers living in Metro housing, and find out what they were doing with their time. She wanted me to assess their needs and how best to serve them. I loved that idea. I also loved the generous fee she was prepared to pay me for the project.

After about two weeks of simply knocking on doors at the Scarborough housing units and getting hostile responses from the residents, I came up with a different strategy. I asked Jean if she would allot me some space on the first floor of one of the buildings. I explained that I wanted to open a resources and education centre. She liked the idea, and arranged for me to have office furniture, computers, telephones, filing cabinets and anything else I needed from a government storage area. I filled two adjoining apartments with three truckloads of office furniture. The resource centre was operative within that week.

Now I had an excuse to go door to door and ask if anyone knew how to work a computer. I found five women in the first week. I took down the names of those women who didn't know how, but were interested in learning. Those who knew taught the others. Before long, we had a support group going, and then a play area, which soon turned into a cost-free, cooperative daycare centre.

We always had tea or coffee on hand. Soon the women started bringing bags of cookies or cupcakes they had made. Within a few months Gordenridge Family Resources Centre was born. All this happened during my single-year contract. It was the most positive professional experience I can remember.

Still feeling the glow from Jean Augustine's Metro Housing project, the best job I ever had, I walked into the embrace of the worst job I ever had. During my search for a new professional challenge, I happened upon an advertisement for the position of executive director for the North York Women's Shelter. It caught my attention, as it was the very shelter I had briefly taken refuge in with Bina so many years before. I applied for the position and was rather surprised to be called for an interview downtown rather than at the shelter.

It was a strange interview. I was candid about my reasons for leaving my last position. I even told them about my own experience at this shelter. Then I was asked what I thought about the women's movement. My interviewers were three white women I did not know, women I did not expect to meet again, and I was by no means desperate for the job, as I was working on another master's degree at the time. So I was forthright about my disappointment with the women's movement in its present state. I said I was put off by people calling others "racist" when they did not get their way, and that I did not consider myself a feminist according to the dogmas of the women's movement.

After about fifteen minutes the interview seemed to fizzle out. I left, and told David that I had wasted my time and gas. The next morning I was shocked to get a call from one of the interviewers, offering me the job.

In Ontario at the time, the women's shelters were all administrated by a collective, a fact I hadn't known (only a few are now). Organizations run as collectives make decisions through consensus. In theory everyone has the same power, and policy is developed through the democratic process of debate and voting. This particular organization was in the process of becoming unionized, which meant all decisions regarding staff were frozen and had to be dealt with through the union.

Before I hired or fired anyone, I went to the shelter to see the situation for myself. Several members of the collective, the old-timers, had resigned before I came aboard, and those who were fired got big payouts. When I arrived, there were three full-time staff, and part-timers were putting in many hours, but nobody was taking responsibility for making decisions.

Women and their children had been left stranded in the shelter, some for up to nine months, with no place to go. The house was filthy. Dirty diapers had been left in the rooms for weeks. The upstairs toilet, supposedly fixed, was leaking into the living room area. In several bedrooms I found human feces on the wall. Tons of food were being thrown out. No one cared. The board members were afraid to meet in the shelter and started to meet off-site.

I packed a suitcase and moved into the shelter for three months. I slept on the floor of my office. Three or four times a week I would go home in the evening to touch base with David and Christina, and let them know what was going on. During the day I cleaned the shelter's kitchen, inch by disgusting inch, and then the rooms upstairs. I did not ask anyone to help me. I hired contractors to renew the bedrooms. After cleaning, I would cook the meals. Slowly, as I had anticipated, the clients in the house became uncomfortable watching me work alone. One by one, the women living in the shelter started to wake up early and help with cleaning. The children would go off to school, after which I shut off the TV and put on loud music to get everyone energized. Soon I found that whatever I was doing, I had two or three helpers, sweeping and scrubbing to the beat of the music. They started to assign themselves cooking and cleaning chores in an organized way. Eventually I did not have to tell anyone what needed to be done.

Finding new board members proved difficult. I got permission from the funders to invite men onto the board for the first time in the feminist movement's history. That was the smartest thing I could have done. The meetings were soon governed by logic rather than emotions. I wanted to set up the agency on sound principles of business management. So I also recruited women from the business world who had no involvement with the feminist movement. Applying business rigour gave the clients more control of their lives. They understood the rules, the expectations they were obliged to fulfil and the criteria for evaluations.

I also made peace with the police. Over the years there had been a great deal of hostility between the police and the "man-hating women," as the police called them, who ran this shelter, and they were not keen to speak to me. So I went to the station, and explained what I had got myself into. I told them I now had men on the board and that I really needed their help to make sure this organization survived, because too many abused women and children needed a safe place. They responded well to my soft-spoken and reasonable approach, and relations improved.

As things began to sort themselves out at work, a national scandal broke out involving June Callwood and a women's shelter she had started called "Nellie's." The black staff women at the shelter were accusing her of racism, a damning slur that, given June's history, was not only cruel, but grotesquely absurd. Calling June Callwood a racist was like calling the Dalai Lama a warmonger. It was, however, a perfect example of how irrational and ideology-driven the women's movement had become.

I could not believe this was happening. I had visited Nellie's. June was so proud as she showed me around the rooms and the beautiful living spaces, everything so calm and clean, the polar opposite of the mess I was living with at North York. We had laughed about exchanging jobs, and she had been warmly supportive whenever I filled her in on my challenges with my board. I called June at once when I heard the news, but she did not respond to my messages. I mailed her a note expressing my outrage and sympathy, but did not hear back.

After a few weeks I sent June another note, saying it had to do with Nellie's and I must meet with her. She responded and we met. The woman I knew as a pillar of strength threw her arms around me and began to cry. She said, "They called me a racist. Can you believe it? Why didn't they call me a 'whore' or a 'thief'? I could handle that. But to say *that* about me – I don't think I can stand it."

June had lost a lot of weight. It was clear she was not looking after herself. We talked about the motivation behind the accusation. I said "June, I have been more racist than anyone I know. I was trained that way from childhood. But you have lived your life fighting this horrible sin. The people who are saying this thing about you know your passion. They knew that this would hurt you, and they did. But they only got to you because you're allowing them to have that power."

Then I revealed that I had been approached to be the mediator between June and the staff at Nellie's, and that I had turned it down. "Why?" June demanded. "You would be perfect. You know both sides."

I explained that I did not feel that I had enough experience to deal with this problem. I was frank in confessing my fears for myself if I took on that role. If she, a person of such status in Canada could be brought to her knees, what would they do to me, a nobody? I confessed that I was not able to deal with the kind of abuse I had witnessed emanating from these militant women. The situation was dynamite, and I greatly feared I might set it off rather than defuse it. In the end, what it came down to was that I was a coward.

June put her arms around me. She said, "I understand perfectly what you are saying, but you are not a coward. You are wise. You know what you can do and you know what you can't do, and you are right, this does seem like dynamite, and who knows where it will end?" I cried so copiously while driving back home that I had to pull over. Like everyone else, I watched the media circus and the lynching of a heroine of the women's movement with sick fascination. The fiasco cemented my decision never again to get involved with any job or political group that gave off the faintest whiff of "women's movement" or "feminist."

Chapter Twenty

Black hole

A combination of the madhouse of the shelter, the politics at work and the shock of seeing a great Canadian brought low by ideological jackals took its toll. I was approaching the completion of my second master's program, but I could feel myself losing the ability to concentrate. I felt enveloped by a cloud of sadness. I was physically present, but spiritually absent. Detached, I seemed to be watching a clever imitation of myself going through the motions of family activities, but without enthusiasm or engagement.

My family didn't need me, I told myself. David looked after Chris perfectly well without me. I started spending more and more of my home time sleeping. When I was awake, I was irritable and combative. I didn't understand what was happening to me. My dormant fear of having inherited my mother's mental fragility awoke and dogged my footsteps. I felt that I was on the edge of falling into a deep, black hole from which I would never find the strength to climb out.

From sleeping too much, I now had trouble sleeping at all. My doctor gave me a prescription for soporifics, but with them my sleep was disturbed by nightmares of wild animals chasing me. I would utter strange noises and David would wake me up. I stopped the pills, but not having enough sleep made me feel worse.

I was desperate to find a reason for my unhappiness, but failed. I had no marital problems; I was doing a good job; my revised board was happy; my master's program was complete; I had put healthy distance between me and my family: By all accounts I should be serene and happy. Instead I felt suicidal, and found myself greedily dwelling on various methods for ending my life.

One evening I came home and went straight to our bedroom and lay down on the bed without a word of greeting to David or Christina. David saw I was disturbed, and was more than usually attentive. He came up and asked if everything was all right. I sat up, and as though I were a puppet mouthing a ventriloquist's script, I heard myself saying things I had not planned to say, and hadn't even known I was thinking.

Very calmly I told David that I wanted a divorce. He looked stunned, but only said, "Are you sure this is what you want? Can you tell me what brought this on?" I said, "You have been trying to change me from the day we met. You have been trying to make me into a person I am not. First it was my father and then it was Ralph. They wanted to control me. You have not wanted to control me; you just want me to change into what you imagine I should be. I think I am having a mental breakdown. You have made me crazy. I am not going to do it any more. I have looked at a few apartments, and I am going to move out. I want you to call ChristIna and tell her that we are getting a divorce."

David was silent for a few minutes, his expression stony and unreadable. Then he said, "If you want a divorce and you think you are unhappy living with Chris and me, then by all means get a divorce. But do not ever put me in the same vile category as your father and your ex-husband. That is the greatest insult, and I will not stand for it."

I had expected – or perhaps I had hoped – that David would be angry, or threaten me, or throw me out of the house. I was filled with self-loathing and looking for punishment. But he just called to Chris to come to our room. He said, "You're going to be the one to tell her." I shook my head.

Chris walked in. As soon as she looked at our gloomy faces, she said in a teasing tone, trying to make light of the situation, "People, whassup? The sky isn't falling."

David put his arm around her shoulders. He looked inquiringly at me, but I remained mute. Finally he said, "Your mother has been very unhappy for a while, and she thinks that she would like to live alone for a bit to think things through. Have some quiet time. So we thought we would tell you about it." She looked at him, then at me, and asked, "Mum, are you talking about a – a divorce?"

I just stared at her in dismay, and wished with all my heart that I were not a puppet, and could say the words I longed to say – "Of course not, Chris, why would I be so stupid as to throw away the best thing that ever happened to me?" – and willed my ventriloquist to come up with good news for her, but he stayed silent, and then David said, "Yes, your mother mentioned it, and if that is what will make her happy, then that is something we will have to discuss."

Instead of bursting into tears, Chris just grinned and shook her head. "People, parents, this is how it is done. The usual way to do a divorce, I am told by my friends, is for parents to fight a lot, for a long time, and then get to hate each other, and then fight some more. And then the child, that would be me in this case, would say something like, 'You two had better get a divorce, or stop fighting.' Parents, get with the program. You love each other and there has never been a fight between you two. You don't have the ingredients for a divorce. So stop it. Just stop it!" By now she wasn't making light of the situation, she was sobbing her heart out like an abandoned child.

David wrapped his arms around her and took her away. I lay on top of the bed and looked at the ceiling. I thought it probably would have been better for me to kill myself then to hurt the people I love so deeply. The dark cloud pressed down on my chest, and I found it difficult to breathe.

A little while later David brought me a cup of green tea. He said, "I heard you coughing. Drink this and go to sleep. You look very tired." I looked at his face. I could see he had been crying. I could not reach out to him. I felt that now that I had detached myself from him and Chris, if I did kill myself, they would find their loss easier to bear.

I slept until three p.m. the next day. Chris had missed school for the first time I could remember, and David did not go to work either. I got up and showered. Chris came in and asked if I would like to have pizza for dinner, and I said yes, that was a good idea. I did not go back to work for a couple of days. I just slept. We resumed a normal routine for a few weeks. No one discussed the divorce or moving out. Both David and Chris seemed to be walking on thin ice, watching my every move.

One day I asked David how Chris was doing, and he just looked at me as if I were an idiot, and coldly said, "How do you think she is doing? You had a five-hour operation to untie your tubes so you could have her. Now, in her last years of high school, she hears about this. You know that if anything happens to you, her life will be totally ruined. All that you have done to protect her will be of no use. You have to get better."

Then David folded me to his chest, and said, over and over, "You have to get better. I wish I knew how to make you better. But you must know that we both need you, and we both love you more than anything in world. I am just so sorry that this love is not enough for you."

I didn't know what to say. I pulled away from his embrace and toiled upstairs, and started writing in my journal. I wrote, "I do not know the person who was in David's arms a second ago. I do not feel any love or warmth or any hurt or any other kind of feeling. I don't want either of them to touch me or love me."

On April 26, 2003, a Saturday, I got up at six in the morning, and without a glance at my sleeping husband or daughter, picked up my car keys and left the house. As in a dream, I got into the car and drove off. I had decided a few minutes earlier that I was not going to kill myself at home. I was going to drive on to Highway 401 and aim my car at the biggest truck I could find in the oncoming lane. As I waited at the side of the road for the right truck to come flying by, I thought I would write a note to Chris and tell her that I loved her. I found some paper, but I could not find a pen. I began frantically looking for a pen in my purse as truck after truck whizzed by. Then I got out and rooted around in the back seat. But no pen.

I got back into the car and drove to the next exit. My plan was to buy a pen. Instead, I ended up driving to my family doctor's office. On Saturday mornings Dr. Dhalla arrived at eight a.m. to do his paper work, and then the office was open to patients from ten to noon. I wasn't aware of his routine. I just knew I had to speak to him. When he arrived shortly after eight, he found me leaning against his door, asleep. He pulled me into his office and talked with me for a very long time. In the end he said I should probably be hospitalized. I left his office with an appointment to see a psychiatrist the following Monday. Then I went back home and went to sleep.

When I awoke, I told David where I had been and why. He was terrified. He made me promise not to hurt myself until Christina graduated from high school. He said I at least owed it to her not to destroy her life before she had acquired a foundation for independence. David had never asked me for anything before. Just this once he asked me to promise him I would keep my word, and I determined I would. Somehow that made sense to my sick mind. It also made sense that I should lie in bed until Chris graduated. So I lay in bed staring at the ceiling for the next eighteen months.

Dr. K. was the first psychiatrist recommended to me. She had no success with me, nor I with her. Dr. K. talked a lot about herself, her life in Poland, her difficulties relating to requalification in Canada and her practice, subjects that were of little interest to me.

In one session Dr. K asked me to name one thing I had wanted most in my childhood. She would not accept "baby brother" as an answer. I could not come up with a single inanimate item I had wanted as a child. She would insist that surely I must have wanted a toy. Every child does. Did I want a bicycle, a dollhouse, a musical instrument? "Close your eyes," she said, "put your head back, return to you childhood and think about what you wanted most." Nothing.

We were communicating across a cultural divide. I continued with her for a while, but eventually saw that she was doing me more harm than good. I reported my frustration to my family doctor, who then referred me to Dr. W. A series of appointments were made for me, all scheduled for one pm. Dr. W. told me that it was his habit to close his eyes during our sessions, but that he would be listening to me. He invited me to pose questions to him if clarification was needed. Dr. W. fell asleep during the first session, but I gave him the benefit of the doubt. When he again fell asleep during the second session, I left him, gently snoring, and advised his secretary to wake him up before his next patient arrived.

I felt doomed to permanent madness. I tried to recall all the symptoms my mother had exhibited before she became ill, but failed, which further terrified me. Practically speaking, I was nagged by the worry that any public knowledge of my situation could seriously undermine my credibility as a therapeutic consultant.

In addition to my depression, I had recurring headaches and vision problems in my left eye that no specialist could find a source for, which gave me further cause for anxiety and pessimism about a good outcome. One evening, because reading was troublesome, I was dozing and mindlessly watching TV. Suddenly I saw a face from my childhood on the screen. Shocked, I sat up and stared in disbelief at the face of a young South Asian girl in a commercial for the charity Save the Children. It was Chandni, a girl I had known over forty years earlier. But it couldn't be. Surprise turned to fear. Now I really knew I was going mad.

Chandni

The name means "moonlight" in Hindi. I met Chandni when our family lived in the industrial Punjabi city of Ludhiana, where Papa was building up a church. I would have been thirteen then. Chandni and her siblings lived on our street – literally on our street – because they did not have a home. Rumour had it that they slept under a nearby bridge. Our parents forbade us to have anything to do with these children for the usual reasons: They were low caste; the neighbours would talk; we'd catch unspeakable diseases …

Chandni and I had what could be called a love/hate relationship. She was about two years older than me. We led similar lives – she had four siblings to look after; I had five – but in the ways that mattered to me, we were different, and I envied her. Chandni was beautiful; I was ugly. Compared to her I was "richer," because we lived in a real house. But boys winked at her, while they called me a "black skeleton" and other ugly names. What really made me fume was that this low-caste nobody had artistic magic in her fingers, while mine were good for nothing but mundane chores and childcare.

Every morning Chandni and her siblings would go to the garbage dump to scavenge for rags. She would wash and dry them, and then she would transform them, with just a bit of wire, yarn and vegetable dyes, into exquisite dolls to sell to passers-by. No matter how many dolls she made, they were all sold by the end of the day, and Chandni would use the money to feed herself and her brothers and sisters.

I hadn't told Dr. K. the truth about never wanting anything for myself. I had forgotten about Chandni and her dolls. I would have loved to own one of them. And that was strange, because I was never a girly sort of girl. I never played house or fancied tea parties with dolls for guests. I was too busy mothering real babies.

But I was enchanted watching Chandni make her dolls. Silently, her head bowed in concentration, oblivious to everyone except her siblings, whom she would occasionally corral and subdue with a sharp command, her fingers flew amongst the rags.

I couldn't afford to buy Chandni's dolls, but my need to get my hands on at least one of them was gnawing at me, so I had to come up with another strategy. I tried begging her for one, but that didn't work. Other times I threatened or bulled her. I finally tried to extort a doll from her, reminding her of the many times during the monsoon rains that I had secretly crept down and opened the back door of our building, so she and her siblings could shelter under the stairs. I even reminded her about the time I got caught unlocking the door for her and was belted for it. This was not true, of course. I did not get caught, nor did I get belted, but I hoped the lie would up the ante in my negotiating power.

Usually she just smiled slyly at my overtures. When she did respond, she might say, "No one asked you to open the door and give us shelter," or "Go bother someone else." Her patronizing tone made me feel that she considered herself of superior status to me – as if I were the homeless urchin, and she a dignified chatelaine. Such arrogance infuriated me.

One day Chandni and her brood were missing from their usual spot near the market. I asked around for them, and the man who ran the tea stall told me she had been "married off." "Oh well, how lucky for her, then," I yelled as I stomped away. I can't say if I was angry because I was going to miss her, or because I would miss her dolls, or because I really thought that she was lucky to have been married. I only remember the acute disappointment I felt that she was suddenly not there.

About a year after that, Ma Ji and I were at the vegetable market early in the morning, and I saw one of Chandni's little brothers, now quite a bit taller than me. I asked about Chandni, and he said, very casually, as if he were talking about a pet cat, "Oh, she died in childbirth," and walked away.

Fury washed over me. I dropped the vegetables I was carrying and launched myself at the boy's back, clinging to him like a monkey, pounding on his head with my fists, biting at his ears and scratching at his face, screaming that I was going to kill him.

Several of the vegetable vendors pulled me off, shouting at my mortified mother to take the crazy girl home and lock her up. The boy's ears and face were bleeding by the time I was detached from him. As Ma Ji dragged me away, I hollered, "And did you murder her dolls as well?" I followed this with a litany of filthy curses.

✳

It was all so long ago. And yet in my fathomless, endless adult depression, it made sense to cry my heart out. I wept for days thinking about Chandni and her dolls. It wasn't that they were so exceptional. It just seemed to me a miracle that they existed at all. What were they, after all? They were garbage, bits of cloth so useless they had been thrown away. Nobody wanted them, not even the poorest and lowest caste of people. But she had seen possibilities in these worthless scraps. With a few dabs of colour and the dexterity of her fingers and her unique imagination, Chandni had made works of art that people coveted, that they would care for and exhibit with pride in their homes. From nothing she created worth and value.

I had not thought of Chandni for all these years, and all of a sudden I was weeping for her. I wept as if the world had come to an end. There was nothing anyone in the house could do to comfort me. I wept for Chandni, and I wept for myself and I wept for my daughters. I wept for burning Kiran and the baby girl who had been thrown away at the side of the road as if she were garbage. And then I wept for all the women I had worked with: the ones I had helped leave their abusive marriages, and also for the ones I could not save, the women who had been maimed and killed by their husbands, and also for the girls and women I had not even met, but knew were prisoners of their families' obsession with honour and shame.

The next morning, for the first time in months, I woke up with a plan for the day. I had never wanted anything as a child except one of Chandni's dolls, and now I realized that the only way I was ever going to fulfil that wish was to make one for myself. I didn't know how to go about it, but I was determined to find out.

For rags I tore up my old t-shirts. I took some wire from David's workshop. I raided Christina's art supplies for paint and glue. I found some old yarn for hair. I got needles and thread from my sewing box. Then I sat myself down and summoned up memories of Chandni's hands at work. I cut the T-shirts into strips, just as I had seen Chandni do. I fashioned a roughly human figure with the wire. Then I started to wrap the strips of cloth around it. First I made the legs and then the body and then the arms, then the head. To make the face, I cut cloth into an oval shape and stuffed it with cotton balls. Then, using a long quilting needle, I shaped the nose. I painted the eyes black and the mouth red.

My first doll was a milkwoman from the central region of India, wearing a typical blue tunic. Her hair was black yarn tied up in a little bun. I didn't know how to make fingers or feet or shoes, so her arms and legs ended in stumps with painted-on nails.

After the milkwoman was complete, I immediately started on another figure. I worked with a terrible sense of urgency, unable to stop. The bedroom furniture was soon snowed under by materials strewn about helter skelter, as I frantically turned out one doll after another. Tired of rags, I cut up my own saris for the dolls' clothing, and I pulled apart my costume jewellery to form doll-sized earrings and bracelets for the tiny ears and wrists.

As I became more competent with my materials, the dolls grew more elaborate and colourful. I made their clothing appropriate to their age (my "old" women didn't wear red) and regions and occupations, with additional niceties like fringed shawls and jewelled headdresses, and accessories like a pile of "wood" (matchsticks) bound up with a strip of rag being held by one hand on the doll's head.

I gave them "moods" too. If I wanted the doll to "smile," I pushed the needle from the back of the head to the right side of the lips, delicately caught it, sent the needle out the back of the head and tied it up. I did the same on the other side of the lip, which produced a semblance of smiling. Depending on my own mood and, I suppose, whatever unconscious memory was motivating me at the time, I coaxed out suggestions of a few other emotions. David described one of my dolls' expression as "horror-stricken."

I was on the kind of binge alcoholics and food compulsives would recognize. I started to research doll making on the Internet and ordered books. None of them taught the method used by Chandni. I had to try and recall what she did. In my head I kept talking to Chandni. I would ask her how to draw the eyes or nose and the response was always the same: "Whatever she wants to be is what she will be."

I sat for three weeks on my bed, day and night, making Chandni's dolls as fast as I could. I created a whole village. I had music going full blast as I worked. Classic mania. One day I told David that I might become a professional dollmaker. He said, "Okay, if that is what you want to do." He meant it. David was very eager for me to leave social work, the source of so much of my sadness, and he would have been relieved to see me take up dollmaking, housepainting, yoga or any other activity that didn't push my emotional buttons.

The dolls helped to heal me. A year later I submitted one of my creations to the Canadian Doll Artists Association competition, and it won second prize in the newcomer's category. People have asked to buy them, but I never sell any. Once in a while I make a special doll for someone I know will appreciate and take care of her. Every time I part with one, I weep. It feels like I am giving away a part of me and one of Chandni's children – the children she would have had if she had lived.

Chapter Twenty One

Goodbye to my father

Once the mania subsided, I knew I needed a competent therapist to help me find a viable route to sanity and productivity. I was lucky to be referred to Dr. L., with whom I felt an instant compatibility. We talked about everything. I held nothing back. Together we discovered that I felt enormous guilt over my inability to parent my daughters properly. I had also not resolved my sadness at feeling unworthy of my parents' love. And most important, my guilt and feelings of unworthiness blocked proper acknowledgement of the treasures I had in David and Christina, and prevented me from finding contentment with them.

Dr. L. helped me explore my fixation on my father's approval, and the ripple effect on everyone around me when he withheld it. We analyzed the responsibility I had taken on for my siblings, and how difficult it was for me to let go of my instinct to protect them. We talked about my culture and how tied up it was with my fundamental problems. Until then, even though my reason told me I had every right to leave Ralph, unconsciously I had accepted full responsibility for my failed marriage. I could not completely embrace my second marriage, because it ran counter to the religious and cultural imperatives I had been brainwashed to believe were absolutes.

It was difficult for me to break away from the clutches of my extended family. As I came to reflect on my family dynamics through my discussions with Dr. L., I realized I have never had what westerners would consider a normal relationship with my sisters or brother. For many years I was more a mother to them than a peer. By the time they were old enough for us to be friends, there was a cultural divide; they were easily Canadianized and I was stuck in my Indian persona as a traditional wife and mother. Rather than treat each other as individuals, each with her own personality and needs and wishes that deserved to be respected, we saw each other as fellow planets fixed in parallel orbits circling our father, the sun, or like the courtiers in eighteenth century Versailles, all vying for the favour of the king, upon whom our status depended. We were too wary of each other to get too close. So our pattern was to form shifting alliances rather than stable intimacies. There was so much that we could not talk about that true honesty with each other was impossible. I was always afraid to confide in my sisters, because inevitably any information I passed to one sister would be prised out of her in a weak moment by another or by my brother. We were all consumed with currying favour with our parents or brother, so if I was in bad odour with my father or brother, I could never count on any of my siblings to stand up for me.

In particular I had to learn finally to say no to the many and frequent pleas for financial "loans" that were never paid back, with no realistic expectation on either side that they would be. (Which didn't mean I wasn't angry about giving them money: I was very angry, but didn't know how to refuse.) But with Dr L's help I eventually learned to develop and maintain boundaries.

The last two years had been hell. As I slowly awoke from my nightmare, I started taking an interest in my daughter's life again. Chris was planning her future and making a point of sharing her objectives with me. She would say, "In four years I will finish my undergraduate studies; then I think I will do this, and then that and maybe after that we could take a break and all of us go travelling and then. ..." It seemed to me that she was telling me that she needed to know I was not going to abandon her again. I gave her that promise.

Professionally I was undecided. The only thing I knew for sure was that I didn't want to go back to social work. I got a job at Durham College in Oshawa teaching in the School of Human Services, and took on short-term consulting contracts. Then, just as I was making my way back into the mainstream of my discipline, my father fell critically ill. This time he really was at death's door.

Years earlier, when I was doing some contract work with the Registered Nurses Association of Ontario, Papa had learned that the arteries on both sides of his neck were ninety-five percent blocked. He was told he could die instantly with little warning. An operation was his best hope, but there was no guarantee he would pull through it.

Word went out to our community that the patriarch was about to undergo life-threatening surgery at the Toronto General Hospital. As our culture dictated, a steady flow of people arrived at the hospital to pay their respects. Dr. L. and David both worried that I would be pulled back into the powerful vortex of family conflict.

We were expected to be at Papa's bedside to greet and talk with visitors. Since I was not working fulltime, I made myself available to drive Ma Ji to and from the hospital. Papa's guests sat with him and buoyed him up with nostalgic talk of his glory days. They reminded him of what a generous host he had been, and how he had supported his family, in particular his siblings. Mention of his brothers, however, would provoke a volley of abuse from Papa.

All the old sibling resentments and grudges, too numerous and petty to mention, surfaced with a vengeance. Sickness and frailty had not mellowed Papa's rivalrous instincts and longstanding grudges. He swore that he would rather die than see or speak to his brothers again.

I doubt that he would have indulged in this histrionic performance if he really believed he was dying. Knowing him as I did, I was sure that he had yet to grasp the seriousness of his condition. Holding pompous court in the Visitors' room, Papa decreed that no one was allowed to mention the names of any one of his brothers, or he would instantly succumb to a heart arrack. He thundered, "Even if they send flowers to my funeral, you must promise to throw them in the garbage."

Of course he was well aware that his brothers and their families had all arrived in Toronto, and were waiting at Chacha Sadiq's house for permission to see him. I was appalled at my father's punitive small-mindedness at such a moment, and distressed at the pain he was so needlessly inflicting on his brothers. But my opinion was not consulted. As the patriarch-in-waiting, only Paul's views would hold sway, and he could be counted on to uphold Papa's honour by denying them access.

With so much at stake for my uncles and for Papa, I could not let my father's foolish pride prevail. On the day of Papa's surgery, I went to Chacha Sadiq's house. All my uncles and their sons were sitting around with drawn faces, waiting for news of the surgery, and wondering what they had done to be exiled in this way. It was humiliating to them that people unrelated to us had free access to their brother and uncle, while they might never have the opportunity to see him again before he died.

They all rushed at me as I entered Chacha's house. I said, "Good, it looks like everyone is dressed. I am here to take you to the hospital. Your brother needs you and your prayers." Chacha Sadiq's eyes welled with tears. He said, "Are you sure? We don't want to cause problems, nor do we want to be humiliated." I

189

hugged each of my uncles and said, "Well, whatever happens, we are all in this together. At least you will know that you tried." So off I drove to the hospital with a carload of chachas, their sons following, praying that we would be in time.

As my uncles and I got off the elevator, we could see Papa on a gurney emerging from his crowded room. When my mother and brother spotted us, they urged the orderly, "Hurry, hurry, take him away." But it was too late. I was at Papa's side. I could tell that he had been given a sedative that was making him dozy, but he recognized me, and asked, "Where were you all this time?"

I told him I had brought someone who was going to pray for him to get better. I stepped over to Chacha Sadiq, hovering uncertainly between the elevator and the gurney. I took his hand, pulled him close to my father, and joined his hand with my father's. Placing my palm over their united fists, I asked Chacha to pray. At first Papa tried to pull his hand away. Then he relaxed, and after the prayer he allowed each of his relatives to kiss him and wish him well.

Just as the elevator doors were about to close, Papa asked the orderly to hold them, and he motioned me to come inside. He took my hand and kissed it, saying, "You know your father so well. You knew I could not die without seeing my brothers. Now go and tell them I am okay." I did as he bade me, and then I drove all my chachas home.

Papa recovered from the operation, but his health remained poor for the ten remaining years of his life. Nevertheless, he was determined to resume his life of social swagger and cultural one-upmanship. I was pleased that he was feeling gregarious, even if he didn't really have the financial means to carry it off.

My father's preferred entertainment was to attend musical parties. It was the custom, if one could afford it, to hire a professional singer from India or Pakistan to the house and invite a hundred or so music lovers to gather in the basement for a nostalgic evening of time-honoured music harking back to the days of the Mogul kings. The plangent arias were guaranteed to produce deliciously intense homesickness for days afterward.

One of the traditions among these music buffs was to throw money at the singer whenever a particular verse gave special pleasure. The men would naturally vie to top one another in conspicuous generosity as a sign of their superior discernment. Papa was himself a fine singer and a poet as well, and at these gatherings his work would be rendered in song, so he had more than the usual reasons for his addiction to these soirées. But if he couldn't fling a respectable amount of money at the singer, he would feel too ashamed to enjoy himself.

So I made a deal with him. I said I would take him to one of these affairs every few months and stay with him. When I accompanied him, it was understood that I would give him enough money to play the role of a rich man, for whom lavish tips to singers were a mere trifle. I didn't begrudge him this delight, as it was clear to me, if not to him, that his days on this earth were numbered.

The summer of 2006 was a good season for my Indian family. Papa's health was stable. I was working more, and feeling stronger psychologically. My siblings were for once all getting along, and I didn't have to be a go-between for them. Then, towards the end of August, Papa became short of breath and had to be rushed to the local hospital. He had high blood pressure, he was severely diabetic and his heart had suffered life-threatening trauma. His lungs needed to be pumped.

After three weeks in hospital, Papa seemed recovered enough to go home, but on the night before his planned release, he relapsed. The doctors told us that they were unable to empty his lungs of fluid. His situation was dire, and we were told to prepare for the worst. I was mentally stable enough to accept Papa's death with equanimity, but I dreaded the family dramas that were sure to follow. I wasn't depressed, but I felt somewhat emotionally fragile, and my headaches and vision problems were still unresolved. Thankfully, this time around Papa was on speaking terms with his brothers, and they all came to pay their respects.

As news of the seriousness of Papa's condition spread, more and more people stopped by. Paul and Ma Ji sat with the visitors every day all day, while my sisters took turns with Papa.

Papa somehow took it into his head that he would be better off at the bigger hospital downtown where he had been treated the last time. The doctors advised against it; they said he might not survive the trip. Paul, determined to play the good son and have Papa's wishes fulfilled as a point of honour, sat on the phone trying to make the necessary arrangements. Time crawled by.

Papa became anxious, then frantic at the delay. When Ma Ji tried to explain why the doctors were reluctant to let him travel, he ordered her out of his room. He did not want any of the family in the room, only me. I told Papa the trip would not be a success unless he calmed down and allowed me to distract him. He meekly agreed. So I soothingly recalled happy events from his life, and asked him questions about his career highlights. I brought up topics I had never discussed with him before. I told him that every time I had to make a speech I felt very nervous, and asked how did he feel when he was translating for all the missionaries – was he nervous too? I asked him how did he get the courage to emigrate, and what made him so determined to be such a success in Canada.

He was having difficulty with his breathing. He would take off the oxygen mask every now and then to give me a quick response and then put it back. I got him to chuckle a few times and he kept nodding. I knew he was hanging on every word I said, because he was determined to be distracted. For the first time in my life, I had my father's total attention.

No, that is not true. This was the first time I had my father's complete and *willing* attention, but it was the second time in my life that I had my father's full attention. The first was at the Toronto Convention Centre in 1991, when I received the YWCA Women of Distinction award. Now I remembered the speech I had given. Not the prepared one I had balled up and discarded at the very last moment, but the anguished indictment of my father that simply erupted from me like volcanic lava. In my speech I had exposed and humiliated my father before hundreds of people. I had spoken as in a fugue, and afterward I couldn't remember what I had said. But now the speech came back to me as if it had appeared on a teleprompter on the hospital room wall.

"Papa, look around you. I am on a stage being honoured by the cream of Canadian society. Imagine that! It seems like just the other day I was one of those immigrant women they said were 'fresh off the boat.' I could hardly read or write. I had two baby girls and a husband who beat me whenever things didn't go right for him.

"Well, I did learn to read and write. My daughters and I have survived. I am remarried to a wonderful man, whose name is David Papp. He does not beat me, and does not want my spirit to be broken, and that is what has brought me to this stage with all these distinguished women – my daughters and David.

"Today is a special day for me, one I will never forget, because my father is here. A man I have loved and adored, a man I have worshipped, and whose approval I have sought all my life. And now I want to say something to him.

"Papa, today is the day when I vow to myself that I will stop trying to be the son you wanted. All my life I have heard you calling me calling me God's mistake. God made a mistake,' you would so often say. 'You should have been a boy.' I know that people born here will not understand this, but I used to love hearing that from you because it told me that you appreciated me as much as you could, that it would be different if I had been born the right sex. I understood that and accepted it.

"Today I stop."

By then the entire roomful of people was standing and clapping. Some women were wiping their eyes. I heard everything as though from a great distance. I looked at David and my daughters. They were all crying. My mother beside them looked confused and deeply unhappy. She spoke only functional English, not enough to follow everything I was saying, but quite enough to realize that what I was saying about Papa to this roomful of important people was humiliating to him.

"Today I realise that those words, God's mistake, are an insult to me and to my womanhood. But I believe with all my heart that it was not your fault you felt you had to beat me. You had no choice. I was not a boy. I was a mistake you did not know how to fix and nor did I. You could not get rid of me. So every time you cracked a rib, every time I fainted from pain after a thrashing, I loved you more. I understood your helplessness. I wanted to make it okay for you, so I tried to be the son I was supposed to be.

"Look around you, Papa. These people paid $150 each for this dinner. They came to tell me I am okay as a female. I and my daughters – where are my daughters? Where are they? Come up here and look at these people! We are okay as God's mistake. So today is the day I stop trying to be your son, Papa. This award, this statue of the woman with wings tells me I can fly as high as I want and I don't have to be a man to do it.

"This is Canada! Not India! And these people are here to tell you and me that you can be anything you want, do anything you like. That's what this award tells me."

Had I really done something so unthinkable as to attack my father and wound his honour in front of so many people? I looked down at the frail and wasted man lying on the bed beside me, and my conscience smote me. It was irrational, of course, but I felt as though it had just happened: that I had attacked him when I was strong and he was as vulnerable as a baby and unable ever to hurt me again. I blurted out, "Papa, I am really sorry I was a difficult child. I think I was trying so hard to be the son you wanted and I did everything wrong. I am sorry I caused you so much grief. I wish I could have done things differently."

At this I saw tears running down his face. He removed the mask with his right hand and grabbed my hand with his left, and gasped, "You should have been … the son… I am… proud of you… what you… accomplished… prizes, awards… way you have lived your life. …"

By now I was sobbing. Prizes! He remembered what I had said and yet he not only forgave me, he… My father had made a very serious admission. In our culture it is the son's *faraz* – the son's role, obligation – to be there for his parents in their old age. That is why people in my community pray so hard for sons. Papa's prayer for a son had been answered, but his son had not lived up to any of his hopes and expectations.

That I had surpassed my brother in my educational and professional achievements hadn't jibed with Papa's projected scenario. It should have been Paul who did well in school, Paul who made steady advances in his career. But he had not, as Papa had fantasized, become the next Billy Graham in the SDA movement. Like many self-made men, Papa put great stock in degrees and professional credentials, but Paul had been an average student, and never got a B.A. Papa rationalized that disappointment by pretending that Paul was by nature born for success in business. In fact Paul eventually did succeed in business, but too late; he was not able to help Papa at the time of his greatest need.

So on the many occasions I had helped my father out financially, I had broken the rule of faraz, even if out of necessity. I felt sure that every envelope of cash I slipped into my father's coat pocket as he left my house was inherently a silent reproach to Paul. We both knew it could not ever be discussed between us.

I told Papa again that I was really very sorry for having caused him so much distress. He shook his head from side to side. "*No* !... I ... I did not know... how to father you. You ... must forgive ... me. I have loved you ... the most... of all. How could I not? ... You knew me best."

I understood that what he was saying was the truth. Every uncle and every aunt and every one of my siblings have told me that Papa always loved me best. Now, in spite of my tormented history with him, I believed it was true. Love is not always kind or fair. Who should know better than I, who have been neither kind nor fair on so many occasions to those I love the most.

Papa put on his mask again and he put his left hand on my head as if to bless me. But then suddenly he took off his mask again, drew my head to his face and kissed my forehead. The heat of his dry, feverish lips was a shock. Since adolescence, I had never felt his naked lips on my skin.

Papa laboured, "You... brought... my brothers to me... you knew..." And then he slept.

When they eventually came to take him to the ambulance bound for the downtown hospital, I saw him off, sobbing, "Papa, I will be right here when you wake up and we will go to the singsong parties together. OK?" Those were the last words I ever said to my father. He died of a heart attack late that night.

Chapter Twenty Two

Black saris and bagpipes

My father's death liberated me. His final blessing meant I had no unfinished psychological business to clear up. I was so at peace with myself that I had no wish to get involved in the mourning and funeral arrangements. Dorothy and I went down to the "India bazaar" to buy nine black saris for myself, my mother and the sisters and sisters-in-law who wanted to dress traditionally. Some of the sisters and all the daughters simply dressed in black western clothing. Everything else I left to Paul to organize.

Paul had still been a child when I married Ralph. To him I was more a mother surrogate than a sibling, which may explain the fact that although he has often quarrelled with my sisters, he and I have never experienced open confrontations. We both had our issues with our father, but our discontents had nothing in common. I struggled to attract my father's attention and approval, usually with no success, while Paul attracted a great deal of attention and approval, but also many burdensome expectations. If I sometimes felt invisible to Papa, Paul experienced him as a constant, looming presence. The unremitting pressure to be a strong and authoritative patriarch-in-waiting took its toll. No matter what Paul did to please Papa, the expectations were continually ratcheted up. Meeting Papa's standards for manhood was a never-ending task.

Many observers and insiders comment on the unfair treatment and physical abuse of girls and women in my culture. But frankly appraised through a western lens, what passes in our culture for training in masculinity might be seen as psychologically abusive. On its face that seems ridiculous. Like other boys in South Asia, in all the superficial ways, Paul was treated like a little prince. His comfort was always considered; ours was not. His education was lovingly planned; ours was haphazard. His mother and sisters hovered over him and ran to serve his every need; we had to fend for ourselves. The habit of service to men is so deeply ingrained in us Indian women, it takes a conscious effort to restrain ourselves. Even late into adulthood, if my daughters dropped in and were hungry, I would point them to the refrigerator and go on with what I was doing. When my son James dropped in hungry, I would jump up to make him a meal (at such times, David would tease me, "Your Indian is showing...").

And yet. And yet. I have spoken to so many unhappy young South Asian men in my counselling practice who have paid a high psychological price for their privileges.

So I had always tried to be supportive of Paul when he looked to me for consolation or encouragement. But after my breakdown, Dr. L. and David urged me to keep my distance from the family, including Paul. I didn't cut myself off, but I did reduce my contact with him.

In retrospect, I think I should have reached out to Paul to help plan the funeral. Like no other of life's passages, funerals tend to retain a rigid fidelity to their cultural origins. The ancient rituals bring solace to people, even those who have integrated into another culture. And of course I knew exactly what the funeral of a humble Christian pastor from India should have looked like. Having left India as an adult, I had been to so many myself. I knew what the older people in my family and my father's peers would expect and feel comfortable with.

Paul didn't. He had come to Canada as a child, and his instinct was both to aggrandize our father in a very unCanadian-like way to indicate his filial love and admiration, and to overdo the element of Indian hospitality that in our culture should be left to others. He simply wasn't attuned to the mood and character of traditional Indian funerals. And so it ended up as a mishmash of contradictory cultural traditions that succeeded in alienating all comers. The ringing reverberations of mockery and gossip over that funeral can probably still be heard throughout Toronto's Indian community.

❋

My parents lived in a small house in one of the newer subdivisions of Oshawa. Paul asked the funeral home to deliver the body to the house for visitation by the family before the church funeral. It is customary in India for the body to be displayed in the home, as there are no funeral parlours there, but our Canadian friends and neighbours, and even some Indians, were shocked to see an open casket where the dining room table usually stood.

In the little backyard of my parents' house Paul had had a tent erected for a mourning-song ceremony. Inside the tent Paul had set out native rugs, and upon them sat all our Christian Indian friends (not just SDA), singing the kind of lamentations you would hear hired mourners performing in my grandmother's village. Neighbours on all three side of the house were subjected to a full day of this loud and plangent keening. Back home in the villages we would have paid for hired singers; here Paul paid with catered food and non-stop tea. But Indian custom dictates that people arriving to pay funeral respects bring food with them, as the mourning family should not be obliged to cook for forty days after the death. As a result we were simply overwhelmed with food, and literally no surface or container to hold it all. Having no way to refrigerate the perishables, I had a nephew dig holes in the backyard and buried them.

In preparation for the funeral service, the family had been mustered into the church basement to line up for a parade Paul had organized. From York Police, where my son James works, Paul had hired a Scottish bagpiper to precede the casket, which was rolled into the church by James and three hired off-duty officers. Immediately behind the casket was Ma Ji leaning on Paul's arm. They were followed by three SDA pastors, and then the sisters and their families. There were a few hundred people in attendance, mostly Indians. Amongst them were several prominent members from our community, as well as Paul's friends, ethnic media personalities and business people Paul hoped could be useful to him.

In the western tradition, funeral speeches are short and to the point. Most western funerals are over in an hour or under. Papa's funeral service was a four and half hour-long extravaganza. First a sixty-minute video was played, featuring friends and colleagues who extolled Papa's many wonderful qualities and accomplishments. It was completely over the top. If a great, much-loved politician or a member of the royal family had died, all the pomp and ceremony might have been appropriate. But since Papa had died penniless, and had even borrowed money from many of the people who were in the room, the excessiveness of the homage was perceived as a kind of parody, and many people could be seen shaking their heads in embarrassment.

Then we siblings were allowed to speak, but we were told to keep our remarks to under five minutes. None of Papa's brothers or other relatives had been put on the agenda. Ashamed of such pettiness, I insisted that Chacha Sadiq play a role, so Paul rather ungraciously allowed him to recite a short prayer. When it was my turn to speak, I said that Papa would have been pleased that everyone was here to give him such a lovely send-off, as he was very fond of parties. I couldn't prevent myself from adding a sly dig, "He would have been even more pleased today as he had not seen many of you for a long time, and he died a very sad and lonely man." This naturally did not go over well with Paul, and he later had my words removed from the videotape of the service.

After the family, three SDA church members who actually knew Papa spoke, and they were followed by almost two hours' worth of speakers who were complete strangers to my father, but whose profile in the community lent status to the occasion.

Eventually it was time to drive to the cemetery to bury Papa. Paul had arranged that the casket be taken out of the car at some distance from the grave in order to maximize the pall-bearing opportunities. Paul had a list with him. Every now and then he would stop and call out names, and those summoned would step forward to take the positions vacated by a previous group, place their hands on the casket and accompany it a short, symbolic distance. All of this well-organized pageantry was filmed. The women followed well behind the men. Conspicuously absent from the list were my father's brothers and their sons, as well as his brothers-in-law.

I could see how humiliated these men felt, as strangers were honoured, while they were walking next to the women. I couldn't stand it. I went up to my uncles and grabbed two of them by the hand and told their sons to follow me. I marched up to the casket, asked the strangers to step away, and before Paul realized what I had done, my uncles were paying their proper respect. My intervention incensed Paul. But I didn't care. I knew that if my father's brothers were not accorded their rightful place by the casket, the insult would haunt them all the way to their own graves.

Chairs had been placed around the gravesite. Paul had arranged for the wives of the attending dignitaries to sit by the widow, rather than Papa's sisters and his brothers' wives. I realized what Paul had done when I saw my aunts at the back of the crowd. I went and collected them and brought them to my mother's side. I asked the women sitting in the chairs to please get up, and then quickly settled my aunts in the chairs, theirs by right and custom. Paul came up to me and hissed, "What do you think you are doing?" But it was too late for him to do anything about it. People were watching. And he had to have known they approved of my action, as I was only respecting the rule he had flouted.

In the ceremony that followed the lowering of the casket into the ground, none of my chachas was asked to participate. Chacha Raja had wanted to sing a farewell song, traditional at such a time, but Paul had already told him before the funeral he wouldn't be allowed to. Chacha Raja was an uneducated man from Chukwal, but he and his sons had done very well in business in Canada. Their success had aroused Papa's envy and resentment, and therefore Paul's too.

Paul had his list for the burial ceremonies too. He called out names, and each man summoned took a handful of earth and threw it on the casket. Then there were more speeches, again by men unknown to my father. After the second one, I called out impatiently, in Punjabi, "But where is my Chacha Raja? Why can't I see him?" I was standing close to the opening of the grave. Raja responded just as loudly from the back of the crowd, "Here I am, Betah Irene, here I am!" He was weeping. Before he could reach me, I said loudly, "Don't you have a song you can sing for your brother? Don't you have something to say to him?" He began to sob, "I have not been allowed. I want to sing, but I have not been asked." To which I responded, "I am asking, Chacha Raja. I am your brother's first born. Where are your sons? Why are they not standing around their uncle's grave? They are the ones who will throw the dirt on the casket as you sing." Chacha Raja threw his head back and began to sing, and the cousins started to throw dirt on the casket as was their right, and as was the custom.

Paul's idea for the post-funeral meal was that rather than mourn in the solemn tradition of our ancestors, he would Canadianize the occasion, and everyone would "celebrate the life" of our father. He had arranged for a grand feast in a banquet hall. He told the hired singers not to sing the usual melancholy hymns, but instead to belt out the life-affirming poetry and celebratory songs my father had loved.

But it backfired. The Indians who attended the feast – for some reason Paul had assumed there would be five hundred people, but only about a hundred and fifty came, most of them extended family – were aghast at the upbeat atmosphere, and the lavish meat meal and fancy desserts Paul had laid on. No matter how westernized our Indian friends had become – and many really were very western by now in their habits and attitudes – a funeral evokes conservative, traditional responses. They wanted simple, vegetarian food and tears befitting the occasion. But they saw no one weeping, not even the widow. This "celebration of life" was too much for my father's sisters. They began to complain out loud that their brother's children were clearly celebrating the fact that he had died, and God would surely punish them.

It was a disaster. Many people left early, hardly anyone touched the mountains of catered food, and we family members stood around feeling awkward and embarrassed. To cap it all, somehow Paul had assumed that no matter what he planned without any consultation, the sisters would chip in to pay for everything. I had always done so for family occasions when father was alive, but I did not consider myself obligated to pay for extravagances I had not signed off on once he was gone. In the end I shared the bill for the food. Paul was disappointed. What kind of way was that to treat the new patriarch?

Chapter Twenty Three

"I always knew you would come…"

With Papa gone, I now had the opportunity to think about my obligations towards Mother. Ma Ji's health had been fragile for many years, but her decline simply hadn't registered for me emotionally. I had been too absorbed in my own problems. Any spare concern I had for others beyond David and my children was for Papa and whatever sibling needed it most.

By May, 2011, my mother was not long for this world. Severely diabetic, she had had a five-artery heart bypass, and suffered from high blood pressure. Three times a week she had her blood cleaned by dialysis. Once a week, Fridays usually, I sat with her in the hospital during the tedious and unpleasant process she stoically endured. I would look at this tiny, birdlike creature (now tinier than her mother, Naani Ji, who took such pride in her ninety-eight pounds of delicate womanhood), and wonder how much longer she could hang on.

It would gratify me to write that these Friday vigils evoked nostalgic memories of mother-daughter intimacy and love. But I have difficulty recalling even moments of pleasure in her company. I was there because it was my duty, my faraz, and because I didn't want to feel guilty when she was gone.

I remember one such visit quite vividly. As if it happened today.

Ma Ji sees me, she grins and reaches up with slack, skinny arms. She pulls me towards her and kisses my cheek with her scaly lips. No matter how long it has been between visits, she always starts the conversation with, "I had a dream that you would come today," or "I was dreaming about the time we went to the market," or "I had a feeling you would come to see me today, I can always feel in my heart that you are on your way."

I find myself tearing up at such moments. The machine she is hooked up to starts to peep. The nurse bustles over and tells me that Mother's blood pressure has gone up. "She was fine until you came," the nurse complains. Ma Ji, who can now speak English after forty years in Canada, reprimands her. "This is my first-born daughter. Never mind the blood pressure." She adds rather triumphantly, irrelevantly, "My daughter, she is a professor." I do not have the heart to correct Ma Ji, to tell her that I stopped teaching after Papa died. It was important to him that I be called Professor. Teaching was a far more prestigious calling in his eyes than the social work I preferred. But I just smile and wink at the nurse, who shakes a playful finger at Mother and says, "Keep your blood pressure under control, Mrs. Abraham. No excitement..."

My sister Dorothy is Mother's other reliable visitor. Dorothy and I report back to each other after every visit. Dorothy usually jokes, "It takes me an hour and a half to get to the hospital, and the first thing Mother asks me is, "Is Irene with you?" Dorothy says she pretends to be insulted: "Ma Ji, you always ask for your first-born. How about being satisfied with your fourth-born?" This teasing reminds us of the times, in our childhood, when the younger girls would vie for the privilege of sleeping with the older ones. Since I was the family storyteller, they all wanted to sleep in my charpoy.

The date of the visit I am remembering is December 6, almost a year to the day since Jessica succumbed to the cancer she had struggled against for years. I am in a blue mood, conscious that I am entering the autumn of life, and that loss has become a more insistent theme of my growing introspection. My father is gone. Jessica is gone. Ma Ji soon will be.

Mother has been living with Paul for the past three years. Since none of the sisters maintains more than necessary contact with him, Dorothy and I are her sole source of family news. So as always on my visits, Ma Ji launches into a stream of animated questions. We begin with my children and grandchildren. She does not remember all the grandchildren's names, but her long-term memory is very sharp. I show her the family photos I always bring with me. Mother then inquires about Mary and her family. I tell her how well they are doing in Texas, that there are plans afoot for Dorothy and my children to go to Texas in a few weeks. She is thrilled. She did not like the idea that Mary had moved so far away from the family.

I brace myself for her next question, sure to be about Jessica, and it is. Mother says, "'Jessica was my lost child. She was so small, so tiny I had to send you to look for her or she would never have been fed. She loved her father." I wonder if her use of the past tense means she remembers Jessica has died. She goes on, "After your father died, I should have died too. That is the proper way. How are your children?" Mother does not remember the details of Jessica's funeral, but she does know that her child has died. I am not in regular contact with Jessica's children, so before each visit to Mother, I check Facebook and am then able to convey some details of their lives. She smiles contentedly as she lays back. She says, "Jessica was a good mother. She really loved her children a lot. She took care of them before she died." She is silent for a while, lost in memories of her departed third-born.

She emerges from her reverie, but there is a sad expression on her face. She says, "Your father should not have hit Mary so hard." Mother is recalling an incident that pains both of us to remember. When Mary was an adolescent, she exchanged a few innocent letters with a boy at Roorkee High School. The boy's father discovered one of them. Since he and my father were mortal enemies over some Church-related grievance, he took the occasion to inflame the situation, implying the letters signified some sexual impropriety on Mary's part. He advised my father to keep a leash on his many daughters, as one of them might "come home with a big belly."

This drove my father mad. His honour had been impugned. He beat Mary quite fiercely, breaking her nose and causing permanent damage to one eardrum. When I threw myself on top of Mary to protect her, I ended up with two broken ribs and more proof, if it were needed, that a child's gallantry was no match for the aroused beast of a patriarch's sense of shame.

I go on hastily to the other siblings, telling her half-truths if necessary to report that all is well with every one of them. I ask Ma Ji if she knows about the new house Dorothy has bought. Isn't that absolutely brave of her? I ask her. Who would have thought that after twenty-eight years, Dorothy would muster the courage to walk out of her abusive marriage, and the strength to stand on her own feet. I remind Mother of how we used to tease Dorothy, calling her 'Dorothy the innocent' or 'Dorothy, our Ellen White,' after the founding prophetess of the SDA church. Dorothy is a dichard SDA, always careful to toe the Church's moral and doctrinal line.

Then I tell Mother about Heather and how much she is enjoying her new job. She still lives in Arizona, I say, and loves the sunshine, and keeps asking us all to move there and enjoy it with her. Mother remembers her visits to Arizona, and agrees that it is much warmer in the winter, but she did not enjoy that area's broiling summers. She'd endured enough heat in India to last a lifetime. Mother does not like the idea that Heather is alone, though, so far away from the rest of us, and I reassure her that I am only a phone call away, and that this is her choice.

As I see Ma Ji fading back into a darker mood, I show her the photos of my grandchildren again. Mother's eyes brighten and soften. "Your father would have loved to have had his photograph taken with his grandsons," she says. "You have four handsome grandsons. You are blessed." I remind her that I have a beautiful granddaughter too. She just laughs at my nudge toward gender equality. "She looks like Christina when she was this age, but she also looks like her mother." At this she laughs loudly, as if she has said something very funny, "Silly me, of course she looks like both of them; they are sisters after all."

Mother then asks, "What is my great-granddaughter's name?" I tell her that it is Margaret Anne. She wants to know who this child was named for, and I tell her that David's mother's name was Margaret. She nods her head in agreement as if to say she approved. "Yes, that is how it should be. David has been very good to you. He was the father when your girls needed one." Mother has always liked David and has always felt grateful to him. She is aware that David has always respected her, while the same could not be said for his opinion of Papa.

Ma Ji is silent for a bit. Then she says, "Just a little while longer, and then you will have to prepare my funeral. I will be with your father again." A cruel impulse overrules tact. I say, "Ma Ji, I will not be attending your funeral. I am here to pay my respect to you, and to tell you that I will do my best for you while you are still here. Once you close your eyes, you will not know if I am standing by your casket or not. I cannot go through the farce of another funeral like Papa's. I would rather say good-bye to you in person."

My mother is not hurt by this admission. She nods and sighs, "Yes, that was too much. I had no control over it. I understand." A mental segue. "You know, and all your sisters and Paul know, you were the one I depended on. Whenever I picked up the phone, you came. I always knew you would come."

I feel a pang of remorse. All my life I have been so consumed with pleasing Papa. It seems to me that every time I gave specific thought to my mother, it was only to figure out how to sidestep her anger, and avoid those strong hands of hers, so quick to clutch and slap and pull my hair.

It now occurs to me that maybe she was angry all the time because she had so little control over her own life. She never even had a real home, one she could think of as permanent. She and Papa were always on the move. Papa served the needs of the missionaries, and Ma Ji served the needs of her husband. I was born in Dasua, near Jullandhar; Mary in Pune in the south; Jessica in Bombay; Dorothy in Jammu in the north, Paul in Jullandhar; Heather in Simla; and Pamela in Amritsar.

Our family lived in Delhi on four different tours. I was married in Indore, in Central India. Moving around so much, Ma Ji had no dependable circle of friends. Papa didn't like her family, so she was constantly thrown into company with his family. And they weren't kind to her. She always lived in a community of Adventists, but she had no deep friendships. She was forever dependent on the good will of people who didn't really know her, let alone love her. And above all, she had not known true mother love. Contemplating my own mother's death and feeling guilty for not wanting to attend her funeral, it struck me for the first time how sad it was that Ma Ji and Naani Ji had been so emotionally disconnected before we emigrated that geography alone was enough to sever their tenuous bond. We had not even known of Naani Ji's death in Lahore until it came to us through the grapevine.

❀

Now that there was so little time left to her, I thought of a hundred questions I should have asked Ma Ji over the years. What did she dream of when she was a young girl? What was her relationship to her younger sisters? Was she in love with Papa? Or with anyone? Why was Naani Ji so mean to her? What were her exact thoughts when she was told, time after time, her new baby was a girl? Did she hate us? And if she loved us, why had she never shown it? Why did she never kiss us or hug us or tell us she was proud of us? How much of her coldness was cultural, how much was personal?

The nurse wants to give Ma Ji a needle. Ma Ji tells her that she doesn't want it. It makes her doze off, and she does not want to sleep when her daughter is visiting. The nurse tells her that she has no choice. I have only been here for a little over an hour, and I had planned to visit for three hours. Yielding to the nurse's wishes as she knows she must, Ma Ji grabs my hand tightly, and pleads, "If I doze off, don't leave. Promise me you will not leave. The medication wears off real fast." I promise to stay, and soon her tight grip slackens, and her eyelids begin to flicker.

But then her grip tightens again. She fights off the drowsiness, determined to suck every vestige of pleasure from my visit. She asks for water. I bring it and she gulps it greedily. Then she says, "So how is your work with women, are you very busy?" She is trying to stay awake and keep the conversation going, but she soon dozes off. I wish she were wakeful. I want to tell her about my work, training people in the helping professions – police, social workers, educators – in cultural competency, teaching them how to deal with South Asian families in distress in ways that are sensitive to their cultural values and customs. I want her to know that the negative experiences in my life have been turned to positive advantage, and that other women from our culture will be helped because of what she and

I went through. I think perhaps it would please her to know that I am listened to with respect by politicians and police chiefs.

Ma Ji wakes up. She is surprised to see me. "Oh, you are still here. I was dreaming. I think I was dreaming that you were coming to see me. And here you are! Mothers know these things. When my children were in boarding school, and if one of them got sick, my breast would swell up and it would hurt, and I would nag your father into making a phone call to find out if any of the children were sick. I dreamt you would be coming. And here you are!"

She is breathless and wants to sit up. She is excited again, and the machine peeps. "Look at all the decorations the nurses have put in this room. Are you all ready for Christmas?" asks Ma Ji. But before I can answer, she laughs loudly and asks, "Do you remember that Christmas when you took the children carol singing? If God had not helped us, then who knows what would have happened to us? God has always been good to us."

I agree with her. She shakes her head from side to side in wonderment. "Who would have thought singing carols would have saved our Christmas? Do you remember how each year your father insisted that we sing carols in Urdu as well? All my children knew the words in Urdu, especially *Silent Night.*"

Moved, I reach out for my mother's hand. I start to sing, "*Ulfat ajeeb, Ulfat ajeeb, pada hua masih. Pada hua masih.*" Then I sing it again in English: "Silent night, holy night, all is calm, all is bright. ..." Several people, all hooked up to dialysis machines, turn their faces to me in astonishment. A rush of joy wells up inside me, and my voice swells to fill the room. "Round yon virgin, mother and child, Holy infant so tender and mild. ..." Tears are streaming down my mother's face. And mine too. We look into each other's eyes and smile our gratitude for this moment. I finish my song to my mother, my voice soft and low now, for her ears alone. "Sleep in heavenly peace; sleep in heavenly peace."

Epilogue

It was during the period of my depression that I confided the story of my childhood sexual abuse to another human being for the first time. To Dr. K, the doctor who couldn't believe any child didn't yearn for toys. Dr. K's advice was to find "closure" by revealing the truth about my childhood rapes to my parents. I balked at that. I explained to the therapist that this might be a good strategy for western women, but it would backfire for someone of my culture. But she was adamant that the acknowledgement of a victim's suffering is a first principle of healing, and disclosure a universally valid necessity for female victims of sexual abuse.

Eventually she wore me down, and I told my family about what had happened. I was not surprised at all to meet a collective wall of revulsion at my revelations: not revulsion against my abuser, but against me for making such a shameful accusation against a kinsman. The result was that my family closed ranks with Aalim. He was invited to all special occasions thereafter, even though, because of church politics and career rivalries with my father, they had become somewhat estranged over the intervening years. My revelation opened a permanent fissure in relations between me and other family members.

Some of my female relations were especially angry at me. The revelations were socially awkward for them, because Aalim was a frequent visitor to their parents' homes as well. One said to me, "Do you think you are the only victim? What do you expect to gain from exposing old history?" The naive therapist's scenario had my family confronting Aalim as the final scene in the "closure" drama, but at this point I listened to my instincts, and resisted further attempts to make that happen.

Dr. K would doubtless have been quite perplexed to overhear a conversation I had with my Aunt Madhu, not long after my father's death, during a visit to her Midwestern American home. I asked Madhu what she would have done if I had come to her on my wedding night and told her my secret about Aalim. She sighed, and said, "I would have had very little choice, Irene. I would have had to help save the reputations of the men in the family." She reminded me that there were five of my younger sisters waiting to be married off as well, and their fate rested on their father's honour. But, she assured me, she would not have fed me the poison herself. She would only have made sure that I had it and that I knew that I had no other choice but to take it.

I hugged my aunt and thanked her for her honesty. I told her that I loved her for that. I told her she would have been my saviour, had she been brave enough to find the poison in time. I would never have held her responsible for my death. It would have been a service to me. I think of this conversation quite often as I brood over my latest area of interest, the distressingly elevated figures on suicide amongst teenage girls from South Asia. I am already immersed in writing a report on that, and can see it could be the subject of a whole other book.

As children, Madhu and I used to play together in Chukwal. Now, as middle-aged women we sat and wept together for the childhood and youth stolen from us for the sake of our family's honour.

✸

When I visited my mother and stared hard at her wizened face, I saw no vestige of the woman I feared so much when I was young. She was a near-stranger. I know nothing of her inner life, and I have never tried to know her. I have never really thought about how much grit and determination she needed to live a life that was chosen for her by others, a life in which a woman's sacrifices, physical suffering and cultural status were wholly governed by men and her reproductive *kismet*. The only way she could have made sense of her experience was by clinging to the moral certainty that life was unfolding as it was meant to for a woman of her time and place.

It's strange to me that my mother and I once shared all the same moral certainties, many of which are so abhorrent to me now. For I too used to be morally certain that men were made to rule over women, weaker vessels, whose duty and pleasure it was to serve them. I too was once morally certain that I really was an "unworthy creature" and "God's mistake," because girls have many functions, but no value. I too was once morally certain that people's status in

208

life was determined by their kismet, that it was neither wrong nor unnatural to consider one superior – or inferior – to others through an accident of birth.

I was once morally certain that a child's body was the possession of her parents: that if she was beaten senseless, it had to be because she had done something to deserve it, and that any punishment meted out by those in authority was beyond criticism. I was once morally certain that sexual gratification was a man's right and only accidentally a woman's privilege; and that sexual jealousy was a sign of love. Most consequentially, I was morally certain that the loss of honour was the worst thing that could possibly befall a family, and that it was up to me to uphold first my father's, and then my husband's, honour. Looking back on my life, I can trace every bad or wrong thing that ever happened to me to this first principle.

I thought that writing my story would be a cathartic and positive experience for me personally. It has been that, but it has also made me very sad. Not depressed, just sad. I am not afraid that I will sink back into a nightmarish catatonia. My sadness isn't personal these days. It has more to do with the world around me. I used to think that the kind of honour-motivated violence I had witnessed and experienced in India would die off in Canada after the first generation, but my education and my career experience have taught me that is too often not the case.

For our family, happily, that was the case. My father no longer beat his children in Canada. Perhaps a fear of legal consequences stayed his hand. It was something that was never discussed amongst us. I know that Papa was eager to be successful in Canada, so I think once he understood that corporal punishment of children might compromise his reputation, that was enough to modify his behaviour. It was the same with my first husband. Ralph knew he could beat me with impunity in India, but not in Canada, so he turned to psychological abuse. At least I knew I could walk away without fearing for my life, as may not have been the case in India.

Over the years I watched my parents change. As my mother began to speak English, and as the children become older, their roles reversed somewhat. I saw that my father's confidence was in kind similar to that of his mother, Dadi Ji. Dadi Ji's high self-esteem was always linked to her cultural status, and to the approval or disapproval of others. It did not come from within. Her confidence would not have survived transplantation to another culture, and nor did my father's. But Ma Ji surprised us, and perhaps herself as well, when she turned out to have inherited something of her mother's spirit and individualism. The momentous change in her circumstances stirred some deep inner reservoir of character and fortitude. She wasn't confused or intimidated by transplantation; rather she was empowered by the drastic change of circumstances. One day, after an argument with Papa about money, off she went, this woman who had never before in her life worked outside her home, and shocked us all by finding herself a job at the Bathurst Street Jewish Community Centre in North York, where she made friends with many women outside her community.

But as my research in the South Asian community, and my work with desperate women convinced me, other families remain dominated by an ancient, deeply entrenched mindset about family honour. Only rarely do the abuses of girls and women in their homes become public knowledge. In 2007 16-year old Aqsa Parvez was killed by her father and brother, because they believed she had brought dishonour on their family. She had done nothing wrong – or nothing wrong by western standards. She was murdered because she wanted to live the life of a typical Canadian girl. She wanted a Canadian-style social life. She didn't want to marry someone chosen for her by her parents.

Aqsa knew she was in danger and she sought help from her school and social services. It cannot be said that the state's resources failed her, and one could say the same about the Shafia girls. In neither case did her teachers or other frontline workers trivialize their expressed concerns. The social services and even the police did what they could. But in the end their families got them anyway.

Fearful of appearing racist, many media people tried to spin Aqsa's tragedy as an extreme form of "domestic violence," the kind of crime that could happen to any girl or woman in our society. They were encouraged to do so by South Asian community leaders. This agitated me. Domestic violence is a phenomenon whose characteristics are actually the opposite of abuses motivated by honour. Domestic violence occurs between partners in intimate relationships, not family members. It is disapproved of in western society. Honour-motivated violence always targets family members, almost always girls or women. It is the product of a community code that is endorsed by the killers' cultural peers. I was not surprised at all by what was going on in Aqsa's household, nor was I surprised that nobody in her family tried to protect her. Aqsa and I are sisters under the skin. I was just luckier than she was. I felt the same way about the Shafia girls and their stepmother. Coverage of the trial gave powerful hints of the bizarre mindset of their killers, their older brother, father, mother and husband. Bizarre to Canadians, that is. But only too familiar to me. One positive effect of the Shafia affair has been the evolution of public understanding, as reflected in the media commentary around the trial. Few observers had the gall to deny the specifically cultural motivation behind the murders, or pretend "it could happen to anyone."

When I started counselling South Asian women, I offered my services to fearful and abused women in the spirit of a village elder, someone non-threatening and empathetic to their culture in general. But as the numbers of honour-motivated crimes began to rise in Canada, I realized that I wanted to do more than counsel individual women. I couldn't change the way people think about honour codes in India or Pakistan, but maybe I could do something to change the way people think about them here. You cannot deal with a problem if it is not recognized for what it is.

I had found my new mission for the autumn of my life. I wanted to educate Canadians. I wanted to tell them that you cannot treat girls and women from an honour culture in the same way you would treat victims of domestic violence. Nor can you offer honour victims the same strategies for escaping their abusers as you would for victims of normative domestic violence. Most of all I wanted to convince Canadians that it is not racist to admit that some harmful social behaviours are rooted in cultural traditions.

Last winter I was the keynote speaker for an anti-abuse group in Vancouver. While there, I was interviewed for a radio talk show. The host challenged me: "There are over a million South Asians living in Canada, and that number is expected to grow in the years to come. There have only been twelve honour killings in Canada, according to your reports. Comparatively, that is a very small number. Why are you making the whole community look bad as if this is a wide-ranging problem?" I was tempted to respond with a question to him: "There are about 35 million people in Canada. Annually about 50 women are killed by their intimate partners. That is a very tiny percentage of the population. Why do we make such a fuss about domestic violence? Why should we make all men look bad over such trivial numbers?" Instead I simply asked him what he would consider an acceptable number of honour killings before we recognized the problem.

On June 10, 2010, the day Aqsa Parvez's father and her youngest brother were sentenced to second degree murder, I was on my way to speak to a group of twenty-one South Asian women. Some had admitted to being victims of domestic abuse. I asked them what they thought about the sentence of these two men.

While one or two hesitated to speak up at first, most soon agreed that it was too bad that the girl "had to be killed." Each one of them felt that murder was justifiable. One said, "She had been told many time by her family to mend her ways." Another said, "She was showing disrespect to the family the way she was dressing." And another that "She was hanging out with the wrong girls – girls the family did not approve of." Yet another, "We have our ways. We have our culture. We don't want our children to be like white girls of black girls. That is not who we are. We have to marry off our girls and they have to be pure for their marriage."

They all affirmed that as mothers, it was their duty to make sure that the girls were kept pure. By the time the matter has been taken up by the father or the brother, then it is too late. Mothers can't do much then. It is out of the hands of the mothers. In these women's moral certainties I heard echoes of my mother's voice and Dadi Ji's voice and all the other women in whose company I had spent so much time listening to complaints about the unworthy creatures they were burdened with.

I am a mother of daughters and now I have a granddaughter. I refused to believe it was out of my hands to break the cycle. I paid a big price for my refusal, so I understand how difficult it is for women in this culture to step away from the brainwashing. For many years my community wanted nothing to do with me. I was accused of betrayal, and on more than one occasion I was even threatened with violence for exposing my community's dirty laundry.

In recent years I have become less of a pariah as, here and there, community leaders have begun to acknowledge and speak out against honour codes. In May, 2011 I received the Grant's Desi Achievers Award for my activism. *Desi News* is an English-language magazine written by and for South Asians all over the world. I was especially happy and honoured to stand amongst so many high achievers of my community and receive their recognition. I consider this award a symbolic opening of a closet door that has for too long remained closed.

Just as I was finishing this memoir, the Supreme Court of India recognized honour killings as a special crime, and only weeks later, West Bank president Mahmoud Abbas pledged to repeal the Jordanian penal code from 1960, which commutes sentences for men who kill or attack female relatives accused or suspected of "dishonoring" their families. These official acknowledgements of culturally-motivated violence against girls and women in places where the need is greatest gladdens my heart and gives me hope that the words "honour" and "shame" will, in my lifetime, take on associations of mutual respect and equality between the sexes.

My beloved Chacha Sadiq died in April of 2011. It wasn't unexpected, but it hit me hard. Chacha Sadiq was the kind of father I wish I had had. Chacha Sadiq and my father grew up in the same culture, but Chacha Ji was as different from my father as night from day. He was humble where my father was arrogant. He was giving where my father was demanding. He was forgiving when my father was punitive. I am grieving for Chacha Sadiq as I could not for my father (and as I did not for my mother, who died a few months after the visit to her I wrote about. I did not attend her funeral.)

At Chacha Sadiq's funeral (simple, unpretentious, the opposite of my father's), old friends spoke of his generosity. One recalled that over 187 people – our family amongst them – stayed with him when they arrived in Canada. Another spoke with awe of the fact that my uncle had cooked for him and his family with his own hands, normally an unthinkable chore for an Indian man.

During the eulogies I thought about my weekly, sometimes twice-weekly visits to Chacha Sadiq over the last six years, which began after my father's death. As an Indian niece, I would walk in and bow slightly before him. He would lay his hand on my head and bless me when I arrived and when I left. "Come in, Betah, God bless you. You bring joy." He would make himself comfortable in his reclining chair and then ask me about my work and my family. But I wanted to ask him about our family history, all the details I hadn't heard before. Now that my father was dead, Chacha and I could talk without fear. It was Chacha Sadiq, our family archivist, who over his last year of life filled in the blanks of my childhood memories, and validated my adult ones.

The loss of the only kinsman who ever loved me unconditionally is wrenchingly sad for me. I knew who everyone was at the funeral, but I did not feel I belonged amongst them. I felt like someone without any roots at all. I do not have any friends who look like me. I have sisters, but we do not often behave to one another as sisters should, and we cannot depend on each other for support. I am no longer Indian, but I am not white. I am a cultural hybrid, like Naani Ji, who was educated into individualism in a British home, and who lived according to her own desires, but paid a big social price for it. Sometimes I feel don't really know who I am at all. Perhaps my fascination with Mr. Popkiss's favourite song, *Nobody's Child,* represented a kind of prescience.

I do not attend a SDA church regularly. I no longer have faith in any man-made dogmas. Yet from time to time, when I am asked about my religious affiliation, I automatically identify myself as SDA. For nearly twenty years I refused to attend any church, because churches reminded me of the missionaries, my father, my ex-husband, and all the beliefs and codes that colluded in the oppression of girls and women.

But I am nevertheless proud to call myself a Christian. What I received from the missionaries was not all bad. Many of them, like Pastor Streeter and Mrs. Burns, did what was in their power to build my self-esteem and persuade me that I was a worthy creature in God's eyes. I have decided that it really does not matter if there is an entity called God or not. What I do know is that for me personally, to feel there has been meaning and value to my life, to feel that everything I experienced was for a reason, I *need* to believe that God exists. I need to feel there was a plan for me. Where I was born, I could easily have been one of the millions of females who end up aborted, or thrown down a well or tossed onto a heap of garbage.

I continue to mourn the loss of social comfort I would have enjoyed if I had conformed to my cultural community's standards of belief and conduct. David asks me, in one of my melancholy moments, "Aren't I enough for you?" And I tactlessly but honestly reply, "No, you aren't. I long to sit at a crowded, noisy, food-laden table, eating and gossiping and laughing and sometimes crying with thirty members of my extended family."

I also miss the fellowship of the SDA community in which I spent so much of my life. A few months ago David, who does not believe in organized religion, but knows how much I love to sing, said to me, "I have watched you sing with your father and your sisters, and you have a lovely voice. You should join the church choir. If you do, I will attend services with you." (He meant our local United Church. Even my wonderful David would balk at SDA.)

And so I did join the choir. And when I sing in church, I don't think about the bad things in my life. I give myself wholly to the intentional moment, joining my own good, strong voice to those of my fellow human beings to sing the praises of our common Creator. At such times I am released from any particularity of colour and caste and gender and religion. I am reminded of the many blessings I have been privileged to receive, not least my citizenship in this beautiful, free and peace-loving nation. When I pour myself into worshipful song, I am just Aruna, at peace with myself and with the choices I have made. I give of myself to God, and it seems to me that He responds, with intimations of healing and strength for the challenges ahead. At such moments I forget my losses and remember my gains, my fears subside and my hopes rise up, I feel gratitude for the love I have given and received, and my heart swells with a joy that is sufficient unto the day.

❋ ❋ ❋ ❋

CPSIA information can be obtained at www.ICGtesting.com
Printed in the USA
LVOW080523261012

304476LV00004B/1/P